The

Daguerreotype

The Daguerreotype

A Sesquicentennial Celebration

Edited by John Wood

University of Iowa Press Iowa City

University of
Iowa Press,
Iowa City 52242

Printed in Japan
First edition, 1989

Design by
Richard Hendel

Library of Congress Cataloging-in-Publication Data
The Daguerreotype.
  Bibliography: p.
  1. Daguerreotype.   I. Wood, John, 1947–
TR365.D35   1989   772'.12   88-27904
ISBN 0-87745-224-5

for

Irving Pobboravsky

with admiration and affection

"I have seized the light."

—Daguerre

Contents

Preface

On the seventh of January 1839 François Arago, director of the Paris Observatory, announced to the French Academy of Sciences that M. Daguerre had succeeded in fixing the objects resolved in the camera obscura. It was probably the first time in history that the creation of an art form was heralded with a public announcement, and especially in an Academy of Sciences. However, the event was emblematic of the technical age dawning upon the world. Science had helped create an art, and it was to scientists, not other artists, that its birth was announced. Few events could have more tellingly foreshadowed the role science was to play in all the arenas of the modern world, including even the aesthetic ones.

Photography is now 150 years old, and there is no aspect of modern life that has not been touched by it. This volume of essays honors Louis Jacques Mandé Daguerre, one of its creators, and celebrates the particular kind of image that bears his name. It is not meant to be a comprehensive account of the daguerreotype's origins or its history. It is a celebration of the form itself. In looking over the table of contents one will immediately think of all the subjects that might have been addressed but were not: the scientific uses of the daguerreotype, the daguerreotype as historical document, and on and on. The ideas rush into the head—as they did into mine, too, in the book's planning stages. I am passionate about the daguerreotype. I love its delicate and exact beauty, its sensuousness and immediacy, and think it unrivaled by any other photographic process. Nothing would have pleased me more, therefore, than a volume of fifty essays and five hundred illustrations. But I had to be realistic, and so I was faced with some difficult decisions.

I might have selected topics and then found the best writers for those topics. It would have made for a neater table of contents. There could have been essays on the American, the French, the German, the English, and other European daguerreotypes, essays on the daguerreotype as art, as documentation, and so forth. But that is rather like the format of books that already exist. I had at once decided not to reproduce daguerreotypes that had been previously published, other than in a few exceptional cases. We all love the famous butterfly collector, Stelzner's wife, and Lemuel Shaw, but to use the same five or six images over and over again makes no sense and also presents a distorted picture of early photographic history. I reasoned, then, that if the illustrations were to be fresh, so should be the text, and so I selected no topics—just individuals, passionate critics, scholars who I felt would have the freshest, most original, and most interesting things to say about the daguerreotype, men and women who would tell me things I had never before heard. And so the mixture of contents, in my opinion, becomes one of the book's most positive features. It suggests the vastness and variety of work those of us who care about our photographic history still have before us, and it proclaims the fact that this is truly a celebratory volume—an intellectual celebration and a visual celebration as well.

Selecting those celebratory daguerreotypes to illustrate was considerably more difficult than selecting the writers. As quickly as I decided to use only previously unpublished images, I also decided to exclude daguerreotypes whose sole importance was their historical, cultural, or scientific significance. I wanted the selection to represent Daguerre's original intent: the daguerreotype as art. Consequently, there are few examples of several kinds of daguerreotypes that are extremely popular with collectors and that command high prices: American scenic views, which are primarily the documentation of someone's house, store, street, gold mine, or farm; occupational portraits, which are often important records of social history but which are usually uninteresting as art; comic and humorous images of people clowning around and having fun, often significant social and cultural documents but, again, seldom great art. In the process of doing this book I learned how very common a great many of the market's so-called rarities actually are, and I confirmed what I had suspected about the true rarity of the fine artistic portrait and landscape. Still, the selection process was quite difficult because many beautiful images have survived.

For perhaps half of the daguerreotypes I chose, I saw others of equal artistic merit that would have served my purposes as well. Sometimes I excluded a piece only because it was too much like another I had already selected, or because it came in too late, or possibly because the copy print simply was not as clear as another. Of course, I have never seen an anthology of any sort—poetry, essays, or whatever—that was as good as the one I felt I could have put together. That's the way everyone feels, and I'm sure it's the way each reader will feel in looking at the images I have selected. If I have disappointed anyone in some of these selections, I hope that at least the majority of them will please.

I tried to contact as many collectors and museums throughout the world as I could, but I'm certain I missed both institutions and individuals with things as wonderful as things here. Two or three collectors chose to hide their daguerreotypes under a bushel and would not even allow their publication credited to "anonymous collection"; however, the vast majority of collectors were generous, open, and gracious—eager to help and to share—and to all of them who assisted me I want to express my sincere thanks. I also appreciate the assistance from the many collectors who sent me copy prints of daguerreotypes I could not use; more often than not they were of rare and lovely things, and I was sorry I could not use them.

I also, of course, owe a great debt of thanks to the scholars who so graciously prepared essays for this volume. Each one of them was involved with his or her own books, articles, exhibitions, or combinations of the three, and I appreciate deeply their having taken the time from their own important projects to work on this one. Grant Romer and Matthew Isenburg, the two most knowledgeable scholars of the daguerreotype it has been my pleasure and good fortune to know, were both wonderfully generous with their time, advice, and help. Richard Rudisill, Hans Christian Adam, Ken Appollo, Paul Katz, and Larry Gottheim made valuable contacts for me that led to the inclusion of important pieces, and I greatly appreciate their efforts. I should particularly thank Ken Appollo, a dedicated scholar and researcher whose enormous energy and enthusiasm for daguerreotypes greatly aided this book.

For years of ideas, suggestions, information, and friendship I must thank Floyd and Marion Rinhart. LaPlaca Productions and David LaPlaca, a fine photographer and major collector, not just of daguerreotypes but of the history of photography, very generously produced over half of the color transparencies and many of the black and white prints used in this volume. For him to have taken so many hours from his schedule to do copy work was indeed generous. To Michael McKinney, another fine professional photographer, I owe thanks for copy work, helpful advice, and much assistance. I feel I should also pay some tribute to Joe Buberger, both in honor of the contribution he has made to furthering interest in the daguerreotype in America and to honor the wishes of quite a few collectors who expressed a desire to see Buberger's efforts publicly recognized.

I must thank the McNeese Foundation, which very generously awarded me two research grants for work on the daguerreotype, and the Reva and David Logan Foundation for a Logan Grant in Support of New Writing on Photography for an earlier version of an essay that developed into my essay in this volume. I am also grateful to the administration of McNeese State University for allowing me time from my teaching in order to complete this book and also for its generous and enlightened attitude toward research and publication. For the past ten years my study and research in the history of photography, which is not the field I was trained in or the field in which I teach, have been supported and rewarded to the same extent that scholarship in my academic field would have been.

John Wood

The

Daguerreotype

A Sesquicentennial

Celebration

Silence and Slow Time

An Introduction to the Daguerreotype

John Wood

Thou still unravish'd bride of quietness Thou foster-child of silence and slow time.
—John Keats, "Ode on a Grecian Urn"

The invention of photography was the most significant event of the nineteenth century. Its cultural ramifications exceed even those of the publication of *Das Kapital* and *On the Origin of Species.* Daguerre altered the world more utterly than Marx and changed our view of man more radically than Darwin. The information provided by photography in conventional photographs, film, television, and now in computer images has revolutionized the world like no social or scientific reformer might have dreamed possible. Photography's most beneficent effects have been in the sciences, and most dramatically in medicine; however, it has also fueled the great engine of greed as few things in history have. Yet instead of driving the already alienated individual to the point of demanding social change, either in the street or at the ballot box, photography has convinced him, just as it did Willy Loman, that the good life, symbolized by material things, by those photographed objects, is close at hand and easily attainable with a little hard work, honest sweat, Yankee ingenuity, and all those other clichés that the fragile architecture of dream and hope is built upon. But all that work, as those who issue the credit cards well know, will provide little more than new televisions, additional photographs and debts, and the next generation's inheritance of the same myth.

Familiarity with photographs, or what we might call photographic literacy, is probably the single greatest threat there is to radical social change. The photographically illiterate rise up because they are inspired solely by the force of a personality and by the power of language, while the photographically literate are bribed into passivity by images of things that will never be theirs. Depending upon one's political persuasion, the glut and welter of photographs might be seen as a source of social stability or social stagnation. But regardless of politics, what is clear is that Daguerre, the second-rate artist, amateur scientist, and clever entrepreneur, more persuasively than any thinker and more effectively than the plots and bombs of Mammon's men, undermined the nineteenth century's most grandiose humanitarian scheme.

However, Daguerre, with equal lack of intention, reinforced the great Romantic notions of man's essential worth and significance with a visual pungency that argued more convincingly than the words of Rousseau, Jefferson, or Marx that the individual was of value and should not be trod upon. Look at a group of daguerreotypes, at those faces penciled to silver by nature itself; see how vigorous, full of life, of muscle, blood, and bone they are as they look out at us with such intense immediacy it is impossible to believe that every one of them is dust. Here is real equality; here is the pure realism of the Romantic movement, rich with feeling and infused with passionate humanity.

Though the camera was not kind to early sitters, and they were sometimes shocked by the honesty of their countenance, the form itself bespeaks a compassion yoked to the century's democratic idealism. These people are worthwhile; they are impor-

tant. Their beauty does not lie in prettiness—just as the beauty of Rembrandt, Goya, and Gericault, those great prephotographic seers of the human face, does not lie in prettiness. The camera's new way of seeing helped humanize our way of seeing: it changed the way we saw ourselves and others. By freezing all faces, even the ugly or deformed, and by being unable, at least at first, to tamper with or retouch them, the camera caused us to look more closely at those around us; to find even in deformity some strength or vigor, the nobility of endurance perhaps; or to find in the familiar, weary, and exhausted plainness of most men and women something urgent and universal, a truth about ourselves; to discover that we are capable of an immediate, individual, and humane response to the faces of our fellow human beings and to the lives that linger beneath them waiting and hoping.

Early photographs of truly beautiful people are as rare as truly beautiful people, but early photographs, especially the daguerreian portraits, the calotypes of Hill and Adamson, and the great social photographs of Oscar Rejlander, John Thomson, Thomas Annan, Jacob Riis, and those commissioned by Dr. Thomas Barnardo, are the nineteenth century's richest artistic documents of man's nobility and compassion. They are aesthetics humanized and ethics made visual, and they touch us in a way no social statement or literary work of even the strongest morality or feeling can. Shaftesbury's political and social activism, Engels's *Conditions of the Working Classes in England* and the influence that book had on its most famous reader, and Dickens's novels written between 1840 and 1855 all contributed to humanizing the face of the nineteenth century, but it was photographers who ar-

Alexander Beckers (U.S.), quarter plate. Collection of Paul Katz.

gued the reformers' position most persuasively and poignantly, photographers who finally popularized it and established it as social doctrine in this century.

That the daguerreotype was primarily an American art form is fitting because it was the United States, more so than Tahiti or any of the other too culturally fragile South Sea Islands, that perhaps best embodied Rousseau's dreamland of noble savages and Romanticism's faith in a middle class and the culture that might spring from it. Of course, America never exactly resembled the Peaceable Kingdom, because finally only Mammon can work the miracles to make Romanticism's most charitable dreams come true, and the open road may have led to the used-car lot. But a goodly portion of generosity and kindness did result from the American drive down it—not as much as there might

have been, because there can never be enough, but enough to turn the sentimental magazine covers of a gifted hack into the self-image of the American people. Though Norman Rockwell's slick covers were no more than prop art and, as such, as dishonest as Thorak's statues or Ziegler's paintings of those healthy, vaguely pornographic German volk of the thirties, the way a people see themselves through their artists can reveal more of their psychology than their actions can. The daguerreotype's popularity and length of survival in the United States seem understandable, given the sentimentalized, Whitmanesque way Americans saw themselves even years before Whitman, and given the great, good, and comforting myth that all men are created equal. Early portrait photography ennobled and made beautiful through the shimmering beauty of its form even those who on the surface might

Thomas Easterly (U.S.), quarter plate. Collection of Paul Katz.

have appeared otherwise, and thus democraticized portraiture, redefined man in a visually democratic context, and established photography as *the* art form of the masses.

Though photography documents history, chronicles greed, and spreads information, it is as art that it possesses its greatest cultural significance. Walter Benjamin, cutting through volumes of gabble, noted that "much futile thought had been devoted to the question of whether photography is art. The primary question—whether the very invention of photography had not transformed the entire nature of art—was not raised."[1] And, of course, the entire nature of visual art was changed by photography, and what was merely a mass art form of the previous century has become the most moving and persuasive visual art form of our century.

Painting has been in decline and photography in

ascendance since Impressionism, which, though indirectly, was also one of photography's artistic gifts to the nineteenth century. Manet's most startling work can be seen as a visual adjustment to photographic realism, an adjustment of eye and palate, a visual and emotional refocusing, and it makes one recall Arnold Hauser's statement that "A work of art is a challenge, we do not explain it, we adjust ourselves to it."[2] Such adjustments are the traditional tasks of the critic but also of the creative artist, who, like Manet, might find himself at the dead end of a tradition. Years of photographic realism prior to photography—and then finally the pure realism of camera and chemical that no painter could hope to duplicate—urged Manet into Impressionism, and along with him those other artists who came to see what his adjusted and refocused eye had seen. The creative painter has continued to re-

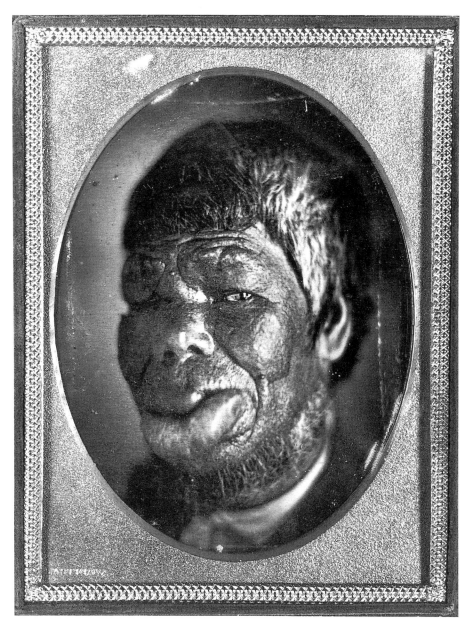

Albert Southworth and Josiah Hawes (U.S.), half plate. Collection of Robert Harshorn Shimshak.

Anon. (U.S.), half plate. Collection of Robert Harshorn Shimshak.

focus the lens of his artistic eye, and we have gone from the Fauves to the Expressionists, to this, to that, and into the complete blur of abstract patterns of color and again back into the precise focus of the camera, which is the painter's symbolic capitulation to photography's dominance.

As perceptive as Benjamin was about the transforming nature of photography, he understated its power. It was not just the entire nature of art that was transformed by photography; photography transformed the entire world. The only event we might compare it to is the invention of writing. I have suggested its role as disseminator of information, historian, and advertiser, in which its effect can be seen as being either beneficial or injurious to society, though I doubt if anyone could find beneficial all the excesses of photographic advertising, especially its reliance on bosoms and buttocks to market any product. However, the most ominous aspect of photography, more so than its engender-

ing a kind of greed that might retard social progress, is that it has become one of the major vehicles for the acquisition of political power in democracies. But apart from all of this, that we live in a transformed world changed utterly by the events of 1839 and that the whole texture of modern life is conditioned by the camera, Daguerre's original dream for his creation is its best, I think, because more sustaining to us than knowledge is that unique and contenting joy that comes from art alone.

Of course, any object can speak to us in ways its creator did not envision or intend, or, put into contemporary critical jargon, there is always at least one subtext and probably several. Photographs certainly do let us see a great many things, and if they are things not immediately perceptible to the eye or intellect, then it is a part of the critic's task to point them out. In general, however, the daguerreotype tells us less than the photograph because it has fewer subtexts. Though daguerreotypy is physi-

*Anon. (U.S.),
half plate.
McConnell's
Miners' Store,
Garden Valley,
California,
1851.
Collection of
Paul Katz.*

cally a richer medium than photography, it is not nearly so rich in terms of the meaning of its content, and I think the individual who would care to view the daguerreotype in some critical context might profit more from reading Sir Joshua Reynolds than from reading Roland Barthes.

We, of course, can draw cultural conclusions from looking at particular groupings of daguerreotypes, but the meaning or text of almost every daguerreotype, if viewed individually, is simple "Here I am," or "Here is my house." A few other equally obvious messages exist, e.g., in the case of erotic daguerreotypes, "Here is my flesh to excite you"; in the case of the so-called occupational portrait in which a carpenter, for example, is posed with his saw, "Here is my work"; in the case of the popular and often dreadful sculpture groups, "Here is art"; or in the case of animals, "Here is my pet or prize bull, hen, lamb, or whatever." Occasionally the message is "Here is a piece of reportage," as in the

case of Carl Ferdinand Stelzner's daguerreotypes of the Hamburg fire or George Barnard's of the Oswego fire. But the daguerreotype's extra-artistic message is nearly always relatively simple, which, unfortunately, has occasionally led critics to dismiss the form as being aesthetically simple, too. This richly physical, poignant form, so quick and sensual that it can disturb, does possess a kind of simplicity, but it is like the simplicity of a sphere. The daguerreotype is so purely self-contained as a work of art that one would expect, if anything, exaggerated claims for the complexity of its aesthetics. Without a doubt, the daguerreotype is the most misunderstood and least appreciated art form of the nineteenth century.

Much of the misunderstanding about the daguerreotype stems from the fact that it is continually confused with the photograph, and for three reasons: (1) they resemble each other; (2) photography supplanted daguerreotypy as the great documenter and keeper of the human face; and (3) photographic history books usually begin with a short, uninspired chapter on the daguerreotype, a chapter often poorly researched, filled with oft-repeated generalizations, and illustrated with the five or six daguerreotypes that are reproduced in every other such book. All this is done in the name of relative importance, of course; the daguerreotype must be quickly dispensed with in order for the critic to get on to the truly important art form of that period, the calotype. Or so goes the conventional wisdom. Lamentable as it might be, it seems a fact that in all fields but the sciences a statement repeated several times and printed several times, regardless of whether it is patently absurd, takes on the aura of authority and is soon thought by everyone to be true.

The lack of critical attention focused on the daguerreotype today and its near second- or third-rate status as an art object is due almost entirely to the prejudices of historians, critics, and curators. Paul Delaroche's often-quoted misjudgment about the daguerreotype's invention, a statement anyone even vaguely familiar with the literature of photography is tired of hearing—that "from today, painting is dead"—was, of course, actually true, or became true within a few months, with respect to the portrait miniature. And just as the daguerreotype displaced the miniature, it, too, was eventually displaced by the photograph. The daguerreotype was popular in the United States longer than anywhere else, but even here it lasted barely two decades. The nature of the daguerreotype, the fact that it was cheaper than a painted miniature and that a paper photograph was cheaper than both, predetermined that the same commercial laws that drive price down along with quality in order to expand markets would determine the future of the great chronicling.

Certainly few events in the history of civilization are any more remarkable than this ongoing chronicling of the human face, this welding of ego to technology in an attempt to record every face, to photograph everyone—and now everything. The chronicle of our countenance has transformed itself into the chronicle of the universe. There is nothing we do not photograph—from the most hidden interiors of the body to those of the atom, and from the most public to the most private of acts. We share our sex and grief like no one ever before us has—and our joys and fascinations and curiosities, too. There is nothing we think unworthy of being photographed. It is one of the most omnipresent of all human activities and, as such, certainly one of the ones most subject to human economic laws. The portraitists abandoned the small silvered plates for paper and a loss of presence and clarity, but their gain was easier to count and measure than matters of quality or questions of aesthetics. And so the daguerreotype is commonly seen not as a unique, vital, though short-lived, art form all of its own, but merely a stage in the development of photography. And therein lie two misconceptions.

The daguerreotype is not a photograph, nor was it a stage in the development of photography. Built into any notion of a stage is the notion of progress. All religions, of course, are based on myth, even the great, true, modern religion of science. Its primary myth is that there is progress and advancement in the world because there is in science. Because of that progress, because it led to the ability to cure, to do the magic and work the miracles we have always demanded of our religions, we deified it, placed our faith in it, and made it the object of our worship. Just as the myths of religion are transferred to the believers' other endeavors and become ingrained with the fabric of their lives and, consequently, their society, a belief in progress has touched every aspect of contemporary life. To deny it, to believe in insoluble problems or to see retrogression of any sort, is to blaspheme. However, nowhere is the fallacy of progress more obvious, more clearly myth and sham, than it is in the field of art, and anyone but the true believer whose eyes are scaled by faith can see it. One need only place a Julian Schnabel beside a Giotto, a Chuck Close by a Hill and Adamson. Many things do progress, but art doesn't; it only changes. But the daguerreotype not

Anon. (U.S.), half plate. Collection of Matthew R. Isenburg.

only wasn't a stage in a progress, it wasn't really a photograph either.

Though daguerreotypy and photography are obviously more closely related than daguerreotypy and painting, and though we do speak of them together, it is not mere pedantry to insist that the daguerreotype is not a photograph. Apart from the obvious—that it doesn't look like a photograph, that it isn't made like a photograph, and that it isn't of the same material as a photograph—the research done by scientist and photographic historian M. Susan Barger on image formation, composition, and particle structure demonstrates that "the daguerreotype is not a direct analogue to conventional photography."[3] One of Dr. Barger's most intriguing statements follows a list of assumptions about image formation; she writes that those assumptions "are based on the premise that daguerreotypes are merely another form of photography and that conventional photographic theory is,

therefore, applicable to daguerreotypy."[4] What is even more interesting than the point she makes is the one we can infer, that it is not merely the technical aspects of conventional photographic theory that have been applied to daguerreotypy but the aesthetics of conventional photographic theory as well. The daguerreotype, like any other art form, demands its own critical vocabulary, its own way of being seen, and its own way of being appreciated.

Though the characteristics of a good technical performance in any work of art can be enumerated, classified, and judged, part of our response to art is something mysterious. We sometimes weep though we are not unhappy, or smile though we have not been amused, or feel good or more complete or more in harmony with everything else. Science, the present-day oracle, may someday choose to reveal why our brains trigger such emotions. At an earlier time and in a more primitive religion, we would simply have attributed it to being in the presence of

Anon. (U.S.), quarter plate. Collection of the J. Paul Getty Museum.

something holy, something sacred. Certainly something must be present in a mass of paint or arrangement of rock or bronze or sound or words to trigger those emotions. And it also, of course, has to do with something special in us that allows such a triggering and makes us different, as far as we know, from other creatures. I hesitate to attribute it to the presence of something sacred in us—that is, if "sacred" is to keep any of its traditional connotations. Art, however, does seem truly sacred, even though it has not done much for the advancement of human kindness, and several centuries of great Christian art has clearly had no effect on human behavior, hasn't made people any kinder than those in cultures with little art other than face painting and body mutilation. If anything, the passion for art usually leads to profane behavior, but clearly something special is present in the art and is present in us. New work in brain science now claims that "human information-processing can be described as *kalogenetic*,"[5] which is to say, the brain likes to create beauty and is pleased at finding it, but I don't think that would come as any surprise to generations of soothsayers, shamen, and priests.

And so, what is certainly the single most important aspect of an intense aesthetic response—our recognition of being in the presence of the sacred—cannot be explained, even by scientists, without resorting to the vocabulary of poets. But among critics there is some agreement as to what makes a statue or a painting or a musical composition at least technically good. Likewise, among those individuals who are serious and passionate about the daguerreotype and who have trained their eyes to respond to its craft and the subtleties of its execution, there is a consensus about what makes a fine daguerreotype.

The daguerreotype is a luxurious image. It is, as one writer described Art Deco, not "for people who are embarrassed by splendor or put off by luxury."[6] Of the thousands of daguerreotypes I have looked at, only a few did not exhibit at least some of that splendor. They might best be compared to those small portrait cameos and intaglios of the Greeks and Romans. Nearly all of those classical gems are beautiful by definition, beautiful merely by being what they are—bits of precious material rendering a face or scene with a detail and exacti-

tude that, oddly enough, might only be termed "da-guerreian." The artists who made them are, for the most part, unknown, though the names of a few have survived. The level of craftsmanship in all of them is surprisingly high, and despite their size, a few, like the Gemma Augustea, must be regarded as being among the monumental examples of classical art. Like the daguerreotype, they have been misunderstood and underappreciated. Books on the art of Greece and Rome have paid scant attention to them, and though museums have acquired them, their curators' true passion was reserved for the larger, splashier things, and so the classical gem has come down to us preserved and treasured primarily by a few collectors who, seeing past their size, glimpsed their monumentality, and, seeing deeper than their crystal contours, looked into the very eye of the age itself.

The quality that distinguishes a fine daguerreotype from one that is merely good is a combination of several characteristics: composition, lighting, focus, the pose, how the plate was buffed, the face itself, but, of course, as in all the arts, it is finally a matter of the indefinable, the genius of the artist,

just as the most essential aspect of our response to the work of art is also indefinable. The nineteenth-century observer was equally aware of this fact. One wrote, "It is often a matter of surprise to some that two portraits of the same person by different Daguerreotypists should appear so unlike, it being supposed, at first thought, that nothing more than mechanical skill was required in the individual managing the instrument, and that it was only necessary for the image of the face to enter the lens and impress itself upon the chemically prepared plate, to have a correct likeness; but this is an error. Unless the daguerreotypist be an artist; or have the educated eye of an artist, he cannot take good pictures, except by the merest accident."[7]

Gabriel Harrison, one of the best of American daguerreotypists, put it more bluntly when he said that the camera, like the pencil, "in unartistic hands will undoubtedly produce abortions," because the daguerreotypist "must observe all of the identical rules necessary of the production of a work of merit that a painter or sculptor would follow to secure graceful position, proper distribution and degrees of light and shade, also tone of picture, arrangement of drapery, etc."[8] And Marcus Root, another of America's foremost daguerreotypists, wrote in his book *The Camera and the Pencil,* "Sun-painting, I was mortified to find, was considered a merely mechanical process, which might be learned in a few weeks, by a person of the most ordinary capacity and attainment. . . . Why . . . should not Heliography be placed beside Painting and Sculpture, and the Camera be held in like honor with the Pencil and the Chisel?"[9]

I was not being flippant when I suggested earlier that reading Joshua Reynolds might provide a better critical context for understanding the daguerreotype than reading Roland Barthes. In his "Address to the National Photographic Association of the United States" in June of 1870, Albert Southworth, who with his partner Josiah Hawes produced not merely the finest daguerreotypes made in America but some of the greatest monuments of nineteenth-century portraiture, echoed the previous writers, but also, and more interestingly, Sir Joshua. Of course, it is not at all surprising that a book as influential as Reynolds's *Discourses on Art,* the single most-respected book of art criticism by an Englishman prior to Ruskin, would have been in the hands of a young artist of the first half of the nineteenth century and that he would have been influenced by it. Whether Southworth actually read Reynolds is unimportant, but what *is* important is that Southworth's aesthetic was imbued with Reynolds's aesthetic; Southworth's ideas were Reynolds's ideas. They may not have traveled to him directly; they might have come through Samuel Morse, his teacher, a man who certainly would have been familiar with Reynolds, but they are present nonetheless, and their presence indicates Southworth's view of himself as an artist and place him in the main tradition of European art. The *Discourses* are a summary of the aesthetics of the three previous centuries, and the view of art and of the artist expressed in them is probably not just Southworth's and Morse's view but the view, though possibly fifth- or sixth-hand, of most American daguerreotypists as well.

The way the early daguerreotypists immediately appropriated the trappings of the artist and the seriousness with which they took their task, their seeing what they were doing as a moral and ethical pursuit of Nature and a quest for Nature's beauty, seems to have been a peculiarly American approach. Though I am of course generalizing, it was as if the English saw daguerreotypy only as a business and the French saw it as part of an ongoing process of discovery. But Americans were true believers—Babbitts, Barnums, schemers, and entrepreneurs, but always believers through and through—and their beliefs were Reynolds's. Southworth wrote:

What is to be done is obliged to be done quickly. The whole character of the sitter is to be read at first sight. . . . Natural and accidental defects are to be separated from natural and possible perfections; these latter to obliterate or hide the former. Nature is not all to be represented as it is, but as it ought to be, and might possibly have been; and it is required of and should be the aim of the artist-photographer to produce in the likeness the best possible character and finest expression of which that particular face or figure could ever have been capable.[10]

This passage might have been taken from Reynolds, who wrote in his Eighth Discourse: "What is done by Painting, must be done at one blow." And in his Third Discourse: "Nature herself is not to be too closely copied. . . . a mere copier of nature can never produce any thing great. ' . . . The works of nature are full of disproportion, and fall very short of the true standard of beauty.' . . . [The artist] acquires a just idea of beautiful forms; he corrects nature by herself, her imperfect state by her more perfect."[11]

Southworth, like Reynolds, was attempting to give advice to younger artists. He spoke of "the immense importance and absolute necessity of acquiring perfect control" of the "principles of mechanics, and of the sciences of optics and chemistry, and the all-important subjects of outline and chiaroscuro" (p. 316). Without such labor, Southworth argued, there can be no art because "there is no high, easy, unobstructed, road to knowledge, but the same long, steep, and toilsome path which has ever led and is still ever to lead to the treasures of learning and wisdom" (p. 321). In his First Discourse, Reynolds had also emphasized the necessity of a solid knowledge of craft, and he chastised young artists who "wish to find some shorter path to excellence, and hope to obtain the reward of eminence by other means, than those which the indispensible rules of art have prescribed. They must therefore be told again and again, that labour is the only price of solid fame, and that whatever their force of genius may be, there is no easy method" (p. 18).

Merely learning the rules, however, was not enough. Southworth wrote, "But the artist, even in photography, must go beyond discovery and the knowledge of facts; he must create and invent truths and produce new developments of facts" (p. 320). In his Sixth Discourse, Reynolds had stated, "Genius is supposed to be a power of producing excellencies, which are out of the reach of the rules of art; a power which no precepts can teach, and which no industry can acquire" (p. 96). Though genius cannot be taught, it can, according to both Reynolds and Southworth, be approached through study. They both insisted that the artist know man, his history, and his art, but most of all he should know nature.

Reynolds wrote: "Nor whilst I recommend studying the art from artists, can I be supposed to mean, that nature is to be neglected: I take this study in aid, and not in exclusion, of the other. Nature is, and must be the fountain which alone is inexhaustible; and from which all excellencies must originally flow" (p. 101). And Southworth's advice was the same: "I would impress upon you the necessity of the most constant and unremitting attention to Nature, her changes, her variations, her moods,

and her principles and productions" (p. 322). This study is necessary to develop the mind, according to Southworth, so that it can be "instructed and directed by impressions . . . emanating from the subject itself" (p. 321). Reynolds's explanation for such study was the same. "The great business of study," he wrote, "is, to form a *mind,* adapted and adequate to all times and all occasions; to which all nature is then laid open, and which may be said to possess the key of her inexhaustible riches" (p. 204).

That "adapted and adequate" mind of Reynolds and the "instructed and directed" mind of Southworth both lead us through Nature to art and then to something more abstract. Reynolds expressed it in the conclusion of his Ninth Discourse: "The Art which we profess has beauty for its object; this is our business to discover and express; but the beauty of which we are in quest is general and intellectual; it is an idea that subsists only in the mind; the sight never beheld it, nor has the hand expressed it; it is an idea residing in the breast of the artist, which he is always labouring to impart" (p. 171). Toward the end of Southworth's "Address," he expressed this same thought: "The artist is conscious of something besides the mere physical, in every object in nature. He feels its expression, he sympathizes with its character, he is impressed with its languages; his heart, mind, and soul are stirred in its contemplation. It is the life, the feeling, the mind, the soul of the subject itself. Nature is the creation of infinite knowledge and wisdom, and it is hardly permitted to humanity to even faintly express nature by a copy" (p. 322).

However, both Reynolds and Southworth and Hawes did at times catch the soul of the subject, did "snatch a grace beyond the reach of art." We can see it in the portrait of "Mrs. Siddons as the Tragic Muse" and in the famous daguerreotypes of Webster, taken by Hawes alone, and the standing portrait of Lemuel Shaw, so reminiscent of Rodin's Balzac, and in the portrait of the girl (plate 1). Those daguerreotypes are three of the great portraits of the nineteenth century, portraits whose greatness arises from that intellectual quest for a beauty beyond the mere physical. To find images of man as penetrating as these, it is not hyperbole to suggest that one can only look to the greatest of Roman portrait busts, to Rembrandt, Goya, and Gericault, to Ingres and Schiele and Rodin. In fact, the portrait of the girl, which Hawes considered his masterpiece and called "the finest [daguerreotype] in the world,"[12] bears so uncanny a resemblance to Ingres' La Comtesse d'Haussonville (1845) that one would think Hawes must have seen it, though it's hardly possible.

There are few such triumphs of daguerreotypy, but there are few such triumphs of painting or sculpture, either. In looking at any great work of art, one can see that the greatness lies beyond what is simply seen; however, most of the insights in the arts are not as mystical as they are technical. The strokes of genius and innovation have nearly always been insights into technique. Asked about inspiration, Henry Moore said, "The word 'inspiration' is an academic term. In reality it does not exist. You either know how to do something and do it, or do not know, and no amount of inspiration can help."[13] Savoir faire of any sort is always a matter of technique, and technical matters can be scrutinized and studied. All of the visual arts share in common several qualities that must be present in any portrait if it is to be convincing; the individual medium, however, places its own specific demands on the artist as to how he might light a face, pose a sitter, or compose an image.

As I have said before, though photography and daguerreotypy share much in common, the daguerreotypist could not approach these matters in exactly the same way the photographer could. The length of the exposure in the daguerreotype necessitated the sitter being quite still for some minutes, though this was eventually reduced to seconds. Metal head clamps were invented to help hold the sitter's pose, and children were often tied into chairs. Were the finished daguerreotype not to look like the portrait of a mannequin, the stiffness

had to be overcome. That stiff, unnatural pose is one of the most common defects found in the daguerreotype; the blurred child is another. The daguerreotypist had to rely on lighting, posing, composition, and obviously his own rapport with the sitter in order to overcome the potential problems of the exposure. Lighting was another problem that made specific demands on the daguerreotypist. Nineteenth-century daguerreian literature abounds with discussions of lighting and techniques for overcoming various problems the daguerreotypist might be faced with. The larger the plate, the more difficult it was to buff properly. Therefore, the larger the plate, the greater the craftsmanship of the daguerreotypist had to be. And finally the size of the plate placed certain compositional demands on the artist. The largest standard-sized plate was only 6½ × 8½ inches, while the most commonly used plate was a mere 2¾ × 3¼ inches. And so the form itself had many restrictions built into it that would not have affected the painter or photographer, or at least not to the same degree. The daguerreotypist had to build a composition that would retain its authority when reduced to a few inches, had to understand the nature of light and shadow on a piece of highly polished silver plate at various distances from a lens, and had somehow to make people clamped and tied down look natural, relaxed, and at ease.

Yet, despite all these constraints, the beauty of the form itself was such that its passing was lamented primarily by those daguerreotypists who had turned photographers. In an article entitled "The Lost Art of the Daguerreotype" written in 1904, Abraham Bogardus, who had been one of the leading American daguerreotypists, said, "Although the photograph on paper has superceded the silver plate, yet, with many others, I consider the latter the best picture yet made with the camera."[14] And John Mascher, inventor of the stereoscopic daguerreotype case, writing in 1858, said, "A plain daguerreotype picture, alone, in my opinion, surpasses in beauty, richness, multiplicity of detail, and intrinsic value, any other kind of picture whatso-

*Jean-Gabriel
Eynard-Lullin
(Switzerland),
half plate.
Self-Portrait.
Collection of
the J. Paul
Getty
Museum.*

ever. What an exalted art Daguerre originated!"[15] The fact that the leading daguerreotypists continued to make daguerreotypes, if only for themselves and their families, and that the process never really died should indicate the esteem its practitioners held it in. What is perhaps an even more interesting assessment of the daguerreotype's beauty came from Ansel Adams. He wrote, "I confess that I frequently appraise my work by critical comparison with the daguerreotype image; how urgently I desire to achieve that exquisite tonality and miraculous definition of light and substance in my own prints."[16]

Adams would have certainly had in mind the work of Southworth and Hawes, whose daguerreotypes are justifiably famous. Their portraits are unsurpassed and some of their scenic views, though not the equal of the very greatest European scenic daguerreotypes, are certainly unequalled by any extant American work.[17] However, much of Southworth and Hawes's fame derives from the fact that a great body of their work has come down to us intact from the Hawes family. Were there similar archives of a dozen or more daguerreotypists (the Langenheims, Williamsons, Roots, and Meades, Martin Lawrence, Mathew Brady, John Whipple, Jeremiah Gurney, Alexander Hesler, Frederick Richards, Robert Vance, Jesse Whitehurst, Samuel Broadbent, Gabriel Harrison, etc.—and these are just a few of the Americans!), though Southworth and Hawes's position would remain preeminent, if only because of their uncanny ability to pose and light the sitter, we would probably recognize that they did have serious rivals, some of whom were greater artists than we presently realize. The ninety-seven Stelzners of Hamburg's Museum für Kunst und Gewerbe are enough to suggest that he was possibly their equal, and the museum's twenty-one Herman Biows certainly establish his artistic greatness. In the limited work of Carl Biewend that survives, it is clear that he also was a great daguerreotypist, but like Alexandre Clausel, Jean Gros, Humbert de Molard, Edouard Dusei-

gneur, and Jean-Gabriel Eynard-Lullin, he was not a professional.

It would be difficult to guess which three or four professional daguerreotypists might come closest to approaching Southworth and Hawes or Stelzner because it was their consistency, the quality of daguerreotype after daguerreotype, that was a large part of their genius. Of course, one could also argue that the day-to-day work and the sheer quantity of it is what perfected their art. I have seen very moving unsigned images that are the equal of some of their best work, though perhaps not their very greatest, and I have also seen great works from the Langenheim brothers, Charles Williamson, Martin Lawrence, Jeremiah Gurney, and several other daguerreotypists, but I have also seen mediocre work by the Langenheims, Lawrence, and Gurney, and even one bad work by Williamson. But what this means in trying to make some assessment about individual artists in the history of the daguerreotype is another and more complicated matter.

The single most significant question the historian needs to be asking is "Who were the masters?" And that is also perhaps the single most frustrating question to deal with. Every student of the daguerreotype has felt that frustration while holding an unsigned image of such power that it raised chill bumps, yet knowing at the same time that the name of the artist was lost forever or was simply one of those hundreds of names we have preserved but know nothing of. We have let part of our richest artistic and cultural history slip away from us. There are few areas in the past five hundred years of art history that we are as ignorant of as we are of the early history of photography. And it isn't just factual history that has been lost; we have actually lost part of our artistic heritage. Hundreds of thousands of daguerreotypes have been destroyed through neglect and ignorance. They have been melted for their infinitesimal amounts of silver and gold, discarded for their cases, irrevocably scarred in attempted dustings and cleanings of their fragile surfaces, or simply trashed as worthless old pictures.

Anon. (France), half plate. Rocks. Collection of the J. Paul Getty Museum.

Of course, one would think that any individual's eye would preserve us from such ignorance, that it would signal, if not the presence of art, then at least the presence of beauty, but unfortunately the signal that more often than not generates the desire to preserve the past is the dollar sign. What may not be revered as beautiful will always be revered if it is thought to be valuable.

But the lack of regard for the daguerreotype's beauty was, of course, just another aspect of the general attitude most people had about photography. A new art form had burst upon the world, but the critics and historians, instead of rushing to the company of men like Hawes and Stelzner and Hill, Adamson, Fox Talbot, and Hippolyte Bayard, failed to recognize what was happening until so long after the fact that vast amounts of a history that should have been chronicled were lost.

And so in the presence of the great anonymous daguerreotype we can only sigh for what we do not know. The chances of our discovering the name of its maker are slim. Occasionally, though, we do have some luck. Erotic French daguerreotypes can sometimes be attributed to an artist if we can see the same studio props in his signed paper photographs from the same period. And though Southworth and Hawes's work is also unsigned, it too can often be identified if certain of their props are present. They were a popular studio for years and produced many thousands of daguerreotypes. The majority have probably gone the way of the majority of other daguerreotypes, though there must be masterpieces still extant but simply unrecognized for what they are—or if not masterpieces, then at least fine examples of their work. The pieces of furniture they most often used—"the Daniel Webster posing chair," as Hawes termed it, the two chairs children were usually posed in, the two columns, the stool, the plant, and the rug—are fairly well known, but there were a variety of other pieces, too. The entire contents of their studio, as far as can be ascertained from their known daguerreotypes, signed photographs, and those several photographs of the studio itself, need to be catalogued and published as a guidebook, along with classic stylistic examples of their work. By comparing the furniture of a particular daguerreotype with that in the guide, a good many Southworth and Hawes's images could probably be identified.

Other characteristics can also suggest their work and, together with matters of style, help build a case for attribution. They seemed to have preferred the black leather, pushbutton case, an oval mat with a simple design around it, the use of wide tape on the reverse seal, and an electroplated or resilvered plate, which resulted in a silvered reverse. Though they did seem to have those general preferences, there are exceptions to every one of them, and I have seen one of their daguerreotypes in which all four preferences are ignored. Myths grow up as misstatements are repeated. It is a commonplace one often hears or even finds stated in books that the whole plate was the most common format in which they worked. But this is only because Hawes's personal collection was composed of a great many whole plates. It is simply unrealistic to assume that any daguerreotypist would primarily make whole plates; one would have to assume that his studio was frequented only by the wealthy and that they returned every few months for another daguerreotype. Though Southworth and Hawes did attract the rich and though their prices were higher than those of other daguerreotypists, a daguerreotypist only to the rich would have gone out of business as soon as the rich had all been daguerreotyped, and Southworth and Hawes were in business for nearly twenty years.

A great part of the popularity and success of the daguerreotype was that it was a middle-class art form with a wide mass appeal. Paintings were still the major vehicle for recording the faces of the rich. The daguerreotype was expensive, but it was within the reach of millions. I think, then, that we can only assume that though much of their greatest work is in the whole-plate format, the majority of Southworth and Hawes's daguerreotypes were, like the majority of all daguerreotypes, sixth plates. The whole plate was clearly an aesthetic preference with them because it is, though not necessarily any more artistic than a smaller plate, a greater tour de force of craftsmanship owing to the more complex buffing and lighting problems involved; however, a good many of Southworth and Hawes's family portrait daguerreotypes are sixth plates and quarter plates, and the two great shirtless portraits of Southworth, certainly two of their finest images, are half plates. They even made the lowly ninth plate, a small and inexpensive image, and at least upon one occasion used it for daguerreotyping a famous individual.[18] I have also occasionally heard it stated that every Southworth and Hawes daguerreotype at Eastman House is electroplated and, thus, has a silvered back, but according to Grant Romer, this too is not the case. Their usual preferences for electroplating, for a specific kind of plate holder that caused a kind of crimping at the top and bottom of the larger plates, for a certain kind of case, and so forth, if coupled with a recognition of their style can help in making an attribution if specific pieces of furniture or props are not visible. But attributions on the basis of style alone are only as reliable as the eye and expertise of the attributor. The eye is a gift that everyone, of course, thinks himself gifted with, but expertise is the fruit of labor, and at this point in the study of the daguerreotype there are only a handful of scholars who have actually worked directly with the archive, and without such experience there is no real expertise.

But even with the difficulties Southworth and Hawes's work poses, there are fewer problems there than in the work of most other major daguerreotypists. If it is possible to be certain that a daguerreotype was the product of the Southworth and Hawes studio, then we can be certain that it was actually made by one or both of them. But such certainty with regard to most other major daguerreotypists' work is not possible. Unlike most of the larger, popular, and famous studios, Southworth and Hawes did not hire operators, men who

Jeremiah Gurney (U.S.), sixth plate. Collection of Julian Wolff.

actually made the daguerreotype or worked on it in some stages of the process. According to Beaumont Newhall, they even boasted that they did not.[19] We know from contemporary reports that large studios employed several individuals to make a single daguerreotype. The operator or cameraman posed the sitter and made the exposure, often being told by the developer when to remove the plate from the camera. The developer then mercurialized the plate, which brought out the image, and fixed it by washing it in hyposulphite of soda. He passed it on to the gilder, who gold-toned it to increase brilliance. It next went to the colorist, if it were to be tinted, and then to the individual who matted it, attached the preserver, and put it in a case.

And so the question of who used operators and who did not is of fundamental importance in attempting to discern who actually made what and to discover who the great daguerreotypists were. The question grows even more complex because it is not merely a matter of who used operators and who those operators were, but of when they were used, during what years, and how involved they were in the process of making the image. Were

they more like apprentices or assistants to the masters, as we know in some cases they were, or merely the cameramen on an assembly line, or the actual daguerreotypists performing the entire operation from posing to casing but at a studio with someone else's name.

In New York City in 1851 there were seventy-one galleries employing 127 operators. In the following year the Meade brothers alone were employing 10 assistants in their gallery. And some galleries like Plumbe's or Whitehurst's, for example, were large chains. The name Plumbe or Whitehurst on a daguerreotype's mat or case not only does not tell you who made it; it doesn't even tell you what state or part of the country it was made in. Attempting to conclude anything definitive about a daguerreotype signed by either of them is clearly a complex problem. But even seemingly simple questions quickly turn into complex problems when dealing with the daguerreotype.

For example, in 1853 Jeremiah Gurney, one of the most famous of American daguerreotypists, won the Anthony Prize, a national competition for the best set of four daguerreotypes. Gurney employed operators, a few whose names are known to us and some whose names have become as famous, or more famous, than Gurney's. Between 1848 and 1852 he employed Albert Litch, who earlier had been a partner of John Whipple. Gurney also used T. Hayes, Caleb Hunt, and the great Gabriel Harrison, who prior to having his own studio had also worked as an operator for William Butler and Martin Lawrence. In fact, Lawrence's famous allegorical daguerreotype "Past, Present, and Future," which won a bronze medal at the London Crystal Palace Exhibition of 1851, was Harrison's work. But in 1853, the year Gurney won the Anthony Prize, he was using as operators three brilliant daguerreotypists: Charles Fredericks, who had just returned from Paris and would the following year be taken on as a partner; Solomon Carvalho, painter, daguerreotypist, and explorer; and William Perry, whom the *Photographic Art Journal* had called "a man of genius" (1851) and "one of the best daguerreotypists in U.S." (1852). Perry had also worked for Plumbe and for George Cook, who had himself been an operator for Mathew Brady in 1851 and a partner of Marcus Root in 1856. Root, by the way, also used a variety of operators, including Charles Williamson, one of the great masters of the mother-and-child portrait. During the year Cook operated for Brady, it was announced that Brady had completely given up daguerreotyping because of his sight and that he relied totally on his assistants; however, Brady had even employed an operator, James Brown, the first year he opened a studio.[20]

If an account of such complexity involving so few daguerreotypists can be pieced together from the fragmentary records that have survived, we can be certain that this early history is indeed a complicated affair. And what are we to conclude about Gurney and the Anthony Prize? If Lawrence felt it was justified to enter the work of his operators in a competition under his name, should we conclude that this was normal practice and a matter of course in the nineteenth century, or that Lawrence was being deceptive? Should the Anthony Prize have

gone to Gurney or to Fredericks or Carvalho or Perry? Or in being given to Gurney, would the attitude at that time have been that it was being awarded to the Gurney studio as a whole?

The entire field of photographic history is replete with such problems. I once saw a fine portrait signed "L. H. Purnell Artist Van Loan Gallery 159 Chestnut St. Phila." on the plush interior of the case. Though Samuel Van Loan was a well-known, respected daguerreotypist who won several awards, Purnell's name appears to be unrecorded. Was he a partner, an operator that Van Loan thought highly enough of to have his name impressed in velvet, or were the operators more autonomous than we had previously thought? Was a position in a gallery more like an independent franchise? The backdrop used in the Purnell image was the well-known one often used by Samuel Broadbent; in fact, it is commonly called the Broadbent backdrop and is used to identify his unsigned works. Broadbent did have several partners, though no Purnell is recorded as having been one of them. What should be concluded from these random facts, especially about Broadbent and his famous backdrop? The slightest study of the daguerreotype brings such problems to light; however, the difficulty is often not one of lost information but of a lack of insight or experience on our parts simply because we have not been able to see enough examples of someone's work.

The only way we can ever know the answers to many of the most obvious questions we can pose will be from studying large collections of individual makers' works. In the presence of several hundred images signed by Gurney and several hundred signed by Perry, we might be able to ascertain something of Perry's role at the Gurney studio. But until museums realize that not just the most spectacular and unusual daguerreotypes are worthy of their attention, that the ordinary American portrait daguerreotype is also an object worthy of being preserved, the research probably cannot be done. There are collectors who have amassed a great many examples of particular daguerreotypists' work, and we can only hope that they will publish monographs on those individual artists, monographs that combine factual research with reproductions of images. That is the only way any comparative study will be done, since our museums have neglected their responsibility to rescue the past and preserve it for the future. Massive archives of the work of almost every major American daguerreotypist could have been assembled during the past twenty years for a relatively small sum of money—and they still could be for only a fraction of their artistic and historical value.

And so at this point we are left having to invoke the concept of "Studio of" quite often, and even that vague expression has to be qualified when we are speaking of the chain studios. "Studio of Plumbe" means something considerably different from "Studio of Gurney." We can assume that there is something of Gurney's taste and eye and personality in each image that bears his name—that if he did not always serve as cameraman, he at least probably exercised some oversight, some quality control. But Plumbe's name on the plush pad in a daguerreotype case means about the same thing as the name Olan Mills on a photograph today. And the same is the case with Whitehurst's name, though the Whitehurst studio work that I have seen has always been quite fine, often remarkable, often better than work I have seen signed by Gurney. However, it doesn't allow us to conclude anything about Whitehurst himself as an artist. We do know from contemporary reports that his work was highly praised and honored, but in order to assess his role, not as entrepreneur and promoter but as artist, we must have a body of work that can be definitively ascribed to him. The fact is that we are stranded at a pre-Berensonian point in our studies. The grammar of daguerreian connoisseurship has not yet been written, and until it is, Berenson's advice is still the best: "You must look, and look, and look, until you are blind with looking, and out of that blindness will come illumination."[21]

Though some museums have not taken the time to look very seriously at the daguerreotype, many individuals have given it serious attention for a surprisingly long time. Writing in 1904 Pauline King said, "The soft, luminous shadows, the melting flesh-tones, the reality of life, are such that they may well excite the admiration and envy of skillful portrait-painters. This has been fully realized by connoisseurs, who have included large collections of daguerreotypes among their *objets d'art,* and the appreciation has extended until now there is a general searching for good examples of the art."[22]

A great many collectors, however, have devoted their energies to acquiring the most unusual or historically important images while neglecting the most artistic examples. Daguerreotypes of famous people, American scenic daguerreotypes, occupational portraits, men dressed oddly or other "humorous" images of people clowning around, photographs of blacks or Indians, images with elaborate painted backdrops or odd objects such as tools, clocks, and so forth, and erotic daguerreotypes are sometimes works of art, but more often than not they are merely records of the unusual thing they have glimpsed and can only be considered as historical artifacts or novelty items. Even with the interest shown in the daguerreotype today, the great portrait still suffers neglect while collectors scramble for curios.

The great portraits and landscapes are the rarest and artistically most important of all daguerreotypes. Though American daguerreotype portraits are of unrivaled quality, our scenic images were primarily documentation of our houses, farms, and shops, or in the case of Platt Babbitt's views of Niagara Falls, our vacations. Babbitt, whose work was quite artistic, was the first to realize the importance of vacation photographs. As Susan Sontag has pointed out, they "offer indisputable evidence that the trip was made, that the progress was carried out, that fun was had."[23] There is considerable historical importance to such images, like the popular but seldom artistic California gold mining scenes. They document a specific historical event, they are rare and costly, they excite many collectors, but few have a place in the history of art. And the same is the case with those other popular novelty images that I mentioned, particularly the occupational images and those with the often garishly painted backdrop. What is missing in them is that indefinable quality that Southworth spoke of and that Reynolds called intellectual beauty. Their oddness, their novelty is their only distinction; nothing else about them is special. However, novelty is not just a problem with the daguerreotype but with much of nineteenth-century art in general.

The Romantic sensibility, noble as its humanitarian aspects might have been, was a sensibility whose aesthetic was deeply imbued with an element of kitsch. Consequently, many of the "artistic" products of the nineteenth century cannot be considered fine art. Hermann Broch went so far as to call the nineteenth century "the century of kitsch" and argue that kitsch was a "specific product of Romanticism."[24] The reason, of course, is obvious and suggests one of Dr. Johnson's famous remarks: "The drama's laws the drama's patrons give." In other words, those with the power determine the art. And bourgeois power makes bourgeois art.

It is clear that in order to appreciate anything we must know what to look at and how to look or listen or judge, and this is true whether we are reading sonnets or watching a football game. Hardworking merchants who spend their hours over accounts might understandably find a Dutch genre painting of a cute child urinating, as Hogarth wittily and viciously shows us in *Marriage à la Mode,* as fine a thing as, for example, a Chardin still life of a copper pot because the untutored eye responds only to content, to meaning. The merchant can readily see the story in the painting of the impish child, but in Chardin's pots he can only see what hangs in his own kitchen and seems in no way out of the ordinary or "artistic," as he would understand the word. This same phenomenon applies in all the arts. The narrative quality of any work is obviously its most accessible, and the more removed a work of art is from narration, the more difficult it is to appreciate with an eye that has not learned how to look. The artistry of many daguerreotypes is, unfortunately, marred by the intrusion of just

such an element of kitsch, an element that attempts to impose a kind of narrative detail on a simple portrait, that offers to tell a story where none is needed.

This primarily appears in the use of the scenic backdrop and occupational materials. Both reflect the Romantic sensibility but at the same time are distracting intrusions. The woman posed against icebergs, an infamous portrait by Southworth and Hawes; the child in the midst of a swamp, complete with Spanish moss; the bare-bosomed woman holding a sickle and sitting before a wall of painted wheat; the nudes on a painted riverbank in front of several painted castles—these inspire more amusement than aesthetic contemplation. The growth of man's appreciation and worship of nature has been well chronicled and is an integral part of the rise of Romanticism. It is therefore understandable that he would want to be photographed in nature. The difficulty of out-of-doors daguerreian photography usually prevented this, and so the scenic backdrop came into being.

It also, of course, was a holdover from painting and its traditions. The daguerreotypist who saw himself more as a miniature painter than as an artist in a new form with a new medium to exploit would be more inclined to rely on the backdrop instead of recognizing the inherent photographic qualities of white, gray, or black space. But that requires thinking of the daguerreotype as daguerreotype, not as an unfinished canvas on which only the sitter has been painted in. It seems very easy for us today to understand that, but it was not so easy in the nineteenth century. The jury of the Crystal Palace Exhibition of 1851, though awarding Mathew Brady a medal, complained that his portraits "stand forward in bold relief, upon a plain background. The artist, having placed implicit reliance upon his knowledge of photographic science, has neglected to avail himself of the resources of art." Robert Taft noted that "In this last sentence, the jury is referring to the custom, introduced by Claudet, the London daguerreotypist, of placing painted backgrounds behind the sitter."[25] One can only admire

Anon.
(Europe),
half plate.
Collection of
Uwe Scheid.

Brady's insights into the aesthetics of a form barely ten years old.

The backdrop is, of course, still in use today; however, its narrative context has radically changed. Other than the crazy icebergs of Southworth and Hawes, I cannot recall having seen a truly false daguerreian backdrop, one that obviously lies about its sitter. I have not seen Spanish moss used by a Boston daguerreotypist, for example, or a castle by any American. I have seen castles in French and German daguerreotypes, highlands in Scottish daguerreotypes, and so forth, all with a kind of authenticity about them, though I am sure there are exceptions. What one usually sees is a sitter in a rather nondescript natural setting; there are some trees, a lake perhaps, maybe the moon, but nothing very unusual, nothing outside the bounds of possibility. Twentieth-century backdrops are all outside the bounds of possibility.

The large chain studios, which produce what we might call Mac-portraits, images of uniform sameness, dullness, and sweetness, pose their clients before Neuschwanstein or on the lawns of great plantation houses or beside rows of Scott novels and Bulwyer-Lytton bound in fake leather. If one looks closely, one will see that not only are the books fake but also the large library they suggest, for the backdrop itself is a composite. There are really only two or three rows, but they have been rephotographed on top of each other to make it appear that there are six or eight, and so the individual is posed before a pseudo-library that could only have been collected by a madman, for who would want two or even three sets of the *Waverley* novels all in the same edition? The narrative that the Mac-portrait wishes to suggest is, of course, one of sophistication and wealth. The Romantic age might have secretly worshiped Mammon while it sang Na-

Anon. (U.S.), sixth plate. Collection of Wm. B. Becker.

ture's praises, but contemporary American society is unashamed of its gods.

The so-called occupational portrait of the nineteenth century also presents a characteristically Romantic but artistically flawed image, because once again narrative has intruded. It is not the butcher's face we are drawn to but the plucked chicken he holds, not the carpenter himself but the saw he flourishes. The daguerreotype of a person actually in the process of his work is another matter. A blacksmith at the forge, the glassblowers in the factory, the cooper making his barrel—these rare and often beautiful images are what the occupational portrait aped, just as the scenic backdrop aped out-of-doors photography. A photograph of a man doing his work is a thing very different from a studio portrait of an individual holding the symbols of his work. What is essential in one is extraneous in the other. Though both have an element of narration, the narrative context is legitimate in one but a mere prop in the other. The man in his shop, even with its greater narrative context than the man posed in the studio, is a more convincing, more moving image because we trust the truth of the narrative; however, both types of occupational image

are more significant as social documents than as works of art. Both affirm the worth and value of the individual and the worth and value of his work. The occupational images are American democracy's best image and the most vigorous photographic statement of middle-class values and attitudes prior to Bill Owens's terrifying view of suburbia. The occupational image created a portraiture of social leveling and the elevation of the common man, and it is not surprising that it was primarily an American genre. What is most interesting in social terms, though, is that such images virtually disappeared from the American scene for a generation and have only recently resurfaced.

As Americans became more affluent in the late 1940s and early 1950s, it was no longer the individual's work he wanted chronicled; it was his leisure. Where the occupational daguerreotype made a statement about social equality based on the integrity of one's work, be he a fireman, policeman, or baker, the leisure photograph and the Olan Mills backdrop suggest equal affluence and equal wealth, a society in which everyone plays, lives on plantations, goes to Neuschwanstein, and reads Sir Walter Scott. Occupational photographs have returned, but it is Avedon and photographers like him who are making them. And it is their vision that desires them and sees a need for them, not the individuals who are being photographed; they still are going to Olan Mills and taking snapshots of wiener roasts. Artists have traditionally understood what was happening in a society before the society as a whole has. Though the new occupational portrait still suggests that the individual has pride in his or her work, it is clearly tinged with bitterness. The faces that look out at us from daguerreotypes are not the faces that look out from men and women working now in the late eighties. Today's faces, however, are not unique; August Sander caught the same expressions, or at least, expressions close enough to them to be unnerving.

Two other uniquely nineteenth-century kinds of images were produced in daguerreotype that also have come down to us with present-day analogues, but only after having gone through several trans-mutations. They are the postmortem portrait and the stereoscopic image, both of which were distinct products of nineteenth-century taste and reflections of the peculiar Victorian psyche. The desire to preserve an image of the dead is historical. The living do not want to let them slip away among the shades of memory, and so we have held on to them as best we can. We have taxidermied them, re-shaped them in stone and bronze, reduced them to two dimensions on paint and canvas, and then down to a few inches of silver, mercury, and light. However, between the Egyptians and the Victorians our natural necrophilia had receded consid-erably. Though death and loss are no less painful at one time than another, the sentimental vision that pervaded so many aspects of Victorian soci-ety seemed to be particularly directed toward chil-dren and death, and the camera's lens became the ideal eye through which to focus that vision. The postmortem portrait, therefore, proliferated. Da-guerreotypists, like embalmers today, took pride in their ability to make corpses appear to be sleeping, and they even advertised these talents!

Though postmortem portraits of all ages were produced, the majority understandably were of children. Even with as many images of death as we in this century have seen and as accustomed as we have grown to watching it televised nightly as news and entertainment, the daguerreotypes of those long-dead children haunt and disturb us like no previous time's images of death, other than per-haps the plaster molds of ash-engulfed Pompeians. And nothing since them but the death-camp photos can so pain us and evoke our pity. The daguerreo-type's brilliant immediacy, that sense of it being a little window into a real room, the sense that flesh is truly flesh and truly living, is probably a large part of the reason for our response—that and, as in the case of the Pompeian casts, death's immediacy; that it is not someone's memory or idealized por-trait of another individual's dying, but that it is death itself, recorded as intensely as a human can vicariously experience it.

But it is not just death alone that so affects us in these daguerreotypes. It is not so much a matter of content as it is of form, not so much a matter of eth-ics as it is of aesthetics. Long-gone children alone are not enough to evoke the painful response the daguerreian postmortem evokes. One can find as many paper cabinet cards, ambrotypes, and tin-types of the same subject, but they never quite so take us to that zero at the bone. The pain is inher-ent in the vitality of the daguerreotype's form, the fact that it looks more like reality than anything else we have ever seen.

Realizing how inappropriate the word *beautiful* must appear in such a context, I am still compelled to say that some of the most beautiful daguerreo-types I have seen are of dead children. Victorian sentimentality may have been the impetus behind the idea of memorializing a dead child in a da-guerreotype, but the images themselves do not come off anything like the usual products of that im-pulse—the dead child poem so popular with the Victorians, the cheap prints of dead or dying chil-dren surrounded by weeping parents, those trite, artless, though well-crafted photographic versions of the same prints, like Henry Robinson's "Fading Away," so *moving* that the Royal Couple them-selves purchased a print. It is the restraint of the postmortem daguerreotypes that elevates them to art. Robinson, whose technical ability was consid-erable, obviously wanted to move the viewer, but he chose to do it not through the simple presenta-tion of death and grief, powerful enough in them-selves to move us, but through all the extraneous trappings of death and grief, through sentimentality and cliché: the sad father with his back turned from the child, the stronger and more stoical mother looking on, braving up to the loss she is about to suffer. Compare "Fading Away" to the most inept daguerreian postmortem of parent and child, and the difference becomes quite clear. In the simple, anonymous, unadorned images of a solemn father holding his grief in his arms is pain so fresh and real that it rushes out from over a century to wrench us. We are left feeling something real and knowing something true about nineteenth-century mortality; we are left with what Robinson and his ilk wanted to convey.

I have seen a great many daguerreian postmortems, and every one of them is a refusal to mourn, a refusal to "blaspheme down the stations of the breath / With any further / Elegy of innocence and youth." Those simple portraits of death compel us in a way those with the more elaborate trappings never can. We believe one but not the other, and not just because we know one actually was real but because its narrative was not devised to move or teach or persuade or explain or propagandize. It is simply present, and there is not the slightest suggestion about how one ought to feel. Our compassion or empathy is not sought; however, we give it freely. And the power to make us do just that is the power of art. It is something even the most compassionate editorial, be it literary, graphic, photographic, or whatever, cannot evoke because we know we are being asked to give something no work of art can ever request, or ever has the right to request.

The postmortem portrait, though distinctly nineteenth century in its feeling, is, in a way, still with us. The emotion the postmortem generates is found today in photograph after photograph. From our vantage point of a century and a half of looking at photographs, we can see things present in them that were never intended by their makers. Time changes context, and its passage can alter the way a work is perceived because it allows us to create a new context for it. Outerbridge's or Zwart's great advertising photographs or Sheeler's industrial work barely suggest their original contexts to us today, a mere half century or so after they were made. Time's passage will continue to distance us from the original context of many photographs and alter our perceptions of them. The allure and meaning of such images lie in the fact that art was not their original purpose but is merely the child of time and our eye. The passage of time creates art as surely as artists create it, and just as time enlarges the eye's ability to perceive art, it also enlarges the eye's ability to perceive other cultural phenomena, such as our responses to sex, death, and money. Time lets us better see the economic demands placed on art by art's consumers, redefines aspects of the erotic, and in the case of photographs has turned them all into postmortems. Susan Sontag in one of her most perceptive remarks observed that "Photography is an elegiac art. . . . All photographs are *memento mori.*"[26] And all of them are sad and all are sweet and it is a wrenching dichotomy perhaps best expressed in metaphor: "It sits on top my desk, but it is faced / So that the sun will not cause it to fade: / The photographs we save are like the taste / Of honey on a sharpened razor blade."[27]

The stereoscopic daguerreotype, like any image viewed in a stereoscope, is an image of the greatest curiosity. Though it is supposed to present a more vivid representation of the real world than a two-dimensional photograph, it really doesn't. It looks like an instant caught between the dimensions, not two-dimensional but not exactly three-dimensional either, or at least not three-dimensional in terms of the way depth is actually perceived. Most stereos look staged and contrived and less like the real world than they do when viewed without the stereoscopic effect. It is as if depth only had two or three points, and they are so singular and striking that everything else appears out of synchronization with reality. The only thing the stereoscopic image looks like that I can recall is one of the strangest images from my childhood, View-Master reels of fairy tales. I still remember the little house of sticks and how oddly it seemed to stand out from the pig and wolf dolls. Of course, View-Master and stereoscope are similar contraptions. The only thing from the real world the stereoscopic effect is comparable to is a stage set. Imagine a flat two-dimensional cactus or two at the front of a stage and a little farther back a flat two-dimensional front of a saloon and behind that mountains painted on a curtain, and you will have imagined a stereograph. The oddness of the stereoscopic effect is diminished in the portrait because less depth is usually present, and so the resulting image is often quite compelling, and that effect coupled with the daguerreotype's physical intensity can make the stereoscopic portrait daguerreotype a powerful image.

The three-dimensional effects of the stereo made it an obvious vehicle for erotica, and though some of the erotic stereos are quite beautiful and their sexuality intense and arousing, a great many are not. The models are often grandly unattractive. One need not have a beautiful face to make a great portrait, but any nude study emphasizes not just the face but the entire body, especially those parts not usually seen. And any portrait of a nude body is in some way a sexual statement and draws attention to the body's sexuality, other than in the case of the very young and the very old, where the point of the nudity is the lack of sexuality either because it has not yet developed or because it has departed. Sexuality cannot be separated from nudity in art, nor should it be. Man's response to sex, to death, and to God (or Nature, since the late eighteenth century) are the three primary subjects of all art, literary and visual both. They are the grand passions and concerns of our existence and are inextricably woven together into the fabric of our personalities and experience. They grow inseparable from one another and become our obsessions and our joys. We yearn after them and fear them, and that fear and yearning animate our personalities and give meaning to our lives. They become, therefore, the subjects of our art, especially photography, which is surely the most sensual and erotic of all the arts—and for many of the same reasons the most elegiac.

And so, if a portrait attempts a sexual statement, as any nude portrait does excepting those I have mentioned, then it must be stated in what might be called a grammar of sexuality. If it is not, then it fails to communicate its sexuality, and that is what happens in many of the so-called erotic daguerreotypes. The models simply do not communicate sexuality; they are images of graceless nudity. Diane Arbus gave us the same figures, but it is clear that she deliberately eschewed a sexual grammar in her nudes, and that fact was a major technical aspect of her art because it allowed her to create a sense of conflict and tension between what she appeared to be saying and what she in reality was saying. Her nudes, though cast in an apparent sexual grammar, are refutations of sexuality. However, Bruno Braquehais, whose work is an accidental equivalent of Arbus, meant no such refutation, and he was not alone in his use of bodies that refute and deny their sexuality while disporting themselves in a sexual fashion. Such works fail both as erotica and as art.

The stereoscopic nude seemed to bring out the worst in many photographers. A profusion of props that could only be termed junk was the stylistic scrawl of Braquehais. I avoid the word *kitsch* in this instance because it has come to confer a kind of artistic legitimacy, albeit a sham legitimacy, on works like Bouguereau's paintings, for instance, which Braquehais's photographs do not deserve. But just as Braquehais was not alone in his use of models that blunted sexuality, he was not alone in his use of props that blunted the potentiality for art. Some daguerreotypists used hookahs and turbans to suggest the pleasures of the harem, or brought straw into the studio to symbolize the pastoral delights, or relied on a variety of tacky backdrops to conjure up exotic spots. Though a painting and a photograph should not be judged in the same way, it is axiomatic that if something would be trite in a painting, it would also be trite in a photograph. We should be no less demanding of photography than we are of painting; nor should we accept as art in a photograph something we would ridicule in a painting.

The Romantic obsession with nature and its worship had led to the invention of photography. The devotee demanded icons for his adoration, and Daguerre's silvered fragments of still nature, foster children of silence and slow time, were as ideal as the polychrome saints an earlier day had demanded. The re-creation of nature was the goal, and the stereoscope brought the daguerreotype and photograph a little closer to achieving it. It was the same nineteenth-century impulse that inspired

Mary Shelley and her priestly scientist, that created television and holograms and the rituals of plastic surgery and chemotherapy, and that now points toward the android, that fruition of the Romantic dream, the living photograph, the final image of ourselves.

NOTES

1. Walter Benjamin, "The Work of Art in the Age of Mechanical Reproduction," in *Illuminations,* trans. Hannah Arendt (New York: Harcourt, Brace & World, 1968), p. 229.

2. Arnold Hauser, *The Philosophy of Art History* (New York: Alfred A. Knopf, 1958), p. 3.

3. M. Susan Barger, "Robert Cornelius and the Science of Daguerreotypy," in William F. Stapp, *Robert Cornelius: Portraits from the Dawn of Photography* (Washington, D.C.: Smithsonian Institution Press, 1983), p. 117.

4. Barger, "Robert Cornelius," p. 115.

5. Frederick Turner and Ernst Pöppel, "The Neural Lyre: Poetic Meter, the Brain, and Time," *Poetry* 142 (August 1983): 284.

6. Alain Lesieutre, *The Spirit and Splendor of Art Deco* (New York: Paddington Press, 1974), p. 7.

7. T. S. Arthur, "The Daguerreotypist," *Godey's Lady's Book* 38 (1849): 352.

8. Gabriel Harrison, "The Dignity of our Art," *Photographic Art Journal* 3 (1852): 230.

9. Marcus Root, *The Camera and the Pencil* (Philadelphia: J. B. Lippincott, 1864), pp. xiv–xv.

10. Albert S. Southworth, "An Address to the National Photographic Association of the United States," *Philadelphia Photographer* 8 (October 1871): 321. Subsequent references will appear in the text.

11. Joshua Reynolds, *Discourses on Art,* edited by Robert R. Wark (San Marino, Calif.: Huntington Library, 1959), pp. 146, 41, 42, 44. Subsequent references will appear in the text.

12. A. Lincoln Bowles, "A Famous Boston Studio," Boston *Sunday Herald,* March 12, 1893.

13. Henry Moore, "An Interview," *World Press Review* 30 (July 1983): 35.

14. Abraham Bogardus, "The Lost Art of the Daguerreotype," *Century Magazine* 68 (May 1904): 89.

15. John Mascher, *Humphrey's Journal* 10 (July 1, 1858): 67.

16. Ansel Adams, *The Print: Contact Printing and Enlarging* (New York: Morgan & Morgan, 1950), p. 2.

17. I am speaking of those monuments of landscape and architectural daguerreotypy, works such as Alexandre Clausel's "Landscape near Troyes" or Baron Jean Gros' "Propylaea from Inside the Acropolis," possibly the two greatest daguerreotypes ever made, or Frederick von Martens' "Panorama of Paris," Lorenzo Suscipj's "Piazza del Popolo," J. W. Pero's views of Lubeck, or Richebourg's views of Rome.

18. See Harold Francis Pfister, *Facing the Light: Historic American Portrait Daguerreotypes* (Washington, D.C.: Smithsonian Institution Press, 1978), p. 321.

19. Beaumont Newhall, *The Daguerreotype in America* (New York: Dover, 1976), p. 46. And Charles Moore in his excellent *Two Partners in Boston: The Careers and Daguerreian Artistry of Albert Southworth and Josiah Hawes* (Ann Arbor: University Microfilms, 1975), making reference to a letter from Hawes and an advertisement of the firm's, writes, "Both Albert Southworth and Josiah Hawes personally posed the sitters and manipulated the plates and camera" (1:13). However, the studio, which also sold cameras and supplies, did naturally employ others, including, as colorist, Nancy Southworth Hawes, Josiah's wife and Albert's sister, and it is possible that some of the employees, such as Asa Southworth, who did become a daguerreotypist, did do some camera work.

20. The information in this paragraph is for the most part pieced together from Floyd and Marion Rinhart's biographies of professional and amateur daguerreotypists that appear in *The American Daguerreotype* (Athens: University of Georgia Press, 1981). Those forty-some-odd pages of tedious details dug from city and business directories, magazines, journals, and the like represent some of the most dedicated daguerreian scholarship of which I am aware. Such research is not glamorous and rewards the researcher with little praise for having done it, but it is what the true spirit of research, the real quest for knowledge, is all about, and it is the necessary groundwork that must first be laid before anything else can be done. The quotations concerning Perry appear in the *Photographic Art Journal* 1 (1851): 124, 191; and 2 (1852): 258; and concerning Brady, *PAJ* 1 (1851): 136. The 1853 date for Fredericks' joining Gurney comes from Newhall, *The Daguerreotype in America,* p. 66.

21. Quoted by J. Carter Brown in "A Personal Reminiscence," in *Looking at Pictures with Bernard Berenson* (New York: Abrams, 1974), p. 18.

22. Pauline King, "The Charming Daguerreotype," *Century Magazine* 68 (May 1904): 81.

23. Susan Sontag, *On Photography* (Farrar, Straus & Giroux, 1977), p. 9.

24. Hermann Broch, "Notes on the Problem of Kitsch," in Gillo Dorfles, *Kitsch: The World of Bad Taste* (New York: Universe Books, 1969), pp. 53, 61.

25. Robert Taft, *Photography and the American Scene: A Social History, 1839–1889* (1938; reprint New York: Dover, 1964), p. 70.

26. Sontag, *On Photography,* p. 15.

27. John Wood, "Elegiac Stanza on a Photograph of Ethel Rosenberg in Her Kitchen," *Poetry* 132 (July 1978): 200.

Rembrandt

Perfected

Ben Maddow

In March 1839 Samuel Morse, in a greatly quoted letter from Paris, wrote that Daguerre's own daguerreotypes were "Rembrandt perfected." Now Morse was no ignorant admirer; he was a painter (his *Death of Hercules* had made him famous), but also the master of a vigorous and balanced literary style, and it was characteristic of the age that all knowledge should be the province of the educated man. Morse had, by his own account, tried as early as the 1820s to fix the image of the camera obscura, that magical inversion of the world; and surely he was not the only savant with a library in the house and gadgets in the tool shed. He, among a score of others, invented the telegraph and gave his name to the Morse Code. So he quite understood what Niepce and Daguerre had wrought, which was a beautiful leap, not of science, but of technology, and the first time that an art was immaculately born of chemistry.

The beauty of the daguerreotype, as he and his contemporaries saw it, was a compound of awe and delight. Of course, there was a strong naturalist bias in nineteenth-century American art—laced with a heavy sweetener of sentiment. Nature and man, each of them the handicraft of God, were best unaltered and unabashed; craggy rocks and craggy foreheads were admired for their own rude force. God gave man dominion, and man, though rendered small by the great verticals and horizontals of American landscape, nevertheless dominated it as a master surveys his still-untamed estate. Our fright at the blind ungovernable force in the heart

of the atom was not to come for a hundred years. So Morse looked at the daguerreotype in his hand with an admiration that did not separate truth from beauty. And not only his peers among the American elite, but the ordinary craftsman or farmer or housewife—or child, for that matter—reacted as he did when they, too, first saw this polished gem of discovery, with a smile of pure and wonderful pleasure.

The literate minority expressed their astonishment in terms that were quite uniform: daguerreotypes were "charming," "enchanting," "exquisitely perfect," "a miracle," "exquisite and delicate," "a piece of fairy work," "marvelous," "brilliant," "wonderful," and "of infinite sensibility." The fact that it was the energy of the sunlight that split apart the bonds of the silver halide was too tempting a symbol to be neglected: " . . . light, the element which gives beauty to our planet, and sheds gladness over all things, by the touch of its Ithuriel wand . . ."[1] Such fancy rhetoric is the expression, in mid-nineteenth-century America, of the unique thrill of seeing photographs of any sort for the very first time. A new pleasure had come into the world, and its unique perfection had not yet had time to be perverted: that would be a job more suited to the last decades of our bloody and cynical twentieth century.

Then how much of this original pleasure remains for us? A great deal, I think. Imagine that here in my hand is a daguerreotype, still closed, waiting for the revelation of its image. It is not famous, it will never be reproduced; it is one of the hundreds of thousands, in the United States alone, made between 1839 and the late 1850s. The plate, as if it were a jewel, is enclosed in a case stamped front and back with scrollwork in the rococo curves common to frames, but in miniature. The image inside is only 2¾ × 3¼ inches, the size of one's palm. Unlike any but the smallest paintings, it is an intimate art, meant for only one person at a time, and just barely that. One undoes the two small clasps and unfolds the case into its two matching parts. On the left is a rectangle of purple velvet, bordered with gold leaves and embossed with still another set of curves. The right-hand panel, seen straight on, is baffling: here is a mirror in which one sees oneself, but only partly, because the face is somehow enlarged and therefore, by its distinctness, just a bit uncomfortable. Superimposed on one's too-familiar face, or floating upon it, are three ghosts, gray negative faces with blank eyes and mouths and the shade of some sort of disembodied clothing. But then the miracle: you turn the mirror ever so slightly and three full characters blaze out at you—a man, his daughter, and his wife. They are not merely an amalgam of mercury and silver on a copper surface, but frozen forever, or almost forever—a piece of the world with all its splendid ambiguity.

And now one is able to see the wonderful, minute gradations of tone from the white of the man's collar, starched and bent like tin plate, through the darker tones of his heavy open jacket, and still darker, his waistcoat in subtle rolls over a middle-aged paunch, to the tie as black as a stroke of ink. And the woman's dark silk coruscates with folds of precise light, and the daughter's gray thick modest dress is a wedge between father and mother. The clothing of these three people occupies two-thirds of the plane, a value natural to the nineteenth century, where clothes marked not merely fashion but a person's place in life, however temporary. Yet it is the cluster of the three faces—husband, daughter, wife—that seizes and fixes one's attention. The girl, perhaps nine or ten, has the tiny frown of anxious childhood; a hand on the shoulder of each parent,

she is attached on either side, needs their support, and bears it.

There are no smiles in this daguerreotype, no false grimace of teeth. The wife is the grimmest of the three. Her frown, her mouth, are curves bent forcefully downward, as if life in this marriage is not joy but duty. Her husband, though, thinks he dominates the scene. His face is almost as broad as it is high; the forehead is a vast cliff; the nose snorts authority from its dark nostrils; the mouth is vast, straight, and firm. His will tyrannizes him most of all. There is a family novel compressed here into the rectangle of this small daguerreotype: a biopsy of how fiercely one had to live in the mid-nineteenth century. Now pry open the frame. On the paper behind it one can read the faded names: "L. M. Spencer, Miss Louise Spencer, Mrs. L. M. Spencer." If the photograph was meant for family and posterity, the wife's first name was not worthy of mention. Put the daguerreotype back in its snug frame, close and shut the two tiny brass clasps; the lives are locked in preservative darkness again, and will outlast those of us who have stared at it, moved and fascinated.

Here in the daguerreotype there is not merely art but a brilliant and novel art, miraculous in its detail of dress and character, of tonality between contrast. Yet it was an art accepted without hesitation by vast numbers of ordinary mankind—not just in Paris, where it was born, but in undeveloped America, Brazil, Russia, and China. It was, from birth, a vernacular art, and vernacular art has a certain constant aesthetic, felt but not easy to define. We may get at it by induction, by examining other popular arts, and they have great variety, but constant qualities.

Children's drawings are surely a vernacular art: the same all over the world, as if the children were in secret international communication. Jazz is another fine example: a compound, almost chemical in its perfection, of African tribal solo and response, French dance tunes of the nineteenth century, and contrapuntal percussion of the slave cultures of the Caribbean. Jazz was segregated for a long time, but

Albert Southworth and Josiah Hawes (U.S.), sixth plate. Collection of George S. Whiteley IV.

burst out of its confinement in the late twenties. Almost as sudden as the splendor of the daguerreotype were the 78-rpm records of Louis Armstrong's "Hot Five" or "Hot Seven": vital, rude, emotional, complex and contrapuntal, performed by musicians who, some of them, could not even read music, but who had been trained in performance since they were teenagers. And again, like daguerreotypes, jazz was always in direct warm contact with its listeners, and not least in the specificity of its lyrics.

> Every night I got me
> Rocks in my bed
> Since you gone and left me
> Rocks in my bed.

Another such vernacular art is the Gypsy flamenco, with its ancient, Mediterranean, ululating lines of melody—expressive, specific, polished by multiple performance. Listen to a woman singing:

> In the street down below
> Goes him whom I love;
> I can't see his face,
> Only the top of his hat.

It's all very visual, like a Rodchenko angle downward. As in the small compass of the daguerreotype in one's hand, one sees the characteristically laconic quality of such arts.

A less obvious vernacular art is the silent black and white movie prior to 1929. Here one can see the process that is one of the unfortunate consequences of the energetic life of the vernacular. The succinct gems like the early Griffiths and Chaplins and Buster Keatons—raw, vital, brilliant, and close to the life of their audience—had to give way, by their very popularity, to the prolixity and sentimentality of mass art. It is inevitable: like it or not we live, and as a species have always lived, in an interactive society; so the life of a pure vernacular art, as it breaks the bounds of its first audience, is certain to be altered and cheapened. Daguerreotypes had that pristine force of a new art, but the later ones became cheap and shabby; and the collodion process, and its even simpler and cheaper successors, made photography the toy of the masses. Since 1840 billions of amateur photographs have been made, and some of these lost and unknown snapshots must have been quite remarkable (evidence,

Anon. (U.S.), quarter plate. Collection of George S. Whiteley IV.

unequally, of obscure talent and simple chance), while the vast majority of all photographs, amateur or professional—or even famous—are aesthetically poor.

The fate of the new art of photography was a classic one; there was a double consequence: while the art was becoming universal and mediocre, it was also taken up by self-conscious artists, many of them refugees from the other graphic arts. By the 1890s the traditional purity of the daguerreotype gave way to manipulation by brush and chemical, and while the results were sometimes especially beautiful in the current mode of secondhand romanticism, they were much more often quite dreadful. In either consequence, the native precision of the daguerreotype was blunted and forgotten. The result is that vernacular art has, characteristically, a brief if powerful life. A good guess would be that within the two decades between 1840 and 1860 some 30 million daguerreotypes were made, mostly portraits, and most of these—another consequence of vernacular art—were fated to be neglected and destroyed.

Because when an art becomes too easy, it loses its energy; it is no longer separated from the amusements of ordinary life. This blur of distinction between art and reality is especially true of the daguerreotype. The very accuracy of its detail, confined though it is to a small rectangle of flat mirror that must be viewed at just the right angle, generates a tension that fascinates and deceives. Small children, as an interesting example of the way we are, read the photograph of a room as truth in miniature, while a model of the same room is useless. And when they grow up, the confusion of truth and art persists, though the story is now part of the folklore of professionals. I was in fact witness to an incident where an elderly woman was complimented on the beauty of her grandson, and replied, "That's nothing, you should see his pictures." We might laugh, but it's part of our mythology, too. There are, in our minds as well as in hers, degrees of verity, and photographs are especially charged with the magnetism of a more truthful truth—partly, one might guess, because once taken they are mysteriously immortal.

Of all the special qualities of the daguerreotype, which it shares with all photographs, the most powerful is its engagement with the inconstant society of its own time. It is impossible to disentangle the subject of a daguerreotype from the abstract black and white pattern on the plate; the facts of history, both public and private, suffuse and vivify daguerreotypes like oxygen. Take a long look in your memory at the earliest portrait of Lincoln, 1847, when he was thirty-eight. We cannot see him as simply a shrewd country lawyer. We project the oncoming tragedy because we already know it; we see Lincoln's face as it will become, as Whitman described it in 1863: "The President . . . has a face like a hoosier Michael Angelo, so awful ugly it becomes beautiful, with its strange mouth, its deep cut, crisscross lines, and its doughnut complexion."[2]

The Lincoln that Whitman describes appears in the marvelous and anonymous portrait of 1860, and again we project the horrors of that bloodiest war of the nineteenth century, even though it has not yet happened.

Equally fascinating, because they reveal the sensuous, carnal aspect of nineteenth-century America, are the studies by the Boston partners Albert Southworth and Josiah Hawes of the then-notorious performer Lola Montez. The people who bought copies of her daguerreotype already knew a great deal about her, but we, more than a hundred years later, know a great deal more: that her true name was plain Betty Gilbert and that she was born in Ireland of an English father and a Spanish mother, that she grew up in Calcutta, married at sixteen, separated at twenty-two, became a dancer (and a miserable one, according to contemporary accounts) under the invented name of Lola Montez, and resorted to prostitution when she was desperate; was expelled from Warsaw by the Russians for a political speech; had a one-month affair with Franz Liszt, and a much longer one with the king of Bavaria, for whom, on their first meeting, she tore her dress open to dazzle him with her perfection, and to such effect that she became a power in the Jesuit politics of the country. With lurid stories about herself, many untrue, and some invented by her, she was enlarged into an international scandal,

until she was banished from Bavaria, arrested in London for bigamy, and fled to America, where she became immensely popular in a play about—who else?—herself.

Did not the partners in this famous daguerreotype gallery know much of this when Lola Montez was invited into their studios in 1851? Very likely they did, and their pleasure in this notorious personality emanates like the rich perfume we imagine she wore; and her sidelong posture, no doubt self-chosen, is somehow far more erotic than a portrait straight on, and even more particularly the dark gloves, the cigarette, and the bold and tilted face. So the portrait, like Lola Montez herself, depicts a calculated and subtle eroticism.

For the underside of all vernacular art is pornography. It is to be found today at any newsstand, no longer hidden, and it obeys the laws of vernacular art by its harsh emotion, its pitiless detail, its rude but precise force. In the more subtle time of the daguerreotype, nudity was not gynecological, merely unclothed. That it was meant to be stimulating, one would have to be truly innocent to doubt, and yet, with the invisible patina of time, such nudes have become beautiful, and even charming. But they have a more sinister quality, too: these plump beauties are all now safely dead, and pathos colors our perception. Indeed, this is true of all daguerreotypes. They are portraits of our common past, and bring to mind both the genius and the bloody crimes of our species; they record the splendor of our poets and the disgrace of our petty patriots. One is tempted, as some have, to think of the body of daguerreotypes as a form of collective American memory.

If only it were true!—but we in this country are famous for the blind destruction of our past. One is tempted to blame the incessant fires of the nineteenth century, when buildings were made of wood and flame from an overturned lamp or sparks from a fireplace or an iron stove turned our silver memories into smoke. Certainly it was that, too, but it was mostly that we didn't care. We no longer lived, as Europeans did, in the houses of our grandparents; we had moved on, hundreds or thousands of miles, dissolving the rich ties of family and leaving the daguerreotypes behind in barrels of trash. Again, one of the terrible laws of vernacular art is that it is fragile, temporary, ephemeral, and often misused and misunderstood by the very audience for which it was intended. Daguerreotypes were not simply works of art; they were souvenirs of those we loved, and when they were dead, and so were their children and grandchildren, the daguerreotypes' use was gone. If they survived, they were mostly nameless, whether subject or artist, or if named, unknown. It's in our time that daguerreotypes are resurrected and their vitality and their beauty—qualities irreversibly intertwined—give us the pleasures of their company.

One is still astonished by their peculiar brilliance. The tones from blinding white to dense black are a great spectrum of fine distinctions. The scale, to use a professional term, is stretched, and the gradations are infinitesimal. The texture of damask, of lace, of sturdy waistcoat, thick white cravat, trousers so heavy they would, one thinks, stand up even when empty, the sheen of silk, of wool polished by wear—all are rendered so marvelously in the daguerreotype that they are more real, in their distinctions, than reality itself. Indeed, one of the astonishments of the daguerreotype is the degree to which one can magnify a portion and still see more, and yet more, as if there were no end to the elaborations of reality and we would come at last to the atoms of silver and mercury locked together. But to call this reality is, of course, an interesting illusion. We know, or think we know, that atoms, or rather the quarks from which they are assembled, are just tiny nodes of energy, separated by the vast space of subatomic fields, and a photograph made of such points is no more than a simulacrum: the geometric projection of the world onto a plane surface, which, in the case of the daguerreotype, is a highly polished copper sheet. Our brains do the rest: we reconstruct reality from infinite and faulty evidence. This illusion, that we know where we are and what we are seeing, is nec-

Samuel Root (U.S.), quarter plate. Collection of Joan Murray.

essary and sufficient; its fractional truth must suffice. And it is one of the high qualities of the daguerreotype that it appears to give us almost as much information as our own eyes.

Yet here, too, in the perfection of this process, there are subtle failures as well as subtle splendors. Why is it that daguerreotypes of the landscape, on the whole, are so mediocre? And those of the urban scene, with some interesting exceptions, not much better? One would expect the same pleasure in the chiaroscuro of leaves or of walls, as in foreheads and lace, but this is rare. It is always difficult, in any of the graphic arts, to compose a convincing landscape, but in photography one cannot, as one can in painting, transpose a tree, lower or raise a hill, shift or cancel massive boulders. One can only crop the margins; the rest is immovable.

But this is not the full or intrinsic explanation for the failure of the daguerreotype with the distant and

Anon. (U.S.), sixth plate. Collection of Julian Wolff.

the impersonal. One suspects that the daguerreotype is somehow more comfortable with the intimate, with the close texture of portraits, with those intricate maps of character: people's faces. Today these nineteenth-century portraits have an intensity unequaled by other and easier means of photography. If we look at, e.g., the portraits of Edgar Allan Poe or of Daniel Webster it's as if we long knew these men, and not merely as chilling writer and mental necrophiliac, and not only as thundering orator, but as neighbors, as close friends or cousins. Through the mirror of the daguerreotype we see, or think we see, into their inexpressible souls.

It's been said that this intensity is only irritation—that the iron half-circle that supported the head during exposure (already in use by portrait painters) was an instrument of mental torture. But was it? It's true that the exposure time in 1839 was a good half hour. None but the anesthetized could sit perfectly still for that long, but by the 1840s the exposure had been cut down by various optical means to three or at most five minutes, and by the end of the decade, to a matter of seconds. The won-

derful daguerreotype we have of young Mark Twain has the direct stare of a perfectly serious boy of fifteen; if he blinked or twitched, the camera never noticed it.

A second and more ingenious explanation of their intensity is that many daguerreotype portraits were of a special class of persons: those of greater achievement or of higher income. Certainly at first, daguerreotypes were relatively expensive: $7.00 apiece, then $5.00, or even as low as $3.00. By 1853 a good daguerreotype could be obtained for $2.00. But to understand what these figures mean, and who could afford them, one must compare them with the cost of living in the 1840s and 1850s. Such figures are hard to find, but one can judge from the pay of a carpenter or a mason in 1850 that it would have been about $1.50 a day.[3] So it would have taken a couple of days' pay for a single daguerreotype—an indulgence not likely to be made. And these figures were for skilled labor; the common laborer earned $1.00 a day or less. Few men would work a third of a week to pay for a daguerreotype at a good studio like Brady's. Of course, eventually there were hundreds of daguerreotype parlors in-

*Anon. (U.S.),
sixth plate.
Collection of
Paul Missal.*

competent enough to charge only fifty cents, but their work was careless and miserable.

To a land-owning farmer, to a doctor or lawyer or businessman, a fine daguerreotype was ten times cheaper than an oil portrait; it followed that the more prosperous classes in the United States were most frequently photographed. It is therefore plausible, if not certain, that strong, confident, assertive men and their families, unashamed, even boastful of their own character, and prospering in the growing nation, would dominate the daguerreotypes we see today. And the more prosperous and thus the more stable families would be rather more likely to keep the pictures of their ancestors we treasure today.

These formidable men appear, often enough, surrounded by wife and children, and one can read quite plainly in these double or triple portraits, in the set of the man's jaw and the frown that protects his direct and powerful eyes, the self-satisfied tyranny of father and husband. And yet occasionally one sees in a family portrait a furious and dominant wife, for mother, too, could be brutal. So the wonderful thing about family daguerreotypes is their frank revelation: it is as though the dazzling and disturbing light of the daguerreotype studio penetrates backward into the shuttered privacy of bedroom and kitchen.

Still a third possible reason for the stern mien and the posture of grim energy momentarily frozen on the plate is the daily expectation of illness and death. In 1850, in as civilized a state as Massachusetts, which already had a settled economy, a man could expect to live only to forty, and a woman a bit more. Children, in fact, were the most numerous dead, and in Massachusetts the death rate for babies under one year was 13 in 100.[4] If death was common, it was nonetheless tragic. The imminent expectation of death can be heard in the mid-century poetry of Emily Dickinson. And American religion, mostly Protestant and evangelical, promised death around the next corner, and Hell shortly afterward. The grand optimism of American character was a product of the energies of the immigration: young, healthy, ambitious people, already bold enough to leave their farms and villages and come to an unknown country—and these optimists did not show themselves in American portraiture until the latter

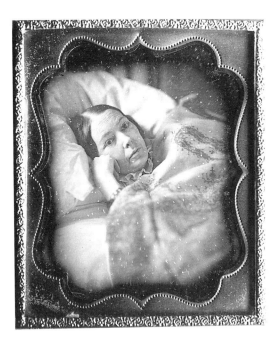

Anon. (U.S.), sixth plate. Collection of Mark Koenigsberg.

part of the century. It is not that illness and death were universally on the minds of the sitters; it is that the hard experience of life had marked the face and posture for years before that brief moment of exposure.

A fourth reason, the most reasonable but the hardest to prove, is that American society of the 1840s and 1850s did not require the use of social masks. Men were what they were; their lifelong decisions, not their temporary emotions, worked like sculptors on their faces. We see what men were because they were proud of their own character and disdained to hide. Who among the American political figures of the last fifty years can match the presence of a Daniel Webster, an Andrew Jackson in his old age, a John C. Calhoun, a Jefferson Davis or William Lloyd Garrison or Frederick Douglass or John Brown? We can read in their daguerreotypes their pride, their force, their integrity—and their vices. These are the faces of giants. That we can see them so beautifully today is one of the great treasures left to us out of the complex American past.

So much, out of much more, can be said of that electric synapse between the object and the viewer, but there was another partner in this experience:

the maker of the daguerreotype. He was often unconscious or even clumsy in his work, but amazingly often he was fully cognizant of what he was after: "A good daguerreotype is by no means a mere machine following a certain set of fixed rules. Success in this art requires personal skill and artistic taste to a much greater degree than the unthinking public generally imagine."[5]

And more technically:

> Those who undertake daguerreotype portraitures, will of course arrange the backgrounds of their pictures according to their own tastes. When one that is quite uniform is required, a blanket, or a cloth of a drab color, properly suspended, will be found to answer very well. Attention must be paid to the tint. . . . It will readily be understood that if it be desired to introduce a vase, an urn, or other ornament, it must not be arranged against the background, but brought forward until it appears perfectly distinct upon the obscured glass of the camera.[6]

It is interesting to ponder, once again, the famous dicta by Southworth:

> What is to be done is obliged to be done quickly. The whole character of the sitter is to be read at first sight; the whole likeness, as it shall appear when finished, is to be seen at first, in each and all its details, and in their unity and combinations. Natural and accidental defects are to be separated from natural and possible perfections; these latter to obliterate or hide the former. Nature is not at all to be represented as it is, but as it ought to be, and might possibly have been; and it is required of and should be the aim of the artist-photographer to produce in the likeness the best possible character and finest expression of which that particular face or figure could ever have been capable. But in the result there is to be no departure from truth in the delineation and representation of beauty, and expression, and character.[7]

What is exceptional in this passage is the virtue

of humility: the admiration for reality, the dependence on what is actually there, and the absolute value of truth—the truth of appearance and the truth of character. The daguerreotypist is humble before the variegated world, but he does not abdicate control. Reverence for the subject and a keen and rapid observation—these are combined with the responsibility of the artist, which is to take hold of, and govern, the apparent chaos of particularity and make order out of the chaos of truth. It was only then, when these double and contradictory powers were balanced by the judgment of the artist, that great daguerreotypes were possible. It is quite wonderful that in a wholly novel art—the creation of beauty by nonhuman means—there should have been so many fine craftsmen. Southworth and Hawes were only two out of hundreds of talented daguerreotypists; most have faded into the past like their copper plates. The brilliance of what we have now is proof of how many people have both creative talent and the faculty of close observation. In the early years their number was great, perhaps because the depression of the early 1840s in America freed them from their normal pursuits.

These men (there were very few women) began the great photographic tradition of humility tempered by control. The best of their successors, though with quite different techniques, have walked in their effulgent footsteps. The infinite riches of the human face, posture, and clothing have been arranged into art, to give some favorite examples, by men as different as Nadar, Paul Strand, Bill Brandt, and Walker Evans, and by the enigmatic Bellocq, who lifted pornography into pathos. And there are scores of others, little-known Americans like Joseph Smith of Kansas, Solomon Butcher of Nebraska, and Adam Vroman of New Mexico, who had this necessary humility before their subjects and yet remained in conscious control of what they made. Still another, and perhaps the greatest and purest of vernacular artists, was Eugene Atget. His reverence before the heavy roots of a tree or the nostalgia of a marble staircase or the confusion of a rag-picker's van or the sturdy whore on her bold

Albert Southworth and Josiah Hawes (U.S.), sixth plate. Portrait of James Jackson Lowell, nephew of James Russell Lowell, who eulogized him in The Biglow Papers. *Here he holds a copy of Charles Dickens's Christmas story "The Chimes." Collection of Dafydd Wood.*

chair in the street was transformed, framed, and composed by a most subtle hand.

The reader will have noticed, in all this, the prejudice of the author, who acknowledges his love for the particular and his contempt for the vague and the symbolic. It is, in the end, a moral issue, and if so, one ought to examine the present state of the photographic arts (as Ansel Adams said he did) by the cruel standards of the daguerreotype. In contemporary work, one can see both arms of the aesthetic lopped off and thrown away. Certain photographers imitate the nihilism of a Marcel Duchamp, as expressed by the immensely influential John Cage: "Our poetry now is the realization that we possess nothing. Anything therefore is a delight."[8] They allow chance to choose its own image on their work, or shoot at random without looking through the finder. This aleatory art, modestly useful in the graphic arts and perhaps in music, but a failure in poetry, has produced some strangely interesting photographs, though a robot could do as well. Images found by chance and chance alone make pretentious the humility before the world that one praises in the great photographers. Yet another mannerism that pretends to respect its subject pro-

Anon. (U.S.), half plate. Collection of Richard and Christine Rydell.

duces photographs of monstrosities that are dangerously close to exploitation; they are an abased and joyless form of pornography.

But far more fashionable these days is the opposite vice: excessive control, which is a distortion of neoexpressionist values. Content no longer matters, or is reduced to the inconsequential and the absurd. Empty sequences of nonencounters at a street corner; blurred self-portraits in hideous color—the reenactment of banal and sentimental personal fantasies; the montage of a hundred evenly boring landscapes: all assert the primacy of the artist and his scorn for the world outside him. This view, sadly, is hardly a new polemic. Whitman said of contemporary poems: "Nothing can be more utterly contemptible. Instead of mighty and vital breezes, proportionate to our continent, with its powerful races of men, its tremendous historic events, its great oceans, its mountains and its illimitable prairies, I find a few little silly fans languidly moved by shrunken fingers."[9]

But the arts, in the long run, are self-correcting. One can expect a decline of the vain and the trivial and a return to the grand values of the daguerreotype. Because just as material of these precious images is an amalgam of mercury, silver, and the subtle tones of gold, so the soul or spirit or essence of the daguerreotype is an amalgam of three elements: the precision of its detail; its great range of lights and darks, with minute gradations from one to the other; and, what is most important, the power of the human image even when, or often because, the sitter is quite unknown. But also there is, unquestionably, something else, something indefinable about the daguerreotype, that gives it such hypnotic beauty, and not quite expressible in words—an epiphany that can be felt only by holding the plate in one's hand and turning it till it strikes fire and becomes visible and alive in its own inner illumination.

Can a photograph, then, aspire to be "Rembrandt perfected"? Sadly, it seems impossible. One step is missing. In photography one controls with the brain,

even in the manipulations of the darkroom, but in painting and printmaking there is another and subtle ingredient: the brushstroke, the trembling line, the mark of the human hand. There are a few, perhaps a hundred or so, photographs that reach the psychological peak of a Rembrandt. One doubts that any vernacular art, with its concise aims and simple techniques, can ever reach the level of the great masterpieces. "Little Mattie Groves," a superb ballad of the seventeenth century, is a vernacular classic:

> Put on, put on,
> Your clothes again.
> Let no one say
> I slewed a naked man.[10]

But it's about a knight who finds his wife in bed with a friend; it is craft in another realm than, say, *King Lear* on a similar subject:

> . . . and the small gilded flies
> Do lecher in my sight . . .

So photography, on the whole, must be accepted at a different level than sublime. Yet it is still a novel art, and for all its perversions, faults, and limitations it is one of the sudden glories of the human mind, and not the least of its accomplishments are the two splendid decades of the daguerreotype.

NOTES

1. Robert Hunt, *A Popular Treatise on the Art of Photography* (1841; reprint, Athens, Ohio: Ohio University Press, 1973).

2. Letter to Nathaniel Bloom and John F. S. Gray, March 19–20, 1863, *Walt Whitman: The Correspondence,* edited by Edwin Haviland Miller (New York: New York University Press, 1961), 1: 82.

3. *Historical Statistics of the United States* (Washington, D.C.: Bureau of the Census, 1975), Pt. 1, pp. 164–65.

4. Ibid., pp. 56–57.

5. E. Anthony, 1849 Preface to Henry H. Snelling, *The

History and Practice of the Art of Photography (1849; reprint, Hastings-on-Hudson: Morgan & Morgan, 1970).

6. Hunt, *A Popular Treatise,* p. 65.

7. Albert Southworth, *British Journal of Photography* 18 (1871): 583, quoted in many subsequent books.

8. John Cage, "Lecture on Nothing," in *Silence* (Cambridge, Mass.: MIT Press, 1966).

9. Letter to William D. O'Connor, September (?) 1866, *Walt Whitman: The Correspondence,* 1: 288.

10. Quoted from memory.

The Genius of Photography

Janet E. Buerger

To the memory of Harrison Horblit

Much of the most sophisticated writing on photography has stressed the idea of an ontological specificity in the medium. A notable attempt in recent years was Peter Galassi's 1981 exhibition *Before Photography* at the Museum of Modern Art, where he examined Heinrich Schwartz's suggestion that the camera had influenced painting ever since the Renaissance and that photography had had an immense effect on painting after 1839. Galassi, however, focused on the kind of cropping that Schwartz and writers after him had seen as a peculiar characteristic of photography and an influence on later painting, and showed that it had already appeared in painting before the invention of photography.[1]

The more fundamental aspect of photography—the classic side of photography's "ontology"—was its illusion of nature, and the true antecedent of the photographic image in this regard, Daguerre's Diorama. The context in which this apparently unspecific ontology inspired the sensation that it did has escaped scholarly attention. But it was not the cropping and other oddities that caused painters like Delaroche to drop their brushes, writers like Baudelaire to pick up their critical pens, and caricaturists like Maurisset to depict engravers hanging themselves in the face of *daguerréotypomanie* (fig. 1). Rather, it was photography's embarrassing ability to accomplish automatically the aim of artists from Euphronios to Ingres, to mimic nature in all its aerial and linear perspective, just as Salon (not boudoir) painting had done before photography, but not as well.

We have heard the phrase "the genius of photography," but what was this genius to the mid-nineteenth-century mind? If we remove ourselves from the quagmires of cause and effect to seek the intellectual position regarding art and nature in the middle of the nineteenth century, things get more interesting.[2] There is a curious concurrence of the works of the German philosopher Arthur Schopenhauer, the British political essayist Thomas Carlyle, and the American writer Nathaniel Hawthorne with the invention of the Diorama and photography that lends additional meaning to both the creation of and the shock resulting from both phenomena.

Schopenhauer's writings on fine arts and on genius and Carlyle's writings on truth that transcends time establish the background for a world in which photography was created simultaneously in different countries. They also provide the background for Hawthorne's main protagonist in *The House of the Seven Gables* (1851), the daguerreotypist Holgrave. Holgrave's position has drawn scholarly attention already,[3] while the novel—or the romance, as Hawthorne preferred to call it—has suffered critical assessment in relation to his earlier work *The Scarlet Letter*. All three of these authors illuminate the nature and genius of photography and the world's reaction to it. At the same time photography can lend a new level of understanding to their works and, through them, to the great issues of the century. The daguerreotype emphasized and served as a mirror not only to the visual world around it but gave test to what that visual

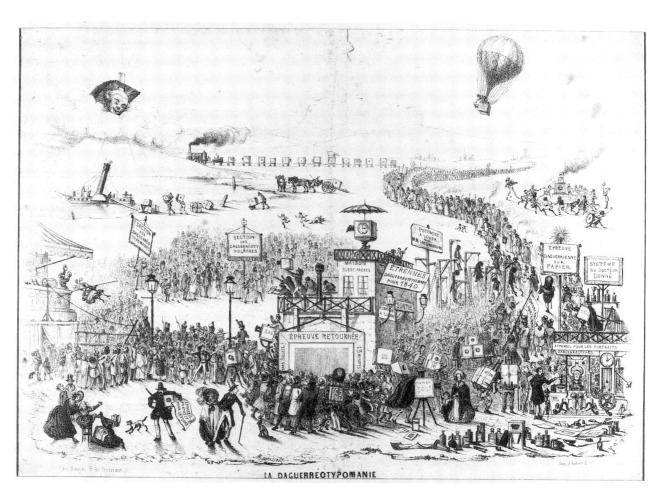

Figure 1.
Maurisset.
Fantasies:
Daguerreo-
typomania,
1839.
Hand-colored
lithograph,
25.4 × 35.3 cm.
George
Eastman
House
68:1322.
Provenance:
Gabriel
Cromer
Collection.
Gift of
Eastman
Kodak
Company.

LA DAGUERRÉOTYPOMANIE.

world meant to society at the time. In Hawthorne, the strength of photographic reality, that vision abstracted from the misleading transience of the matter of life into an objective and transcendent form, remains a symbol of ultimate insight. But what was the background to such an interpretation?

The great precedent for this power of the daguerreotype was the Diorama. Louis Jacques Mandé Daguerre was the inventor of the first practical photographic process that bears his name, but before that he was a noted painter. Lack of serious scholarly attention to the daguerreotype and to Daguerre's significant career as a prephotographic artist is a detriment to our understanding of some of the central issues in the development of Realist art.

Some photohistorians minimize Daguerre's achievement in the invention of the daguerreotype in relation to the contributions of his partner Nicéphore Niepce. Niepce died before Daguerre made his process public in 1839, and his heirs received less of a pension from the French government than Daguerre (4,000 francs, as compared to Daguerre's 6,000). While Niepce enthusiasts cite the outcome as unjust, Daguerre's extra sum was in fact in return for the revelation of his method of achieving his spectacular Diorama effects. Not only had each Diorama showing run successfully for months on end in Paris, but either Daguerre's own work or imitations ran in the provinces, in London, in Germany, and, if the broadside advertisement for a showing at City Hall in New York is to be believed, "these Magnificent Pictures" were barraged with "crowded audiences which attended this exhibition nightly," causing "their removal to be deferred."[4] It is the Diorama that gives the proper red carpet approach to *daguerréotypomanie.*

Le Dyorama... port de Boulogne.

Lith. Marlet

Figure 2. Unidentified artist. Audience viewing the "Port of Bologne" at the Diorama, ca. 1835. Lithograph (Marlet), hand-colored, 16.7 × 26.7 cm. George Eastman House 82:929:2. Provenance: Gabriel Cromer Collection. Gift of Eastman Kodak Company. No Diorama of the port of Bologne has been identified in the literature.

After a celebrated career as a stage designer for the Théâtre de l'Ambigu-Comique, 1816–22, and for the Paris Opera, 1820–22, Daguerre embarked on this most important prephotographic invention.[5] In 1822, with the painter Charles-Marie Bouton, he opened an entire building called the Diorama for the exhibition of two 45½ × 72½-foot canvases. The huge Diorama paintings were remarkable achievements of optical illusion. They were shown to an audience in a darkened auditorium in the specially designed Diorama building (fig. 2). Each scenic picture was larger in width than a normal house lot—larger, in fact, than most galleries devoted to photographic exhibitions today, and larger by far than most movie screens. Each painting magically changed when carefully placed, filtered light from both in front of and behind the picture "decomposed" one or the other of several superimposed atmospheric or time-lapse "effects" on the same canvas.[6]

It is almost impossible for us to imagine what this spectacle was like; the photographically derived movie of today is the closest parallel we have to it. Until 1839 Daguerre's reputation rested on his naturalistic stage designs (1816–22) and Diorama paintings (1822–39), but most if not all of these were destroyed by fire before his death in 1851. All we have today is a handful of drawings related to the Diorama paintings (fig. 3), a few inadequate woodcut or engraved reproductions from contemporary magazines (fig. 4), handouts given at Dioramas (fig. 5), and images from toy *diorama portatifs* like polyorama panoptiques (figs. 6–9).

Daguerre's genius dazzled connoisseur and public alike by combining the tricks of art and science, of fantasy and reality. He and Bouton received med-

Figure 3. Louis Jacques Mandé Daguerre. The Inauguration of the Temple of Solomon, ca. 1836. Brown ink and wash study for the Diorama, 25.5 × 34.8 cm. George Eastman House 83:2415:1. This was a double-effect Diorama. First the scene was dark and moonlit; then, gradually, the scene lightened as worshippers gathered in the courtyard and music played. "Here is a new marvel of M. Daguerre," one contemporary wrote. "This is almost the sole praise that one can give to the Diorama, in order not to say the same thing every time. . . . One really doesn't know anymore how to express one's surprise in the presence of such astonishing results."

als of the Legion of Honor when they exhibited small copies of Diorama subjects at the Salon.

In 1831 one critic wrote this of the latest Diorama painting:

A new Diorama is offered for the curiosity or rather for the admiration of the Parisians; and this time the illusion is carried to such a high point, that one might defy the artist to surpass it henceforth. Entirely accustomed to occupying myself with the seductive effects of the perspective, I believed myself, I admit it, more difficult of erring than spectators who had not been forewarned, and I went to the Diorama, thinking that I would discover the game of some secret machines. Error; presumption. . . . I saw the beautiful basin of Ghent fed by the Lys and carrying a number of ships with masts and riggings; I saw the quais adorned with rich buildings of stepped gables, decorated and painted, and presenting a picturesque and original sight; I saw the gothic churches; the old towers; a revolving bridge; I saw all the baggage of a commercial and active population that glittered in the sun, while a gentle vapor seemed to await the breath of Zephir to balance it in the air. But of machines, of canvas, of paint, I saw nothing. After a few minutes of surprise and ecstasy I began to see that the waves in the water had become still, the clouds thick, and the people *fallen asleep* as in the palace of Sleeping Beauty. Then an unexplainable sadness seized

me, and I shuddered as at the sight of some prodigy; for it was a singular mixture of life and of death, of illusion and disenchantment; but little by little a somber color spread about; night deployed its veils, and soft rays of the moon silvered the oblique roofs of the Oratory and the lions and dolphins of the house of the boatmen. Then everywhere lights shone out and projected their rosy reflections in the interiors of shops, on walls, through windows. . . . Then I hear among the spectators exclamations of joy, of admiration, of surprise. . . . I wouldn't know how to say where reality ends or where the painting begins, or from whence came that mysterious day that the artist had modified to his will.[7]

The Diorama suspended ordinary reality and presented a heightened and abstracted reality that the viewer perceived in the same way that he or she saw true nature. Daguerre and his protégé Hippolyte Sebron introduced the most sophisticated Diorama, the double-effect Diorama, in 1834; their "Mass at Midnight at Saint Etienne du Mont" and "Basin of Ghent" were the first examples. The double-effect heightened the illusion by employing transmitted as well as reflected lighting (lights from behind as well as in front of the canvas) for greater effect, increasing the number of visual changes possible in the picture.

Here as before, however, the experience did not rely on narrative, as did many of the 360-degree panorama paintings that had been in vogue earlier

*Figure 5.
Prospectus for
the Diorama
"Vue Générale
de la Ville
de Rouen"
(shown
February 1824
to April 1825).*

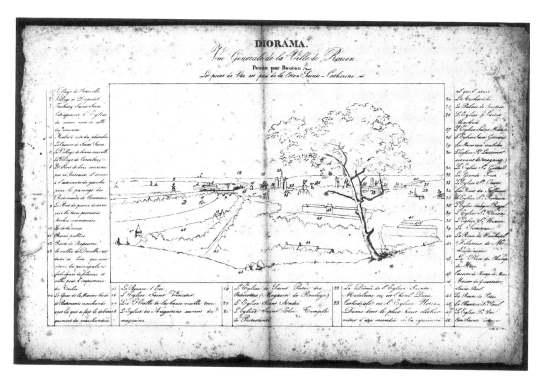

in the century and admired for their realistic detail.[8] Daguerre's Diorama depended on the total absorption of the viewer's senses into his illusion of reality. It took the viewer unawares. One was not to stand in a well-lit auditorium discussing the scope and accuracy of the work; one was in a darkened gallery away from worldly associations and was to be grabbed by the experience of the illusion. The departure from narrative and reliance on complete illusion of nature were inextricably interwoven. The impact of the Diorama was not in its storytelling (which was an incidental adjunct to its central power); it was in its direct experiential spatial illusion. A critic reviewing Daguerre's Diorama of the "Tomb of Napoleon at Saint Helena" remarked: "Before this admirable painting emotions are more rapid than thought: never had something so true, so marvelously true lured the audience of the Diorama. But one regret you have in leaving it: you would like to cut a branch of willow, snip a geranium flower."[9]

Art historians are as reluctant to accept the Diorama as a major force in the development of Realist art as to admit the demise of Romanticism until long after something else had replaced it. It takes scholarly as well as mental archaeology to reconstruct the lost Dioramas. But it is clear from reviews that they represented not Romanticism but Realism, not painterly academicism or bravura unto itself, but a goal of complete illusion. Without accepting this, it is difficult to discuss accurately the only real precedence for the impact of daguerreotypy and photography. The daguerreotype, with its distillation of volumetric (apparently cubic) illusion—completely unlike that of early paper photography, which was tied reluctantly but surely to its interfering surface—was the sequel to the Diorama. Painter Gustave Courbet's arrival on the scene in 1848 was the second phase of a movement already in existence, and one already with a great deal of potency. His works were compared to the daguerreotype, which by 1848 was the standard for Realism.

The reference to the suspended ambience of Sleeping Beauty in the review of the Diorama of Ghent is an interesting one on several levels. The preoccupation with time in the middle of the nineteenth century is a curiously ill-studied subject in art history.[10] Tennyson's first "Sleeping Beauty" (1830, 1845) ends: "She sleeps, nor dreams, but ever dwells / A perfect form in perfect rest," leaving her in suspended time. The seventeenth-century story of Sleeping Beauty, however, was later taken as an allegory for earth awakened after her winter sleep by the kiss of the sun. Here there are the obvious references to renewal and the passage of time, which was of such interest to the nineteenth century in general, and to divine control, which was later to characterize symbolic thinking pertaining to photography.

The author of the story of Sleeping Beauty, Charles Perrault, has another interest for mid-nineteenth-century photographica. Perrault, in his position as an academic, took a leading role in the controversy over the Ancients and the Moderns, pointing to the superiority of the writers of his own day (the Moderns) over that of classical authors. Jonathan Swift's satire of this popular controversy, "The Battle of the Books," is certainly the source for the nineteenth-century version of it by Champfleury where, in his battle of ten daguerreians and ten artists in *Le Realism* in 1857, the New Art fights the old. The best-known sequel to Sleeping Beauty in America combines both the time-suspension element and the passage from an ancient to a modern culture: Irving's Rip van Winkle (1819), in falling asleep for twenty years, wakes not only to the passage of time but to the new world of American independence in which George Washington replaces King George. Such ideas of suspended time and an awakening to an enlightened new world hover around the history of Realism.

Indeed, the slumber of the Ghent dusk relates to both the period's fascination with time and its suspension of time for dissecting analysis, and it foreshadows the forthcoming and newest version of the Battle of the Ancients and the Moderns. Daguerre chose to show two canvases in each Diorama performance (the gallery rotated 180 degrees after the performance of the first canvas to face a second canvas on the opposite side of the building); one painting showed a landscape view representing a

creation of God, the other a building or an urban view, the creation of man. In such juxtaposition was a recognition of the development of civilization, of the passage of time from the virginity of Creation to the marvels of modern man. But it was in his deftness in suspending life, in re-creating nature on his own terms, in enforcing a pause in reality as a way of seeing it more effectively that Daguerre showed his greatest insight.

It was Daguerre's attempt to perfect his duplication of the illusion of nature that brought him to seek a way to fix the image of the camera obscura. He and his partner Bouton employed the camera obscura and camera lucida in their studies of nature, enlarging the results scientifically for use as the compositional structure of the huge Diorama designs. The gridwork on Bouton's drawing of Fountains Abbey, used for the London Diorama and preserved at George Eastman House, illustrates the technique. These drawings are hardly distinguishable from the ones copied from daguerreotypes by engravers as guidelines for their reproductions in various publications of the 1840s and 1850s that featured views from Paris and around the world.[11] The result of Daguerre's research into fixing the image of the camera permanently was the daguerreotype.

About the same time that Daguerre created his Diorama concept a German philosopher, Arthur Schopenhauer, produced one of the most important philosophical works of the nineteenth century, *The World as Will and Representation* (1819). Two sections of this work are of particular interest in relation to the invention of photography: those on art and on genius.

Schopenhauer's thesis was that the selfish will of man motivated all his activity. His one exception was the artist, who rose above will to objectivity. Art was a work of genius.

Art . . . is everywhere at its goal. It plucks the object of its contemplation from the stream of the world's course, and holds it isolated before it. This particular thing, which in that stream

Figures 6–7. Unidentified artist. Gothic church interior, ca. 1840. Hand-colored lithographic view for the polyorama panoptique, 14.4 × 20 cm (slide size). George Eastman House. Provenance: Gabriel Cromer Collection. Gift of Eastman Kodak Company. Reflected light shows a daytime scene; transmitted light reveals a nighttime mass.

was an infinitesimal part, becomes for art a representative of the whole, and equivalent of the infinitely many in space and time. It therefore pauses at this particular thing; it stops the wheel of time; for it relations vanish; its object is the only essential, the Idea . . .[12]

This could easily apply to the curious Realism of the Diorama or even to the time-distilling daguerreotype. But Schopenhauer becomes specific in his description of the way an artist succeeds in such a representation:

Only through the pure contemplation. . . , which becomes entirely absorbed in the object, are Ideas comprehended; and the nature of genius consists precisely in the preeminent ability for such contemplation. Now this demands a com-

plete forgetting of our own person and of its relations and connections, the *gift of genius* is nothing but the most complete *objectivity*. . . . Genius is the capacity to remain in a state of pure perception, to lose oneself in perception . . . to discard entirely our own personality for a time, in order to remain *pure knowing subject,* the clear eye of the world.[13]

In a later series of essays he repeats more clearly the same thoughts: "A genius has a double intellect, one for himself and the service of his will; the other for the world, of which he becomes the mirror, in virtue of his purely objective attitude toward it."[14]

In a startling reversal of the dominant Romantic eighteenth-century view of genius, where genius, exempt from rules, is the antithesis of imitation (either of nature or of earlier artists),[15] Schopenhauer suggests that the artist's objective imitation of na-

ture *is* genius. In his apology for visual realism, he offers motive for a number of nineteenth-century artists and photographers, and a further explanation for powerful effect on society of the classic illusion of the Diorama and the daguerreotype. The early daguerreians, like the artist of the Diorama, mimicked a fully defined boxlike illusion or considered the result imperfect. Such illusion, according to Schopenhauer, was enhanced by specific and precise detail, which, "by a careful and detailed preservation of a single individual, person or thing, . . . aims at revealing the idea of the genus to which that person or thing belongs."

Even in its specificity, this duplication of nature in art remained an abstract Platonic idea for Schopenhauer. It was the form, taken away from the matter that existed in a constantly incomplete, constantly fluctuating world with subtexts of interfering references. Art was the form alone, as if it were taken out of its incompleteness and made whole.[16] Thus, abstract thought was already inherent in the most apparently and unrelentingly Realist position.

Inherent in Schopenhauer's artist-mirror is the potential of the ultimately objective art—photography—for making a major contribution in the pictorial arts. At the very minimum, his position opens the field for the artist to use the camera as an artistic tool. Schopenhauer's work was better appreciated outside of Germany when it was translated into French and English in the 1850s; the full extent of his influence would be felt even more when the whole text of *The World as Will and Representation* was translated in the 1880s, just before the art photography movement emerged.

Thomas Carlyle, like Schopenhauer, would enjoy a *fin-de-siècle* vogue and, like Schopenhauer, wrote his major works at about the time photography was invented. His *Heroes, Hero-Worship, and*

Figures 8–9. Unidentified artist. The painter before nature, ca. 1840. Hand-colored lithographic view for the polyorama panoptique, 14.4 × 20 cm (slide size). George Eastman House 77:562:21. Provenance: Gabriel Cromer Collection. Gift of Eastman Kodak Company.

the Heroic in History, originally given as a series of lectures in 1840, was published in 1841. Like Schopenhauer's work, it was philosophical and primarily concerned with truth. It essentially suggested that if truth were to be achieved, it would be discovered by considering the entire scope of history. His heroes from all ages represented the best ideas of their time. To combine their knowledge, he asserted, would give a closer idea of truth than to take any time-bound partial truth of the current day.

The mid-nineteenth-century man, facing the increasing knowledge of his time and, more particularly, an overwhelming sense of the elusiveness of truth, was fully aware that he was entrapped in a complex world of partial realities. His age—the age of man and the age of earth—was being adjusted by new geological and evolutionary studies. Charles Lyell's uniformitarian *Principles of Geology* was published in 1830–33; Darwin's *Origin of Species,*

drafted in 1842, was published in 1859 after being anticipated by Alfred Russel Wallace in 1858. The new astronomy epitomized by Sir William and Sir John Hershel's nebula catalogues, begun in 1786 and concluding with the addition of the Southern Hemisphere in 1864, put forth the vastness of a universe in which light just reaching human eyes was older than the oldest rocks on earth. It made previous views of age and vastness pale into insignificance. And even the Catholic church was being undermined by biblical higher criticism, which suggested that the Bible be interpreted in the context of Ancient Near Eastern literature. Man was seen increasingly as a tiny speck in a vastness of space and a longness of time; truth—even religious truth—became a relative matter rather than an absolute.

To get a hold on a suddenly relative and overwhelming reality, keen insight was needed to fortify stern observation. Carlyle's trick was to combine the

wisdom of all ages. In *Heroes, Hero-Worship, and the Heroic in History* he reminds:

> Poet and Prophet differ greatly in our loose modern notions of them. In some old languages, again, the titles are synonymous; *Vates* means both Prophet and Poet: and indeed at all times, Prophet and Poet, well understood, have much kindred of meaning. Fundamentally indeed, they are still the same in this most important respect especially, That they have penetrated both of them into the sacred mystery of the Universe; what Goethe calls 'the open secret'. 'Which is the great secret?' asks one.—'The *open* secret,'—open to all, seen by almost none! That divine mystery, which lies everywhere in all Beings, 'the Divine Idea of the World,' which lies at 'the bottom of Appearances' . . .[17]

In this quote from his lecture on "The Hero as Poet" Carlyle raises the artist from genius to priest,

giving him extraordinary powers of insight. His position on the value of the past at the artist's disposal comes at the end of his lecture on "The Hero as Divinity," where he presents an apology for taking Odin as one of his subjects and suggests the absorption of earlier heroic stances into the repertoire of artistic observation as an aid in the search for truth:

> Neither is there no use in knowing something about this old Paganism of our Fathers. Unconsciously, and combined with higher things, it is in *us* yet, that old Faith withal! To know it consciously, brings us into closer and clearer relation with the Past,—with our own possessions in the Past. For the whole Past, as I keep repeating, is the possession of the Present; the Past had always something *true,* and it is a precious possession. In a different time, in a different place, it is always some other *side* of our com-

mon Human Nature that has been developing it-self. The actual True is the *sum* of all these; not any one of them by itself constitutes what of Human Nature is hitherto developed. Better to know them all than misknow them. 'To which of these Three Religions do you specially adhere?' inquires the Meister of his Teacher. 'To all the Three; for they by their union first constitute the True Religion.'[18]

In such a view of the passage of time and the value of every age, the stopping of time for the act of observation was just a method of examining its drift by getting, as Coleridge would have it, "the be-fore and the after," to make the succession of prog-ress intelligible. The world of the 1830s, more than any other period in history, was acutely aware of it-self as an element of this progress. It is in this cli-mate that the arresting illusion of the Diorama and the daguerreotype captured a fleeting moment of a precisely observed world and fixed it into a time-transcendent form. A daguerreotype of a landscape (fig. 10), an event (fig. 11), a family (fig. 12), a child or a famous man, living or dead, or even of a piece of the universe all proved their position in the flux of time. A painting of the same thing could be ad-justed to—or could be the figment of—the imagina-tion of the artist. It proved nothing. The daguerreo-type was the ultimate symbolic triumph over time, done in the ultimate style of precise duplication.

From the beginning the daguerreotype was thought to be a mysterious process. After all, the

Figure 11. "Cromer's Amateur." Organ Grinder. Sixth-plate daguerreotype, ca. 1848. George Eastman House 76:168:50.

plate was sensitized and developed with fumes! One had to be a chemist of sorts to be a daguerreian. Antoine Claudet's panorama of London, which was made on several daguerreotype plates from the top of the column of the Duke of York and copied as a *tableau monstre* engraving for publication in the *Illustrated London News* in 1842, elicited the typical reactions. One critic likened Claudet to Asmodeus (the evil demon who appears in the Apocryphal book of Tobit, the Talmud, and Milton's *Paradise Lost*). Most critics, however, likened the extraordinary power to more benign intervention: "The picture must be correct since it was delineated by the glorious sun itself." [19]

By 1851 the daguerreotype stood not only for the *ne plus ultra* of exact imitation of nature, but for some superhuman, even divine insight into the nature of the world. In this "solar phenomenon where the artist collaborates with the sun," as Lamartine would later call photography, the sun was associated with divine power.

Nathaniel Hawthorne's main protagonist in *The House of the Seven Gables,* the daguerreian Holgrave, was a symbol himself of the principles represented in the daguerreotype. The daguerreian image of Judge Pyncheon, who had inherited the nasty nature of his ancestor, showed him in his true evil character, which his relatives could not see by looking directly at him.

The revelation of this New Art paralleled Holgrave's advocacy of a new way of life for the Pyncheon family, which included his urging of the

Figure 12. Unidentified photographer. George James Webb, Mrs. Webb, and daughters Mary Isabella and Caroline Elizabeth. Whole-plate daguerreotype, ca. 1850. George Eastman House 79:3297:1.

spinster Hepzibah to give up her old-fashioned ideas of class structure and act like a New American, where the Jeffersonian aristocrat was one who succeeded by hard work and talent rather than inherited rank or position. Hawthorne's interest in the sins of the ancestors visited on their heirs, and the position of the daguerreotype as a symbol of modernism and an aid to stopping the evil succession, is a reaffirmation of Carlylian history and a striking example of the daguerreotype in all its symbolic power. The daguerreotype represented accurate insight, just as Holgrave represented enlightenment.

Now the artist had passed from genius to priest to divinely inspired, without reverting to the Romantic image that opposed imitation. This step was an important one to the *fin-de-siècle* artist's self-portrait as Christ, where the artist looked inward to seek the revelation of truth.

Daguerre, in his classic illusionistic theater designs and Diorama, and then his subsequent daguerreotype process, set a powerful standard in 1839 and one that essentially, in its traditional classic composition, form-defining modeling, and natural linear and aerial perspective, as well as in its automatic record of precisely defined detail, remains the standard even today. Throughout the 1840s and 1850s, both the public and the photo-

Figure 13.
Unidentified
photographer.
View at the
Crystal Palace,
London.
Stereoscopic
daguerreotype,
ca. 1853.
Collection of
Wm. B.
Becker.

graphic community revered this standard; paper photography continually strived for that transparent surface and that sharp-edged detail. The demise of the daguerreotype, which is signaled by the decline in commercial offerings of daguerreotype plates and other equipment around 1863 (and not earlier, as is often supposed), was the result of the successful replacement of the metal plate with the more desirable repeatable process of the collodion negative and the paper print with shiny albumen emulsion. Both negative and positive had attained a practical enough comparison to the sharpness and illusory quality so admired in the metal plate that society, reluctantly, gave up the daguerreotype.

During this early period, photographic realism was enhanced by degree through various inventions that we mostly ignore today or regard as odd aberrations, but that together emphasize the seriousness of the period about the imitation of nature. These include the introduction of stereoscopic photography (mostly after 1851, fig. 13), the life-size photograph (popular already in the 1850s), and photosculpture (introduced in 1861). The ultimate form of this total photographic realism was the hand-colored stereoscopic daguerreotype. But total realism lasted little longer than the daguerreotype.

One of the great passages in the history of photography was the demise of the daguerreotype standard itself, however, which was carried on for decades in slightly diminished form by the glass-plate negative and albumen print. This passage was triggered by Muybridge's motion studies in the 1870s and 1880s, which undermined the sense of adequacy of straightforward observation. The subsequent art photography movement of the 1890s, with its subjective vision, was a full-blown manifestation.

The passing of the standard was a major event. The acceptance of soft-focus photography, of manipulated photography, of rough-surfaced paper, was coupled with a total collapse of mid-nineteenth-century empirical Realism. The illusion that had characterized the Diorama and the daguerreotype stepped off the pedestal of style. It is beyond the scope of this essay to discuss the significance of the return of straight photography in the twentieth century, but a study of the relation of that to the standard of the daguerreotype and the reappearance of Schopenhauerian ideas like equivalency and "the thing itself" in the artistic philosophy of f.64ers like Edward Weston might be worthwhile.

The daguerreotype, whether from God or not, gave a picture of precise matter–absent reality/abstraction directly to the viewer as if evading its necessary trip through any human genius. Mathew Brady called it "the concentrated truth of counterfeit presentment." Hawthorne said that when his writing was at its best it was "a neutral territory . . . where the Actual and the Imaginary may meet, and each imbue itself with the nature of the other." Among Otto Brendel's 1930s discourses on the "visible idea" was the thought that "the strangest self-pronouncements in history arise where the boundary between appearance and inner meaning become a razor-thin line which is easily crossed," and that these "ceaselessly strive, if not to overcome, at least to direct the mutability in every human situation into the permanence of the spiritual and religious existence of images and symbols."[20] The daguerreotype's success in these areas—and not in minor technicalities such as cropping—enabled a spell-bound public and artistic community to witness the goals of Euphronios achieved after 2,300 years.

NOTES

1. Peter Galassi, *Before Photography: Painting and the Invention of Photography* (New York: Museum of Modern Art, 1981). Since this exhibition, a selection of Schwartz's essays has been edited by William E. Parker, *Art and Photography: Forerunners and Influences* (Rochester, N.Y.: Smith/Visual Studies Workshop, 1985). An excellent review of the issues raised in the exhibit followed. See Gene Thornton, "The Place of Photography in the Western Pictorial Tradition: Heinrich Schwartz, Peter Galassi and John Szarkowski," *History of Photography* 10 (April–June 1986): 85–98. Galassi for the most part discusses what might be called private studies, which would not have been the paintings shown at the Salon, although this interesting factor is not discussed as such. The notable exception he includes is the example of panoramic painting (and photography), which was a very public art. Curiously, he does not mention the Diorama, though it was among the most popular phenomena of the prephotographic period. He recognizes that the basis for photography is ultimately fifteenth-century "linear perspective," but like many historians still seems embarrassed at the boredom of such a fact. The difference between the neoclassical pictures of David, which correctly employed Renaissance linear perspective, and the Dioramas of Daguerre, which used essentially the same boxlike constructions, was that Daguerre grabbed the "soul" of the viewer in the true Albertian sense while David only captured the viewer's intellectual comprehension. This reach to the soul, also characteristic of photography, can be added to the theory of Renaissance perspective as a recognized goal of Renaissance painting. As Schwartz pointed out in the title essay of Parker's edition of his work, Erwin Panofsky has warned that the Renaissance dogma for a work of art to be the faithful representation of a natural object is "the most trivial and actually is the most problematic dogma of esthetic theory."

2. The shift in the primary ontology of photography, from cropping and such things to perfect classic illusion, severely affects the cause-and-effect arguments regarding photography's influence or lack thereof on painting. If the "fugitive, contingent and fragmentary qualities" previously claimed as ontologically elemental to photography are seen only as minor in relation to the more important classic illusion, not only does Galassi's position become more a matter of illuminating side-currents in prephotographic painting than an argument for dismissing photography's effect on painting, but Kurt Varnedoe's earlier articles dismissing the influence of

photography on Impressionism become irrelevant as well. See *Art in America* (January 1980): 66–78; (June 1980): 96–110. There is no question that after 1839 every painter who raised a brush was profoundly affected by photography.

3. See Alfred H. Marks, "Hawthorne's Daguerreotypist: Scientist, Artist, Reformer," in *The House of the Seven Gables,* edited by Seymour L. Gross (New York: W. W. Norton and Co., 1967).

4. This was for "The Remains of Napoleon in the Church des Invalides at Paris on the 15th of Dec, 1840," "The Valley of Goldau," "The Church St. Etienne du Mont at Paris with the Midnight Mass," and "Venice with its Carnival at Night." The broadside of August 1842 is now preserved at George Eastman House.

5. Barry Daniels has done a number of interesting studies on this phase of Daguerre's career and on the work of Daguerre's collaborator at the Paris Opera, Pierre-Luc-Charles Cicéri (1782–1868): "Cicéri and Daguerre: Set Designers for the Paris Opera, 1820–1822," *Theatre Survey* 22 (May 1981): 69–90; "L. J. M. Daguerre: A Catalogue of his Stage Designs for the Ambigu-Comique Theatre," *Theatre Studies* (no. 28–29): 5–40; "A Footnote to Daguerre's Career as a Stage Designer," *Theatre Survey* 24 (1983): 134–38. See also his "Notes on the Panorama in Paris," *Theatre Survey* 19 (November 1978). I am grateful to him for drawing my attention to these studies.

6. See L. J. M. Daguerre, *An Historical and Descriptive Account of the Various Processes of the Daguerreotype and the Diorama,* edited by Beaumont Newhall (New York: Winter House, 1971).

7. "Diorama: Bassin de Gand," *Journal des Femmes,* Deuxième Partie: Mélanges, Nov. 11, 1831 (?) (clipping from the Bibliothèque de l'Arsenal, Collection Rondel, Rt. 12,659, f. 15). My translation. Cromer's handwritten list of the sequence of the Dioramas, preserved at Eastman House, cites Le Bassin Central du Commerce à Gand as on display from March 1834 to September 1836 and specifically notes it as "vue à double effet."

8. Daguerre had arrived in Paris in 1804, the year the panorama painting opened, and in 1807 he apprenticed to its author, Pierre Prévost. The best overview of Daguerre's life is Helmut and Alison Gernsheim, *L. J. M. Daguerre: The History of the Diorama and the Daguerreotype* (New York: Dover, 1968). Also see

my "Daguerre: The Artist," *Image* 28 (June 1985): 2–20.

9. "Diorama Tombeau de Napoléon à Sainte-Hélène; effet d'un soleil couchant, dessiné d'après nature au mois de juin 1829, peint par M. Daguerre," *Cabinet de Lecture,* May 14, 1831 (clipping, Bibliothèque de l'Arsenal, Collection Rondel, Rt. 12,659, f. 14). My translation.

10. For the appearance of certain issues of time in nineteenth-century literature, see Jerome Hamilton Buckley, "Symbols of Eternity: The Victorian Escape from Time," in George M. Young, *Victorian Essays* (London: Oxford University Press, 1962), pp. 1–16; Buckley, *The Triumph of Time* (Cambridge: Belknap Press, 1966). I was also aided by material delivered by Buckley in his course "From Darwin to Decadence" at Harvard in 1985.

11. The most important of these was N. P. Lerebours's *Excursions Daguerriennes,* 1840–44.

12. Arthur Schopenhauer, *The World as Will and Representation,* trans. E. F. J. Payne (New York: Dover, 1966): 1: 185.

13. Ibid., pp. 185–86.

14. Arthur Schopenhauer, "On Genius," in *Essays of Schopenhauer,* trans. T. Bailey Saunders (New York: A. L. Burt, n.d.), p. 363.

15. Examples of this "conversation" on genius are included in *The Norton Anthology of English Literature,* edited by M. H. Abrams (New York: W. W. Norton and Co., 1975), pp. 2432–42. The notable disputant, Sir Joshua Reynolds (*Discourses* VI, 1774), evidently was an advocate of the use of the camera obscura (Schwartz, "Art and Photography," p. 113).

16. "The Metaphysics of Fine Art," in *Essays of Schopenhauer,* pp. 279–88.

17. Thomas Carlyle, *On Heroes, Hero-Worship, and the Heroic in History* (London: Chapman and Hall, 1841), p. 80.

18. Carlyle, *Heroes,* p. 41.

19. In a whole page of reviews that were reproduced in the *Illustrated London News* of 1843, p. 48, the majority of the critics seem confused as to how much invention there was in the image.

20. Otto Brendel, "The Shield of Achilles," in *The Visible Idea: Interpretations of Classical Art,* trans. Maria Brendel (1936; reprint, Washington, D.C.: Decatur House Press, 1980), p. 67.

Whatever new object we see, we perceive to be only a new version of our familiar experience, and we set about translating it at once into our parallel facts. We have thereby our vocabulary.
—R. W. Emerson, "Art and Criticism"

Mirror in the Marketplace

American Responses to the Daguerreotype, 1839–1851

Alan Trachtenberg

In the salon of a Broadway hotel on December 4, 1839, the first French daguerreotypes made their initial New World appearance. In the preceding months American examples of the fledgling art of picturing had already been seen in New York shop windows,[1] but here were specimens from the hand of the inventor and master himself, Louis Jacques Mandé Daguerre, offered to the public by his ingratiating agent François Gouraud. With impeccable references as "friend and pupil of Mr. Daguerre," Gouraud announced his "charge of introducing to the New World the perfect knowledge of the marvelous process of drawing, which fame has already made known to you under the name of 'The Daguerreotype.'"[2] Already known by name, the curious objects with their flickering images of Parisian boulevards and monuments nevertheless challenged the credulity of the select audience. Seeking an appropriate language to describe "their exquisite perfection [which] transcends the bounds of sober belief," Lewis Gaylord Clark, patrician editor of *The Knickerbocker,* struck upon a perfect solution from the apparatus of everyday life: a looking glass:

Let us endeavor to convey to the reader an impression of their character. Let him suppose himself standing in the middle of Broadway, with a looking-glass held perpendicular in his hand, in which is reflected the street, with all that therein is, for two or three miles, taking in the haziest distance. Then let him take the glass into the house, and find the impression of the entire view, in the softest light and shade, visibly retained upon its surface. This is the Daguerreotype! . . . There is not an object even the most minute embraced in that wide scope, which was not in the original; and it is impossible that one should have been omitted. Think of that![3]

Like Plato's whirling mirror, Clark's panorama of Broadway beguiles the mind with flashing images of the real. Of course, Plato's conundrum of appearance and reality, in which the mirror induces a kind of inebriation in the deceptive pleasure of mere illusion, is hardly the case here; Clark's mirror stands simply and unambiguously for exactitude, and the author's quite anti-Platonic awe at imitation itself: "Think of that!"

Exuberant awe and fascination prevailed at the inauguration of photography in America, as it did everywhere in Europe. Here was proof again, like lithography, the steam engine, the railroad, of an age of "progress," of enlightened reason prevailing over dark superstition, and science over magic. But the chorus of celebration was not without its discordant notes. The very wonder excited by first sight of the new objects occasionally harbored a more reserved, disbelieving response, such as we hear from Philip Hone, another visitor to Gouraud's exhibition, who included among his words of praise this flickering hint of uncertainty: "One may almost be excused for disbelieving it without seeing the very process by which it is created. It appears to me a confusion of the very elements of nature."[4]

This note of discomfort, quickly muffled in Hone's hymn of celebration, finds an answering echo in the reaction of Phoebe in Hawthorne's *The House of the Seven Gables* (1851): "I don't much like pictures of that sort,—they are so hard and stern; beside dodging away from the eye, and trying to escape altogether."[5] Phoebe's unease invokes a little-regarded moment in the early career of photography in America, a moment of shudder, suspicion, and refusal. "I don't wish to see it any more," she cries. To be sure, most Americans proved eager enough not only to see but to possess a specimen of the new art, and a thriving trade in daguerreian images developed rapidly. Photography fit so neatly the rhetoric of the "technological sublime" common in the age of steam in America, how are we to understand the few but insinuating signs of a countervailing response?

For the cultural historian such rifts within the linguistic environment of a technological innovation provide telling signs of an uneven process of change. In regard to photography, the process of acclimatization was neither as spontaneous nor as unequivocal as is often assumed. The compacted overlay of implication within the language of response can help us reconstruct and understand a climate of mind within which photography achieved its initial cultural identity in America. Language in its figurative uses especially—images, allusions, metaphors—preserves nuances of meaning that can be read as indices to the cultural effects of historical change. The figures by which people represent new phenomena to themselves and each other is especially valuable to the historian, for by such language the new is brought into relation with the old and the familiar—in Emerson's words, is perceived "to be only a new version of our familiar experience." By familiarizing new objects, tropes such as Clark's mirror on Broadway serve as more than descriptive terms; they signify an entire process of ingesting new experiences, making a place for them within existing systems of thought and feeling, and in the process modifying old structures in ways only a sensitive attention to language can reveal. Particu-

larly apt and promising for close attention, then, is the metaphor of the photograph as mirror, especially as Clark imagines it: a mirror in the New World marketplace of Broadway.

I

"Talk no more of 'holding the mirror up to nature'—she will hold it up to herself, and present you with a copy of her countenance for a penny." Thus exclaimed N. P. Willis in the first published news of photography in the American press.[6] He had not set eyes on an actual specimen, had only read William Henry Fox Talbot's account of his experiments in the English *Literary Gazette* (February 2, 1839), but instantly imagined the medium as a kind of mirror-press by which nature imprints itself as a cheap picture. Seizing the Englishman's remark that the invention would abridge "the labor of the artist in copying natural objects," and that "by means of this contrivance, it is not the artist who makes the picture, but the picture which makes *itself*," Willis calls up a scene of panic among displaced craftsmen: "Steel engravers, copper engravers, and etchers, drink up your aquafortis, and die! There is an end of your black art—'Othello's occupation gone.' The real black art of true magic arises and cries avaunt. . . . The Daguerreoscope[7] and the Photogenic revolutions are to keep you all down, ye painters, engravers, and, alas! the harmless race, the sketchers."

The cleverness of the conceit was not entirely a joking matter. New York in the winter and spring of 1839 still felt the worst effects of the catastrophic Panic of 1837: financial collapse, ruinous defaults and bankruptcies, uncontrollable deflation, and an economic slowdown of an order never before experienced in the United States.[8] Over the next ten years, virtually until the discovery of California gold in 1849, the city remained gripped by unemployment, rising pauperism and homelessness, sporadic riots, and an increase in violent crime. In light of what one writer in 1843 called "these Jeremiad times," in which "only the *beggars* and the *takers of likenesses by daguerreotype"* can survive,[9] Willis's "real black art" reveals a distinct social meaning.

Among the early writers on the new medium, mostly gentlemen scientists and artists like Samuel F. B. Morse, Willis is virtually alone to imagine a point of view of practicing draftsmen, engravers, printers.[10] Not that he himself refers explicitly to the hard times visible on the streets of New York, but his imaginary scene of discarded craftsmen, their "occupation gone," serves as a sharp reminder that photography appeared in America in the midst of the first modern depression and mass unemployment, the first signal of an unstable economic system keyed to the mysterious vagaries of capital, of money. It seemed to many at the time that blame for the depression lay at the hands of private banks and their issuance of paper money not backed by species, a practice which encouraged unrestrained speculation. While this is difficult to prove, it is not improbable that loss of the authority of printed money and the consequent widespread perception of instability in society's basic token of exchange affected the reception of photography, a new technique which itself threatened, as Willis foresaw, to destabilize the entire craft of picture-making, and not least, to deflate another kind of standard currency: the representational value of hand-crafted pictures.

Willis imagines further ambiguities and encroachments in the realm of daily life.

What would you say to looking in a mirror and having the image fastened!! As one looks sometimes, it is really quite frightful to think of it; but such a thing is possible—nay, it is probable—no, it is certain. What will become of the poor thieves, when they shall see handed in as evidence against them their own portraits, taken by the room in which they stole, and in the very act of stealing! What wonderful discoveries is this wonderful discovery destined to discover! The telescope is rather an unfair telltale; but

now every thing and every body may have to encounter his double every where, most inconveniently, and every one become his own caricaturist.

Beneath the witticism lies a vein of serious contemporary worry, the telling linkage of anxiety over losing one's "image" by stealth and one's property by theft. The doubled fear results in a paradoxical predicament: what the magic mirror seems to offer on one hand—security of possessions through an invisible system of surveillance—it removes on the other—the security of self-possession, the danger of appearing in public as a caricature of oneself. Owners and thieves stand equally naked, undefended, against the scrutiny of a newly ubiquitous social eye, a gaze belonging to an invisible body; the implacable mirror is simply immanent, part of the room. Thus the inconvenient "double" is itself doubled, representing two apparently distinct but distinctly connected objects of anxiety: personal goods and public "image." Are owner and thief, then, two sides of the same self? Willis seems to grasp, at least in the unconscious vibrations of his language, that he stands at the threshold of a major turn in culture, toward a condition in which mechanically reproduced self-images will emerge as a new form of marketable, and thus vulnerable, personal property.

This is not to claim any special prescience in Willis, but to identify implicit concerns and fears betrayed by the linguistic resources that lay ready at hand to a Broadway writer in 1839. In the following years numerous writers will include, in their list of "applications" of photography, protection against crime both by direct surveillance (anticipating the autoptic functions of the camera) and by physiognomic identification of criminality, or revelation of "character" through "image."[11] Willis's fantasy of self-indicting thieves in the night, slight as it is, can be seen as answering to the sort of tense nervousness in middle-class New York we detect by noticing what lies on either side of Philip Hone's diary entry about his visit to the Gouraud exhibition. His glowing account of the French daguerreotypes appears between two entries of disturbing acts of violence. The first tells of drunken street brawls and stabbings, "some even in Broadway," signs that "the city is infested by gangs of hardened wretches, born in the haunts of infamy"; the second, of "a most outrageous revolt" of tenants near Albany, "of a piece with the vile disorganizing spirit which overspreads the land like a cloud."[12] The social turmoil within which photography appeared in America, and the perceptions of crisis among the earliest elite patrons of the new medium, could hardly be made more graphic than this location within the private discourse of his diary of Hone's appreciation of "one of the wonders of modern times."

Even more graphic and dire are scenes depicted in a slim novel of 1846 by Augustine Joseph Hockey Duganne, suggestively titled *The Daguerreotype Miniature; or, Life in the Empire City.*[13] The earliest appearance of photography in American fiction, this otherwise unremarkable pulp fiction puts into dramatic motion many of the covert concerns and perceptions dashed off in Willis's brief essay. By plot and theme the story belongs to the genre of "city mystery" popularized in the 1840s by the labor radical George Lippard.[14] A country lad appears on Broadway and falls into the clutches of two confidence men who scheme against his life as well as the inheritance of which he himself is ignorant. While their elaborate plans proceed, the innocent hero wanders among the "gorgeous" shop-window displays of Broadway and falls in love with a daguerreotype portrait he sees in the window of the "Plumbe National Daguerrian Gallery" at Broadway and Murray streets (an actual place; indeed Duganne dedicates the book to "Professor Plumbe"), recognizing it as the very image of the beautiful young lady he had glimpsed his first day on Broadway, when he risked his life to stop the runaway horses of her carriage. He procures a copy of the daguerreotype in exchange for allowing Plumbe to take his own likeness, and wears it in

his bosom as an amulet; indeed it proves its magical powers in the end by deflecting a knife blade aimed at his heart by one of the villainous crew, and leads him to marriage with the appreciative young heiress.

But the plot alone provides only a fraction of the interest of the tale. Life in the Empire City, which takes place chiefly on Broadway, appears as a never-ceasing drama of *eyes,* of watching, observing, gazing. The plot itself centers on acts of deception, of false identity, disguise, and betrayal; its villains are gamblers, speculators, conniving lawyers—a predictable Jacksonian cast of enemies of republican virtue. Duganne opens the narrative upon the "river of life" of Broadway, in which the crowds go about their business mindless of a certain set of "men with cunning eyes . . . watchful and observing, glancing at each and all" (p. 5). They are all "robbers," though "some were called merchants, bankers, brokers, aldermen, judges, lawyers, and gentlemen—others were designated as speculators, sportsmen, bloods, and beggars." What they have in common is a certain kind of eye, "in the expression of which were cunning, and uncharitableness, and cruelty, and deceit" (p. 6). The text overflows with terms of seeing: survey, glance, gaze, observe, view, detect, penetrate, look, behold, inspect, stare, scrutinize, appear and disappear. Moreover, a number of reflective surfaces—the large plate windows of a saloon, the waters on the bay, the gloss and glitter of the arch confidence man's sartorial splendor, and not least, the eyes in which the united lovers at the end "beheld . . . the light of first love"—provide a *mise en scène* of glinting mirror effects. A paradoxical place of heightened visibility and counterfeit appearances, Duganne's Broadway resembles a hall of mirrors, where selves encounter each other as images, as doubles, and "robbers" disguised as respectable men of business lie spying on unaware victims.

And in the midst of Broadway, at the still center of this swirling spectacle, Duganne inserts a picture gallery. The very site of both image-making and exhibition, it is a place above the street where "ladies and their attendant gentlemen" "promenaded the floor, or paused admiringly beneath some elegant frame." Duganne's description of the actual Plumbe gallery corresponds strikingly with a newspaper account by Walt Whitman in the Brooklyn *Eagle* in the same year: "The crowds continually coming and going—the fashionable belle, the many distinguished men. . . . What a spectacle! In whatever direction you turn your peering gaze, you see naught but human faces! There they stretch, from floor to ceiling—hundreds of them. Ah! what tales might those pictures tell if their mute lips had the power of speech![15]

The pictures, mainly of the famed and celebrated, engage Whitman in speechless conversation, their silence together with their vividness "creating the impression of an immense Phantom concourse—speechless and motionless, but yet *realities*. You are indeed in a new world—a peopled world, though mute as the grave." A "new world" of images conveying a new order of reality: Whitman thus discovers in Plumbe's gallery of daguerreotype portraits unsuspected powers in the eyesight alone. The eye, he writes, "has a sort of magnetism. . . . An electrical chain seems to vibrate, as it were, between our brains and him or her preserved there so well. . . . Time, space, both are annihilated, and we identify the semblance with the reality."

Duganne evokes a similar mystic sense of the gallery as a new kind of electrical power which "chain[s] the attention of the passer-by." Its function in the tale, moreover, is not merely to embellish the story with a contemporary reference or to provide the *deus ex machina* to resolve the plot— the physical daguerreotype which saves the hero's life. More than this, the gallery holds the key to the symbolic action of the melodrama, for it holds up a mirror of truth in the place of deception. It provides images that counteract those of the street: portraits of "statesmen, the renowned soldiers, the distinguished *literateurs* of the country, [who] looked down, life-like, from their frames." With its

irresistibly compelling pictures of presidents, governors, poets and preachers, "Lecturers, Lions, Ladies and Learned Men," the gallery was "a perfect study of character" (p. 35). In a world of rogues and false-seemers, the gallery above yet within Broadway offers itself as a paragon of character, a mirror of what ought to be as perceived in the faithful representation of the best that is—what a few years later, following Plumbe's lead, Mathew Brady will call his "Gallery of Illustrious Americans." Just as the hero assures his own salvation by fixing "indelibly within my bosom" the "image" of his love, so citizens can save themselves and their city by gazing on these still, magical images. Thus the "daguerreotype miniature" represents more than an incident and a device of plot but a pedagogy, a kind of "mirror of magistrates," to "the life of the empire city."

Duganne's fiction alludes to a cultural program for photography already established in public discourse by 1846. The photograph represents a different kind of image from that which catches the eye in the crowded flux of the street, and in its difference lies a hope for control, for a moral pedagogy from above: a teaching by images of the virtues missing on city streets and in shops and halls of public office. In the same year an article in the *Christian Watchman* spoke of daguerreotypes as "indices of human character," providing "so many exponential signs of disposition, desire, character," and thus accomplishing "a great revolution in the morals" of portraiture.[16] Unlike a hand-drawn or painted portrait, most likely designed to flatter, the daguerreotype offers a genuine mediation of a living presence, thus making it possible for the moral leadership of the society to make itself felt as immediate experience. In a world where money transactions prevail, where the marketplace and competitive individualism encourage a traffic in false images, the emerging discourse implied, the daguerreotype portrait offers an especially potent corrective. For it too belongs to the market; it competes as image with image, as true image driving out false. The quasimagical mirror of the daguerreotype miniature seemed to offer, then, an amulet against the menace hidden within the Broadway spectacle, the threat of counterfeit transactions at the market center of the Empire City.

II

Within the overt appropriation of the mirror image as an emblem of security, a paragon of character, a pedagogy of republican virtue lay less hopeful, more murky implications in the new technology of picturing. Variants of the mirror image—from exactitude to enchantment, from accuracy to necromancy—disclose a fascination that cannot be explained by reference to rational political motive alone. Like Willis's "the real black art of true magic arises and cries avaunt," Phoebe's turning away from the shadowy image as if it possessed a will or spirit of its own revives ancient taboos against graven images and likenesses, against icons, simulacra, imitations—any reproduction of the world's appearances. It may be that reproduction as such excites subliminal unease, as Jean Baudrillard writes, for "it makes something fundamental vacillate."[17] A closer look at uses of the mirror metaphor offers some clues to its staying power.

The trope seems to have, for example, a basis in physical fact. As an object the daguerreotype indeed resembles a looking glass, the image floating on the surface of a silver-plated copper sheet burnished to a bright mirror effect. By a mere shift of optical focus from the image to the ground upon which the image appears, beholders have a personal hand-mirror, their own mutable reflections mingling with the primary image. The result is a doubling of image upon image: the beholder's fluxional image superimposed upon the fixed daguerreian image, most commonly a portrait of someone known to the viewer. The effect is apparitional: at the merest tilt of the plate the photographic image flickers away, fades into a shadowed negative of itself entangled in the living image of the beholder. The primary image comes to seem evanescent, suspended in a depthless medium. Moreover, as in actual mirrors the daguerreian portrait appears reversed right to left, thus allowing the sitter viewing his own finished image the curious experience of catching sight of himself in the past, as if in a mirror-once-removed, coexisting with one's present and immediate mirror image.

But by themselves literal associations only partially explain the pervasiveness and power of the mirror metaphor. In its semantic depths lay resources answerable to needs less articulate than those of physical description, or of the cultural needs to which the emulatory theory of the daguerreian portrait responds. By tradition a paradoxical symbol both of the mind's encyclopedic capacity to depict the sensible world (Plato's whirling mirror) and of the mind's severe and fatal confinement to its own self-image (the Narcissus myth), the looking-glass image was at the same time a folklore motif of wizardry, black magic, occult divination, forbidden encounters with the dead or absent, and it projected alternative, elusive, and contradictory interpretations upon the new mode of picturing by light. Standing at once for truth and deception, the trope of photograph-as-mirror returned to its users their own confusions and incomprehension, a modern version of old suspicions aroused by images and icons. No matter how well intentioned as a term of praise, "mirror" transfers to the photograph the duplicity traditionally suspected of pictures and picture-makers.

Of course, no more need be made of such figures than to take them as a sign of linguistic resourcefulness before the unfamiliar. But their persistence into the first decade and beyond of American photography, particularly in popular fiction and verse, suggests something more complex and revealing: oblique or unconscious recognitions of an uncanny and possibly disruptive power in the new medium of mechanical reproduction. In popular fiction of the 1840s and 1850s, daguerreotype likenesses appear not only as amulets but as objects of unique obsession, as if they were living presences. In sentimental and celebratory verse they are indeed living spirits, animated shadows, or souls of the dead.

Most often they appear in Gothic settings of preternatural fantasy, wrapped in the same cloth of motifs and imagery examined by Otto Rank in his study of the "doppleganger" and by Freud in "The Uncanny."[18]

Like Freud's "uncanny," which arises out of a relation between the familiar and the unfamiliar, the *heimlich* and the *unheimlich*, animistic descriptions of the photograph often arise in an "enlightened," even scientific and technical, discourse in which the invention of photography represents a major event in the progressive liberation of mankind from superstition, magic, and mental tyranny. Animism may seem a minor note within the rhetoric of "progress" which greeted photography, but its effect is acute. The coexistence of discourses suggests that the process of assimilation of photography within the broader culture shaped itself as a dialectic between familiarizing and defamiliarizing languages, between images of science and images of magic. Writers employed the rhetoric of enlightenment to make a home for the new medium and its unfamiliar images within a familiar ideology, just as practitioners tried by a steady current of "improvements" to make the image seem familiar as "fine art." At the same time, and often in the very same pages of journals, other writings reveled in uncanny sensations which, as Freud observed, arise when something novel comes to seem already known, "once very familiar." It is the meeting again, unexpectedly, of "something familiar and old-established in the mind that has been estranged only by the process of repression" (p. 148).

One of Freud's major examples is the recurrence of an emotion associated with "the old, animistic conception of the universe," which supposed that "the world was peopled with spirits of human beings" (p. 147). Thus animistic tropes in written accounts of photography can be taken as a return, at the site of an image, of guilty, repressed beliefs in the old animistic universe expelled by Christianity, reason, and science. Uncanny sensations such as Phoebe experiences would thus represent the unconscious recurrence, charged with guilt, of the

long-repressed belief and feeling that likenesses—shadows as well as reflections in mirror surfaces—are detached portions of living creatures, their soul or spirit. Freud's insight into the way the psyche allows itself the pleasurable terrors of the uncanny in order to reinforce its defensive repressions helps us to better understand the function of figures of black magic as reinforcement of the authority of "reason." It suggests that the progressivist view of the origin and development of photography allowed space for "irrational" figurations as a way of reinforcing itself, confirming its own authority to speak for the future of the medium, especially its application to the fine-art genre of portraiture.

The social history of the medium supports this supposition. While commercial practitioners in the early 1840s were often transient entrepreneurs and itinerants, photographic communities began to consolidate in the major cities, and by the beginning of the 1850s a distinct "profession" emerged, complete with national journals, associations, competitions, and awards.[19] A key element in this process was a differentiation between the "mechanics" (including the practical science) and the "art" (including the theoretical science) of photography, as well as between "cheap" and "artistic" pictures.[20] The early journals took as their major cause the need for theoretically knowledgable and artistically cultivated practice as the prerequisite for professional status. The mix of articles of history, science, and art, chronicling the history of research leading to photography and combining theoretical discussion of the nature of light and optics with arguments for the fine-art possibilities within the medium, conveys the ambition for the public acceptance of commercial photography as a *serious* and not merely a marketplace endeavor.

Henry Snelling, founder and editor of the *Photographic Art Journal*, titled his lead editorial in the first issue, January 1851, "The Art of Photography":

> At the present day it [photography] is viewed, too much, in the light of a mere mechanical occupation to arrive at any high degree of excel-

lence. In too many instances men enter into it because they can get nothing else to do; without the least appreciation of its merits as an art of exquisite refinement, without the taste to guide them, and without the love and ambition to study more than its practical application, neglecting the sciences intimately connected with it, and leaving entirely out of the question those of drawing, painting, and sculpture, sister arts, a knowledge of which must tend to elevate the taste and direct the operator into the more classical and elegant walks of his profession.[21]

The initial step in the walk toward "profession" is clearly to promulgate standards of excellence. Too many practitioners lack essential qualifications of theory and sensibility. The scene surveyed by Snelling has its beginnings in the economic depression of the late 1830s and 1840s, when to set up as a daguerreotypist seemed relatively free of risk, requiring minimum capital and mechanical skills. While what Snelling most deplores is ignorance of the finer points of the craft and crass commercial motives, he also wants to dispel an aura of quackery and the hint of sorcery clinging to the medium. Robert Taft notes that the earliest photographers, often local blacksmiths, cobblers, dentists, and watchmakers with an eye to expanding their income, "made their work appear mysterious, especially those in smaller towns: that is, they imposed themselves as magicians," a deception made credible by the darkened closet into which the daguerreotypist slipped to prepare and develop his mysterious plates.[22]

In the 1840s the popular press had made much of the perils of having a daguerreian likeness taken, a running comedy in which the humor cuts both ways, toward the primitive devices of the medium and toward the wounded vanity of a public increasingly aware (and the new medium fostered this to an incalculable extent) of "image," of social self-presentation. Shadows were a particular blight. "'Can't you take me a likeness without these dark places?' asks a lady who sees, with surprise, a dirty mark

under her nose, around her eyes, under her chin, or on the side of her cheek. 'There is nothing like this on my face.'" T. S. Arthur, who recounts this misreading of the image in a humorous essay in 1849 in *Godey's Lady's Book,* also tells of a farmer so frightened by the photographer's preparations that he "dashed down stairs as if a legion of evil spirits were after him," and of sitters who suffer the "illusion that the instrument exercises a kind of magnetic attraction, and many good ladies actually feel their eyes 'drawn' toward the lens while the operation is in progress!"[23]

Thus tremors of apprehension, of the "uncanny," survive the humor, a strong enough hint for us to venture that by knowledge of science and art Snelling meant precisely the skills to produce an image so true to conventions of flattering portraiture as to be free of disturbing traces of the unfamiliar, the *unheimlich.* The onus for producing a "true" picture lies with the photographer, his sensibility, his cultivation. The alternative would be surrender to the mechanical apparatus, to the camera as automaton—another image, mirror-like, steeped in the "uncanny." The lesson of those early grim images in which sitters cannot recognize themselves as they imagine themselves to be is that "no one can be a successful Daguerreotypist unless he is an artist, as well as a manipulator."[24]

Snelling argues obsessively in the early years of the journal that professional status for commercial photographers requires that they take their lead from the fine arts, which themselves in just these years developed distinct institutions, schools, art unions and associations.[25] Everything depended on how the photographer saw himself: artist or mere technician, creator or mere manipulator. Snelling supported his defense of photography as a potential fine art by drawing on the rhetoric of progress and enlightenment which ruled public discourse in America. He enlists photography in the master plot of "progress": the struggle between light and darkness, science and the black arts, reason and barbarism. "The faculty of language," he writes, voicing the commonplace middle-class ideology, "has gradually worked a most wonderful change in the relations between man and all other created things," letting loose "a flood of intellectual light" which washes away "old established opinions and theories" and establishes "others more truthful, more natural, and more intrinsically valuable." A key event is the defeat of superstition: "those things which once appeared . . . marvellous are no longer so, but the mere effects of natural causes." Thus the "progress of knowledge" leads "from the barbarism of former ages to the present civilized state." And from the same civilizing process behind the Copernican Revolution and the discovery of the invariable laws of physics, "the photographic art was brought to light." "At once the cynosure of all observers" for the "beauty of its conception, and the importance to which it must ultimately arrive in the world of art," the universal enthusiasm at its birth gave rise "to a class of artists who must one day become as famous as the great masters of painting." Guided by art, photography will inevitably advance toward the goal of the perfectly realized resemblance, as it has already progressed from the "mere half distinct development of the daguerreotype plate" to "the full drawn, bold and clear impressions" of recent improved processes.[26] Thus, as Snelling wrote in the opening number of the journal, in the not far distant future "our best Daguerreotypists will wonder how they could, for so long a time, be content with the specimens of their art they now put forth, as much as they do at this day at the shadows of six and eight years ago."[27]

III

To illuminate the shadows, to dispel the aura of sorcery and deception, to exorcise demons still haunting the medium: these motives Snelling shared with the photographic community emerging in the 1850s. Yet, like ghosts and blurs and other inexplicable appearances which frequently marred the most carefully executed of pictures, those demons refused to disperse; they continued to assert themselves in the very diction representing the medium

in popular expressions. The term "shadows" may, for example, represent the primitive state of "half indistinct" images, but in the common coin of daguerreian lingo other meanings survived. "Take the shadow ere the substance fade," the popular slogan of daguerreotypists, calls up the notion of shadow as soul, as animate extension, double, and immortal part of self.[28] Of course, such figures of speech had long lost original force, diluted of any distinct supernaturalism. But is it only fanciful to suggest that just as, according to Freud, experiences of the uncanny in tales such as E. T. A. Hoffmann's "The Sandman" represent a recurrence of repressed psychic anxiety (chiefly about castration), so the reappearance within the public discourse of photography of a diction of shadows and shades, spirit lands, mirrored doubles, represents the return of a barely repressed animism comparable to (surely a sign of the same development) the eruption of Gothicism at the height of the age of "enlightenment," "reason," and "revolution"? That in the daguerreian period photography rejuvenated a debased diction of light-and-shadow, reinvested it with new anxieties provoked by mechanical images of automatic reproduction, the evocation of the visible from the invisible, but just as surely in response to rapidly changing social relations, the displacement of an older system of propertied wealth and deference by an urban market economy of money and its deceptions?

No matter how conventional and formulaic, how drained of literal belief, magical and animistic figures of speech signify strains, tensions, and fears within the culture. Why, for instance, so widespread an association between daguerreotypes and death? Providing a lasting image of departed "loved ones" was among the very first possibilities imagined for the medium. "Take the shadow ere the substance fade": the very taking of a likeness, fixing a transient appearance of flesh as an image, evoked death, cessation, ultimate fixity.

Here is a genial, smiling, energetic face, full of sunny strength, intelligence, integrity, good humor; but it lies imprisoned in baleful shades, as of the Valley of Death; seems smiling on me as if in mockery. Doesn't know me, friend? I am dead, thou seeist, and distant, and forever hidden from thee; I belong already to the Eternities, and thou recognizest me not! On the whole it is the strangest feeling that I have . . .

Thus Carlyle writes to Emerson about a daguerreotype likeness of his American friend, and goes on to request that "you get us by the earliest opportunity some living pictorial sketch, chalk-drawing or the like, from a trustworthy hand."[29] A poem published by Snelling, "On Seeing a Daguerreotype Portrait," more literally associates death with the unique look of the daguerreian image:

> What means this vain, incessant strife,
>   To hide thyself in fitful gleams—
> Now standing like a thing of life?
>   Then fading like a poet's dreams.[30]

The flickering which disturbs Carlyle becomes an emblem of the passage between "thing of life" and "dreams," between life and death. The poem goes on to say that the daguerreotype's "visioned form" is like "a fiction," or a trace that "memory leaves / Upon the tablets of the mind," or the "flitting of a thought" that rises from "secret depths" and is quickly "vanished" by "reason sage." It is precisely this tendency toward unfixing itself in the mind, seeming familiar and unfamiliar at once, which gives the image its uncanny power to evoke death. Thus its "semblance" is "airy," "it speaks of forms in spirit land," of "that better state, / Where sin and sorrow never come," and promises that "those we love / . . . Shall wear those well known forms above."

The easy absorption of daguerreotypes into sentimental thanatoptic diction may say more about sentimentalism than about the medium, but it tells of a cultural association of photography with death that we cannot discount as mere convention. In addition to sublimating natural fear of death, consolatory verses appearing in the early photographic journals in the 1850s also address more public concerns, at a time of economic recovery but increased agitation over slavery, about the death of leaders and heroes, the "fathers" of the republic. "Stanzas, Suggested by a Visit to Brady's Portrait Gallery" invokes the "soul-lit shadows now around," the pictures of "illustrious Americans" Brady and other leading photographers exhibited like charms on their gallery walls: "They who armies nobly led, / They who make a nation's glory / While they're living—when they're dead, / Landmarks for our country's future." After reciting the names of Brady's pantheon—Taylor, Jackson, Frémont, Houston, Webster, Clay, Audubon, Bryant, the poet concludes:

> Like a spirit land of shadows
>   They in silence on me gaze,
> And I feel my heart is beating
>   With the pulse of other days;
> And I ask what great magician
>   Conjured forms like these afar?
> Echo answers, 'tis the sunshine,
>   By its alchymist Daguerre.[31]

The rhyme breezes through figures of magic, alchemy, and conjuring spirits without blinking, but even the doggerel conveys an authentic wish that photography preserve not only the appearance but the actual presence of authoritative fathers so badly wanted by a generation bereft of the moral guidance of the founders.

No surprise, then, that for all his enlightened rationalism Snelling indulged himself in sentimental verse, let alone Gothic tales in the German manner of E. T. A. Hoffmann. In at least two striking instances he opened the pages of his journal to unadulterated fictions of the uncanny. One is an actual tale by Hoffmann, "The Empty House"; the other, in the same mode but in a manner close to Poe, "The Magnetic Daguerreotypes."[32] Identified only as "A German Tale," without mention of the author, "The Empty House" (1817) bears many similarities to "The Sandman" (1815–1816), upon which Freud bases his discussion of "the uncanny." Ambiguity of perception lies at the heart of both tales: in

"The Empty House," apparitional visual experiences which produce strange "indescribable" feelings of "delightful horror," "at once uneasy and delightful," "full of anxiety and ardent longing." In both tales optical devices, possibly magical, magnify the ambiguity of the visible and heighten anxiety: Nathaneal's pocket telescope in "The Sandman," Theodore's opera glasses and pocket mirror in "The Empty House." Powerful erotic feelings affect the bedeviled heroes in both tales, and wizard figures with green catlike eyes appear in both, imagos of the wicked father. And by use of skeptical, disbelieving characters who insist the hero can free himself from his morbid obsessions, each tale leads the reader to the unanswerable question: are the uncanny experiences self-willed delusions, signs of the hero's mental derangement, or the product of an external cause such as black magic, or both?

The presence of the pocket mirror, so like a daguerreotype in size and intimacy, probably accounts for Snelling's publication of "The Empty House," which he ran serially in four successive numbers. Not only is Theodore able, as he discovers accidentally and not with unalloyed pleasure, to conjure in his mirror the image of the mysterious lady at the window of the empty house—it is never clear whether she is an apparition of the young Edwina, the ancient witch in the seductive form of the young woman, or a painted portrait!—but the mirror also induces in him a strange fixation. While using it to make himself inconspicuous when observing the tantalizing image in the window, Theodore suddenly feels paralyzed as if in a "waking dream." A clue to the mirror's power appears in the confession he then makes, "with shame," that he thought at once of a story told by his nurse when she found him "staring at the large mirror in my father's room." His nurse warned him that "if children looked into the glass at night, a strange ugly face would peep out, and that the children's eyes would at once become fixed." Naturally he could not resist looking, saw "hideous fiery eyes sparkling in the glass, and fell down senseless."

"The Sandman" concludes with Nathaneal's destruction, a victim of his obsession with "the uncanny." Theodore survives, however, aided by a doctor who helps him recognize "the deeper connection between all these strange things." His survival, and the apparent victory of rational explanation, may also account for the story's appearance in Snelling's journal—an example, we might put it, of the mirror image purged of its diabolism. But the tale can be taken as well as an explanation of the persistence of an animistic aura in the daguerreotype. For an "empty house" actually housing strange creatures, including a lascivious witch, translates easily into the unconscious itself—"the dark, mysterious region which is the home of our spirit," in the words of one of Theodore's learned friends. This same "physician" explains that dreams, with their "extraordinary peculiarity" to deposit in the waking mind "dim recollections" that make strangers seem "so astoundingly familiar to me," dispose certain persons vulnerable to influence by "some external psychical principle," "a magnetic relation" that one mind might exert over another. Thus the tale might be read as teaching that animistic representations of the daguerreotype derive finally from propensities within human consciousness itself, from the "empty house" we people with ghosts and wizards and seductive ladies who in the moment of the first embrace draw back the mask to disclose the rotting flesh.

Was it part of Snelling's program to insinuate magic in order to purge it by a kind of homeopathy, a therapeutic reading? "The Magnetic Daguerreotypes," which appeared two years earlier, reprinted from the New York *Sunday Courier,* speaks more directly to the uncanny effects of the photographic image as a *living* presence. Also set in Germany, the tale has a narrator—nameless until the final paragraph—who visits the studio of Professor Ariovistus Dunkleheim (the first name signifies prophetic eyes; the last, dark home) with his betrothed, the lovely Elora, to have likenesses taken by the professor's new process. The sitters place themselves each before a highly polished plate of steel, "a perfect mirror," and by "electro-galvanic" or "magnetic" action their likenesses are fixed instantaneously.[33] That night the narrator learns that the portrait of his beloved, upon which he gazes with mounting desire, is "a faithful mirror of the absent Elora's features," an animate picture in which he sees her as she is at the moment (asleep in bed, as it happens). "How superior to the cold, ghastly, shadowy immobility of the mere daguerreotype, were these living portraits of Dunkelheim's."

The pleasure is short-lived, however, for the narrator remembers that Dunkelheim himself had retained copies of both images, and even now, with his "bottle-green eyes" and his diabolic look of "critical penetration," might be enjoying the look of desire on his face, able to "watch every change in the expression of my face, to read my every thought, as in an open book." He feels himself "forever subject to an excruciating moral espionage! to be denied for life, the security and luxury of privacy," particularly as he grows more excited with "a fever of impatient love" and continues "to gaze and gaze with an intense and burning ardor" on Elora's living portrait. He informs Elora of their predicament ("A detested stranger can, at will, become a witness of our most rapturous moments, our most secret delights, our—") and pledges to regain the copies or to slay their tormentor. Dunkelheim eludes his grasp; they marry after all, "but a spectre haunted us. . . . Night and day, his terrible green eyes were upon us." The hero resumes his pursuit, destroys the fiend, and recovers the telltale plates. "'Henceforth we are at least our own masters,' cries Elora, 'and not puppets, acting for the amusement of a detestable old necromancer!'" Still, the "cold green eyes" of Dunkelheim return at times to "haunt our fancies."

Only at the very end does the narrator reveal his own name, and we grasp at once the reason for his withholding it until now: Ernest Darkman. The correspondence, slant as it is, of Darkman to Dunkelheim adds a hint of a familial (and oedipal) conflict between hero and villain to the tale's already strained eroticism and prurience. The network of echoes, doublings, parallels through which the tale works toward the frisson of its final revelation serves as a charged setting for its theme of visibility, the fears it raises, in order homeopathically to expel them, of the camera as an all-seeing eye, a disembodied invasive gaze in a system of scrutiny extending through the bedroom into the mind and soul. In this most stunning instance in the early literature of the photograph as mirror we have a graphic diagnostic chart, as it were, of premonitions that among the many ways life would never again be the same after photography, the transformation of self into an object of surveillance as well as an image for manipulation and consumption by others might be the most consequential.

Thus we see that Clark's mirror on Broadway hid within its shadowed depths a far less simple, more troubled—and thereby far richer and more challenging—cultural response to the photograph than we have yet recognized. In part the conflicted structure of response I have described reflects divisions in the early social practices of the medium, including the quite early application of the daguerreotype to the study of criminality.[34] The largest significance of the pattern lies, however, in the ambivalence it represents within the dominant middle-class acceptance of the medium—an ambivalence which suggests a pervasive insecurity about newly gained property and status within a rapidly changing social and political order. Particularly, the homeopathic process of evoking fear in order to allay it which appears in the professionalizing rhetoric of early commercial photography provides a not-inconsiderable clue to forces shaping a modern culture within the passages of antebellum American society.

NOTES

1. William Welling, *Photography in America: The Formative Years, 1839–1900* (New York: Crowell, 1978), pp. 7–15. Exhaustive information about the establishment of the daguerreotype in America can be found in

Floyd and Marion Rinhart, *The American Daguerreotype* (Athens: University of Georgia Press, 1981). Richard Rudisill, *Mirror Image: The Influence of the Daguerreotype on American Society* (Albuquerque: University of New Mexico Press, 1971), the first attempt to place the daguerreotype within a cultural history, has been a touchstone for all subsequent studies.

2. Quoted in Robert Taft, *Photography and the American Scene: A Social History, 1839–1889* (New York: Macmillan, 1938), p. 41.

3. *The Knickerbocker* 14 (1839): 560.

4. *The Diary of Philip Hone, 1828–1851,* edited by Allan Nevins (New York: Dodd, Mead, 1927), p. 435.

5. Nathaniel Hawthorne, *The House of the Seven Gables,* edited by Seymour L. Gross (New York: Norton Critical Edition, 1967), p. 91.

6. *Corsair,* April 13, 1839, pp. 70–72. A week later, on April 20, 1839, the New York *Observer* published Samuel F. B. Morse's eyewitness account of Daguerre's invention in a letter from Paris.

7. It remains unclear how Willis came upon this misnomer, which implies that he had already heard of Daguerre even before Morse's letter of the following week.

8. Edward K. Spann, *The New Metropolis: New York City, 1840–1857* (New York: Columbia University Press, 1981), chaps. 4–5. See also Samuel Rezneck, "The Social History of an American Depression, 1837–1843," *American Historical Review* 40 (1934–35): 662–87.

9. Welling, *Photography in America,* p. 41.

10. Depressed conditions did in fact create a favorable climate for the commercial development of portrait daguerreotypy. To set up on one's own required only a minor outlay of capital and small expenses; thus photography took up some of the slack among unemployed craftsmen. See Taft, *Photography and the American Scene,* p. 39.

11. *Living Age* (June 1846): 552.

12. *The Diary of Philip Hone,* pp. 434–36.

13. Duganne, *The Daguerreotype Miniature; or, Life in the Empire City* (Philadelphia: G. B. Zieber & Co., 1846). Page references are to this edition.

14. See, for example, Larzer Ziff, *Literary Democracy: The Declaration of Cultural Independence in America* (New York: Viking Press, 1981), chap. 6.

15. Walt Whitman, *The Gathering of the Forces,* 2 vols., edited by Cleveland Rodgers and John Black (New York, G. P. Putnam's Sons, 1920), 2: 113–17.

16. Quoted in *Living Age* (June 1846): 552.

17. *Simulations* (New York: Semiotext(e), 1983), p. 153. Page references are to this edition.

18. Sigmund Freud, *On Creativity and the Unconscious* (New York: Harper & Row, 1958), pp. 122–61.

19. This process is well documented in Rinhart, in Taft, and in Welling. See Burton J. Bledstein, *The Culture of Professionalism: The Middle Class and the Development of Higher Education in America* (New York: W. W. Norton & Co., 1976).

20. Insight into the competitive framework within which this distinction appeared can be gleaned from the following double-entry meditation on the trade by publisher S. D. Humphrey in his *Daguerreian Journal* 1 (1850): 49: "We find 71 rooms in this city, devoted solely to this art; independent of the many stores and manufacturies engaged in the making and selling of the materials. In these rooms there are in all 127 operators, including the proprietors and persons engaged in the Galleries, also 11 ladies and 46 boys. We find the amount of rent paid by these artists to be $25,550 per year. Let us allow $10 per week for the 127 operators; this is certainly a very low estimate, we find the amount $1,270 per week, or calculating 52 weeks per year, the result is $66,040. For the 11 ladies engaged, we estimate $5 per week, making $2,860 per year. The 46 boys, at $1 per week, $2,392. Thus we find the total amount necessary to defray the above expenses to be $92,842, per annum. It is seen by the above that we make no estimate of the materials used (such as plates, cases, and chemicals,). . . , and we forbear to make any estimate of this last, as many artists are now taking pictures at such reduced rates." Humphrey also forbears citing gross intake, but is patently alarmed at the price-cutting tactics of "cheap" competitors. For an invaluable discussion of the changing economic and social structures of the nascent industry in these years, see Reese Jenkins, *Images and Enterprise: Technology and the American Photographic Industry, 1839–1925* (Baltimore: Johns Hopkins University Press, 1975), especially chap. 1.

21. *Photographic Art Journal* 1 (January 1851): 1.

22. Taft, *Photography and the American Scene,* p. 48.

23. T. S. Arthur, *Godey's Lady's Book* 38 (May 1849): 352–55.

24. J. K. Fisher, "Photography, The Handmaid of Art," *Photographic Art Journal* 1 (January 1851): 19.

25. See Neil Harris, *The Artist in American Society: The Formative Years, 1790–1860* (New York: Braziller, 1966), especially pp. 90–122.

26. *Photographic Art Journal* 3 (May 1853): 316–17.

27. Ibid. 1 (January 1851): 2.

28. See Sir James George Frazier, *The Golden Bough,*

Abridged Edition (New York: Macmillan, 1951), pp. 220–25.

29. Quoted in Welling, *Photography in America,* p. 55.

30. *Photographic Art Journal* 1 (March 1851): 179. The author is Mrs. G. H. Putnam.

31. Ibid. 1 (January 1851): 63. The author is Caleb Lyon.

32. Ibid. 7 (1854): 316–18, 350–51; 8 (1855): 20–23, 51–52.

33. See Welling, *Photography in America,* pp. 25–27, for discussion of actual experiments in electrogalvanic processes.

34. See Allen Sekula, "The Body and the Archive," *October* 39 (Winter 1966): 3–64.

Southworth and Hawes

The Artists

Matthew R. Isenburg

Southworth and Hawes daguerreotypes have a subtlety and sophistication beyond any other daguerreian images of their time. Why should this be?

To begin with, Josiah Johnson Hawes, the artist, and Albert Sands Southworth, the promoter, made an ideal partnership. Southworth's public relations and promotional ability and his connections brought the influential, the powerful, the rich, and the famous to the studio at 5½ Tremont Row where Hawes handled most of the photography. An advertisement read: "One of the partners is a practical Artist, and as we never employ *Operators,* customers receive our personal attention." [1]

Josiah Johnson Hawes was a master in three areas: lighting, composition, and posing. All three are reflected in the daguerreotypes with a consistency that is startling. The more one sees of this body of work, the more one realizes that it was no happy accident; each plate is a true masterpiece. Add to this the unusually large number of full plates produced by the firm, and one is even more amazed.

Most daguerreian artists shied away from the full-plate size for numerous reasons. First and foremost, the clientele could not afford it. Nor were they made to think of the results as works of art requiring the larger and much more costly format. Observation of daguerreotypes seen at shows, in private collections, or in museums leads one to surmise that better than 60 percent of those extant are 2¾ × 3¼ inches, or sixth-plate size, while whole-plate-size images, 6½ × 8½ inches, represent far less than 1 percent of the total output.

One of the reasons why relatively few of the whole-plate daguerreotypes were made is that the large camera needed to make them was more cumbersome to operate. Fine-focusing a far forward lens knob with fully outstretched arm while simultaneously trying to check the results in the ground glass at the rear of the camera without jarring or moving the instrument was difficult at best.

The sensitizing and developing equipment was also large, volumetrically requiring much more chemical preparation, and physically harder to use as compared to that needed for the more popular smaller formats. Some daguerreians even bragged in their advertisements and broadsides about having a full-plate outfit, which leads the reader to assume that many operators did not possess one. [2] In those days before enlargers, no large camera meant no large picture. Much more care and time, as well as much more attention to the uniform sensitizing of the plate, went into evenly buffing a 6½ × 8½-inch plate than a 2¾ × 3¼-inch plate. And the surface of the plate was so fragile that anything coming into contact with it could cause less than perfect results.

It is astounding that so many whole plates were produced by one firm. It is a gift from Josiah Johnson Hawes to our photographic heritage that so many were preserved intact.

The three areas that set Hawes apart from being just another good technician are best described in an ad, probably worded by Southworth, to explain the success of the firm: "Our plates are the largest, most highly polished, and have a more perfect surface; our pictures have a surpassing delicacy in their finish; there is no sameness in our positions and use of the light, it being adapted to the design of showing every face in its best view. As far as possible we imitate nature in her most beautiful forms, by a mellow blending of lights and shades, an artistic effect of drapery and figure, a pleasing air, forcible expression, and startling animation; representing thought, action, and feeling or soul." [3] To this day, almost 150 years later, a more accurate and explanatory statement would be difficult to make.

To explore the areas of lighting, composition, and posing more closely, it is necessary to go through the studio experience step by step. A visit to the Southworth and Hawes studio included much more than just having one's picture taken. After a climb to the top floor, there was an indoctrination as to dress, shawl, jewelry, or other articles to enhance the women in their sitting. Hair had to be arranged in as complementary a fashion as possible. Advertisements read: "We have in attendance two Ladies and Females can have assistance in arranging their dress and drapery, and consult them as to colors most appropriate and harmonious for the Daguerreotype process." [4] Gentlemen were also groomed to reflect their attitude, outlook, and station in life.

Hawes, reminiscing about old times in an 1893 interview with A. Lincoln Bowles of the Boston *Sunday Herald*, was quoted as saying, "They were all ladies and gentlemen who came here then, sir. They were men and women of family, and with names. We could tell a commoner very quickly. It wasn't necessary for him to say more than a half dozen words." [5] Hawes seems to have had no trouble expressing his impatience for those he felt of less breeding than his normal run of distinguished, famous, or powerful clients. Southworth, writing in the *Lady's Almanac* for 1855, expressed the idea that a daguerreotype sitting was an occasion not to be taken lightly, but rather a time-consuming affair between artist and sitter that required mental preparation as well as proper attire. He wrote:

"The hour of departure on a tour of travel, a few hasty moments snatched from a shopping excursion in town, or between hurried morning calls and dinner, will not be likely to find one in a sufficiently fresh and quiet mood to yield to the hints the Artist may desire to throw out expressly for the sitter's benefit. . . . On your own account, as well as for the sake of those who will value a correct portrait of yourself, choose the most favorable opportunity, as already suggested, and afford the Artist ample time, without haste or nervousness, for his labor." [6]

This professional approach to artist and subject was most laboriously spelled out at a time when other daguerreian studios were boasting of as many as five hundred sittings daily [7] and advertising images for as low as twenty-five cents apiece. [8] No other practitioners charged what Southworth and Hawes did. By pricing their daguerreotypes at fifteen dollars, [9] they catered to the carriage trade. They also considered themselves artists, and this is reflected in all their advertising. "Daguerreotype Artists" and "Artists' Daguerreotype Rooms" were constantly recurring themes of self-description for themselves and their studio. [10] Even their studio location, Tremont Row, was in the heart of the artists' colony in Boston, as opposed to the business district of Washington Street where most photographers rented their rooms.

In an article published in the November 1896 *McClure's Magazine* it was described thusly: "In the old days, when this studio was opened, Tremont Row was the center for the artists of the city. Here fully one-third of the portrait painters of Boston lived; here, too, were most of the sculptors, several engravers, and a goodly number of art supply stores. In the building where Southworth and Hawes took their quarters, Greenough and Story both had studios, and in this same building Harriet Hosmer worked. All of the fraternity up and down the Row were deeply interested in the new discovery and were constant visitors at the gallery." [11]

A mid-1850s Southworth and Hawes ad read:

In extending a cordial invitation to all who

chance to peruse these pages, to visit our exhibition gallery, it is proper to state in a plain and comprehensive manner what we would have visitors expect, especially those who are judges of pictures. We aim in our profession to please Artists, and those whose taste for the fine arts has been cultivated and refined. Our patrons and customers have uniformly been of this class; and as we have aimed to do superior work, our services have commanded much higher prices than others in the same business are able to obtain.[12]

One should remember that there were few accidents with a three-second exposure. Much more thought went into a quality photograph in those years, since no daguerreian cameras were hand-held and the proper plate preparation was a ceremony in itself, thus making each exposure far more important than that of today's motorized camera.

Due to the lack of artificial light, Hawes's first concern after the subject left the dressing rooms and moved into the sitting rooms was to place the person in that always gray soft northlight that filled the studio as the sun described its eternal arc across the earth's sky.[13] Of course, the props such as chairs, tables, columns, and rug were all movable. Once the proper positioning for subject lighting was found, Hawes then set his mind to a very important operation: the distance from his camera to the subject. This composition required a thorough understanding of the spatial concepts of the plate about to be exposed. Whether to come in close with the camera, thus filling the plate intimately, or to pull back with the camera and tripod, thus composing the portrait with more dignity and formality, reflecting the stylized portraiture of that time, had to be considered with each plate. The space between camera and client was in a direct relationship to how Hawes perceived his subjects, commingled with how he felt they perceived themselves. This sensitivity to people's moods, as well as his keen awareness of their social position in the rigid social structure that was Boston of the 1840s and 1850s,

allowed him unerringly to set the tone for those portraits that to this day make us feel we know and understand the sitters in this cavalcade of personalities that spans almost one and a half centuries. This strength of presence is so overwhelming and so powerful that a modern-day viewer is transported and feels as if he or she were present in the studio during the actual sitting. No other daguerreian artist achieved this with such consistency.

As important as the positioning of the camera to the subject was, so was the vertical placing of the camera, the raising or lowering of the tripod to set the mood of composition. The subtlety of looking up or down at the subject in the ground glass again changed the composition on the plate. Some portraits were made from eye level, others from slightly below or above, thus shifting the message conveyed, yet always with a feeling for the subject being photographed. The classical pyramid was evoked in group sittings whenever possible. The interplay created between group members by composing them into each other rather than at the camera gave group shots a uniqueness hitherto unknown in the photographic arts. Composition on the plate was the first consideration of Hawes the artist.

Posing, as opposed to composition, was the fine-tuning of the portrait. Particularly obvious was the way hands were posed to describe still further the sitter's character. Adolescent female hands were so delicately handled by Hawes that a special gentility crept into these portraits and gave them a sensitivity all their own. Men's hands were posed more rigidly, or grasping a book, and, thus, set a more masculine tone to the portrait. Throughout all the known daguerreotypes by Southworth and Hawes, one never sees a head rest or neck brace. Posing was made to look natural since the artist could not possibly suffer the intrusion of artificial aids or devices to detract from the portrait as a work of art. The male neck and head were set alert and sometimes even firm, while the female neck and head were usually turned and relaxed, almost in a reclining position, all of which served to bring grace to the female and resolve to the male figure. This again delineates the ideal roles played by family characters in the typical upper-class New England household of the 1840s and 1850s and reflects a belief in and a reaffirmation of a social order long lost to modern society. Through the wonderfully artistic work of Hawes, a very real social statement took form, and its message from another age and another time is still frozen clear.[14]

The use of light both on the subject and as background was the third ingredient that went into making these jewels of the daguerreian art. The first concern seemed to be the way light fell upon the subject itself, but just as important—and very advanced for its time—was the masterful way background lighting was controlled from light to dark. Through a series of backgrounds, shades, reflectors, and diffusers, the background lighting was always in contrast to the subject, thereby giving a depth to the portraits unequalled by any other artist of that day.

It would not be enough to say Southworth and Hawes utilized background lighting; they invented it! They carried its subtleties to an area unreached by any other daguerreian firm. Dark hair could be highlighted with a very light background, while light skin tones could be contrasted with a darker background, all of this in the same daguerreotype. The presence of the gray scale was much more prominent in Southworth and Hawes daguerreotypes than in the much harsher black-and-white images of other operators. When personality, pose, or demeanor called for high contrast to describe a sitter's inner self, that plate shifted from shades of gray to stark black and white. This was accomplished by a change in time of exposure, time of development, or both, and thereby created a purposeful contrast to portray the subject's personality. The combination of subject lighting and skillful backlighting no doubt reflected Hawes's discipline through years of painting with oils and his appreciation of fine art.

Attention to detail as seen through an artist's eye, the approaching of all sittings with the same thoroughness used for portrait painting, and enough time to do the total job gave us an unmatched legacy of images on silver. Hawes's final touch was the taking of three proofs, of which the sitter had his or her choice of the best. And here, once again, Hawes was doing something almost a century before it became common practice.

To sum up the entire visual experience of Southworth and Hawes's work, I return to their own words about themselves, written at the peak of their creative period: "In every possible application of the Daguerreotype we have led the way beyond all competition. . . . This will seem extravagant to all who are strangers to us; and yet we ask Artists to expect to see something superior to what they have ever seen at all, and we will risk their being disappointed."[15]

NOTES

1. A. D. Jones, *The Illustrated American Biography* (New York: J. Milton Emerson & Co., 1853), 1: 222.

2. "Only Whole Size Camera in the County," broadside, L. V. Staffer & Co., Allen's Block, Ravenna, Ohio, author's collection.

3. Jones, *Biography,* 1: 222.

4. Original invoice, author's collection.

5. A. Lincoln Bowles, "A Famous Boston Studio," Boston *Sunday Herald,* March 12, 1893.

6. A. S. Southworth, "Suggestions to Ladies Who Sit for Daguerreotypes," in *Lady's Almanac for 1855* (Boston: John P. Jewett & Co., 1855), p. 117.

7. Original trade card for Tyler & Co., Boston, author's collection.

8. Original trade card for B. D. Maxham, Worcester, author's collection.

9. Bowles, "A Famous Boston Studio."

10. Jones, *Biography,* 1: 222.

11. Mrs. D. T. Davis, "The Daguerreotype in America," *McClure's Magazine* 8 (November 1896): 16.

12. Southworth and Hawes, descriptive advertisement clipped from unknown publication, author's collection.

13. "Light and Skylights," *Daguerreian Journal* 1 (February 1, 1851): 177.

14. "Daguerre's Art Preserves 19th Century Bostonian

Faces," Boston *Evening Transcript,* November 7, 1934, Pt. 3, p. 1, col. 4.

15. Southworth and Hawes, descriptive advertisement clipped from unknown publication, author's collection.

Southworth and Hawes

The Studio Collection

Ken Appollo

Josiah Johnson Hawes was a dedicated photographer and a devoted, loving husband and father. He was at once an itinerant artist and a man who kept the same business location for fifty-eight years. He was gentle, upright, patient, and generous. He enjoyed his work and took an interest in the work of his colleagues and of younger artist friends. It is our good fortune that Josiah Hawes was also a collector. Visiting the famous studio in 1896, five years before the photographer's death at ninety-three, Mrs. D. T. Davis reported what she witnessed firsthand:

> Here are a half-dozen rooms furnished with ancient apparatus and appointments, and cluttered with the daguerreotypes and photographs of a half century of active work. . . . Mr. Hawes has in the specimens of his work an almost complete gallery of the eminent residents of Boston in the 40's and 50's, and of the prominent people who visited the city in the same period. The collection is of rare historical interest, and should be kept intact in some Boston museum, though it is doubtful if any one else would give it the reverent care that its white-haired owner does.[1]

It was to the unmarried children of Josiah and Nancy Southworth Hawes that the duty of closing their famous father's studio passed in 1901. Josiah's only son, Edward Southworth Hawes, the youngest of his three children, was the heir apparent of the studio collection.[2] In that the collection coincidentally contained much in the way of family photographs, personal correspondence and effects, it

seems likely that the Hawes daughters, Alice Mary and Marion Augusta, shared this inheritance. Marion especially, together with Edward, would later take an active role in placing selected daguerreotypes with the Boston Museum of Fine Arts and Metropolitan Museum collections.

The responsibility of caring for the Southworth and Hawes studio collection was no small undertaking. At various times during his long life, Josiah Hawes claimed to be the custodian of as many as 20,000 daguerreotypes and 40,000 glass negatives.[3] To be sure, he was determined and single-minded in his preservation of these materials. Copying his old photographs was part of his trade. As late as 1897 he renewed the copyright on a large albumen copy of his favorite daguerreotype of Daniel Webster.[4] His careful treatment of the studio archives, combined with the strength of his personal recollections, influenced their preservation after his death. But the collection was large, and its relocation, let alone appraisal and redistribution, demanded considerable attention.

In 1901 the Hawes children were already middle-aged. Edward, the youngest, graduated from Harvard in 1880 and lived in Brooklyn, where he taught Greek and Latin at the Polytechnic Preparatory Country Day School. Meanwhile, his sisters lived on in the family home at 90 Bay State Road and actively pursued their own interests and careers. Alice, the oldest, active in the fields of religion, literature, and the arts, was a spokeswoman for various philanthropic enterprises. Marion, the middle

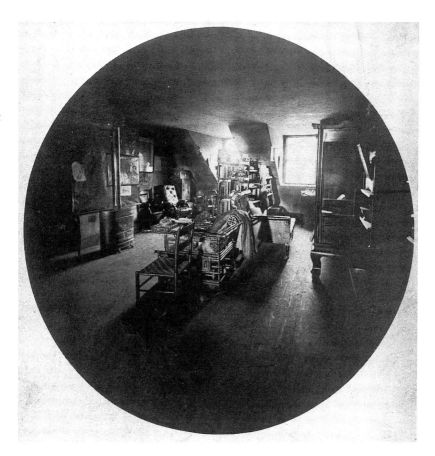

Inside the Studio. Paper print. Collection of International Museum of Photography at George Eastman House.

child, was a Brighton High School teacher whose distinguished career would span forty-five years. All three children were cultured, well educated, civic-minded, and devoted to church and public charities. They were also aware of their family history and shared a typically New England preoccupation with genealogy. They were members of the Massachusetts Society of Mayflower Descendants and traced their ancestry to John Alden.[5] To such worthy and conscientious children passed the duty of preserving the studio legacy.

It is noteworthy that the Southworth and Hawes studio was a family business. Josiah married Nancy Niles Southworth, his partner Albert's sister. She was close to her brother and was a participant in the work of the studio, both before and after her marriage in 1849. She helped women and children sitters prepare for their portraits and arranged clothing and drapery for best effect in front of the

camera. She also tinted daguerreotypes with remarkable sensitivity and understatement. At different times, other Hawes and Southworth siblings worked at the studio as well. With additional help from hired assistants and apprentices, the needs of a sitter at the famous Boston studio were well attended. Posing sessions were collaborations. With both parents and other family members working at the studio, 19 Tremont Row figured significantly in the early education and family experiences of the Hawes children. They were Josiah's frequent models and infrequent child's scribblings, most likely Edward's, embellish the photographer's *carte de visite* era scrapbook.[6] Personal family history combined with studio history and the mix was complicated and extensive.

Exactly what happened in 1901, when the studio was closed, is uncertain. In all probability decisions regarding what to keep and what not to keep were

made in various stages, and at first the bulk of the studio contents were removed to a family storehouse of unknown location and to the family home at 90 Bay State Road. It is likely that the Hawes children, busy with their own lives, warehoused these materials for over three decades until, with their careers behind them, they were better able to devote time and energy to this particular project.

During his lifetime Josiah Hawes had greatly prized some of his daguerreotypes. One full plate of a beautiful Salem girl, aged sixteen or seventeen when she posed for her picture, was insured for $1,000 when it was originally exhibited at the fair of the Massachusetts Charitable Mechanic Association.[7] Such valuations of the studio's best work reflected the fact that they were unique and irreplaceable. In 1893 the elder Hawes maintained that the above daguerreotype was still worth $1,000, which at that time was another way of saying that it was not for sale. The first public sale of Hawes daguerreotypes in 1934 would realize less than $1,000 for thirty of the studio's finest plates.[8] If Josiah Hawes had somewhat overestimated the contemporary market value of his daguerreotypes, he nonetheless coincidentally influenced their preservation by pricing them for some future art market.

The aging Hawes children might well have been overwhelmed by the prospect of disposing of the studio collection had it not been for the timely assistance of a younger man, Louis A. Holman, Boston print dealer. Inadvertently, Josiah Hawes had played a part in this association. As a young man, Holman was befriended by the kindly Mr. Hawes, who on one occasion rewarded him with a lot of large photographs for helping to clean the studio.[9] Louis Holman would play a significant part in the distribution of the studio collection, and maintained warm and friendly relations with the Hawes children that extended beyond their business dealings. With them, Holman shared artistic, aesthetic, and academic interests. In fact, Marion Hawes liked his son, Richard, well enough to provide for him in her will a gift of two hundred dollars.[10]

On August 29, 1934, in a letter to Dr. Edward Hawes, Louis Holman offered to make as much wall space available as needed in the main part of his shop at 5A Park Street during November, so as to offer for sale daguerreotypes and photographs from the studio collection. Terms of the sale provided that Dr. Hawes would assume advertising and framing expenses and that sales receipts would be divided equally.[11] In the November 1934 issue of his *Within the Compass of a Print Shop*, Holman announced a sale of eighty-two "Daguerreotypes of Famous Persons by Josiah Johnson Hawes." The *Compass* that issue ran twenty-eight pages, the first eighteen of which concerned the Hawes exhibition. There was an illustrated biography of Hawes the "daguerreotyper" from autobiographical notes, a "List of Hawes Daguerreotypes on Exhibition and Sale," and a biographical sketch of Louis Jacques Mandé Daguerre. In the closing paragraph of this essay, Holman stressed that an original daguerreotype was unique: "The daguerreotype process was more suited to copying the human face than to copying other daguerreotypes."

While Holman was a little overenthusiastic in assigning authorship of all the daguerreotypes in his care to Josiah Hawes, it is clear that Hawes was the principal cameraman at the studio. Early business accounts and correspondence preserved with the studio collection provide details of Albert Southworth's business activities before his partnership with Hawes. In establishing his first studio, Southworth formed a company with "two first rate mechanics."[12] From the outset, Albert Southworth was more personally involved in selling daguerreian equipment and supplies and in instructing other daguerreotypists than in taking portraits. In a later advertisement for the studio, circa 1850, the point was stressed that "One of the partners," referring to Hawes, "is a Practical Artist."[13] Southworth's talents were scientific, organizational, promotional, and social. While both partners shared an interest in artistic theory and experimented with technical improvements to perfect their art, Hawes clearly lived to take pictures. It was Hawes, while Southworth was in California, who would

Albert Southworth and Josiah Hawes (U.S.), whole plate. Collection of International Museum of Photography at George Eastman House.

suggest, through his wife Nancy, that perhaps taking daguerreotypes would be more profitable than mining during the rainy season.[14] Southworth, for whatever reasons, had neglected to take a camera along to California. Any lingering doubts regarding primary authorship of the studio daguerreotypes can be resolved by studying Hawes's large body of later signed work.

Because of his Gold Rush adventures, much has been made of Southworth's restless nature. He was at times impatient with the photography business and its uneven rewards. He would leave the studio in 1862 and return to Blood Brook Road, West Fairlee, first to settle his father's estate and then to run the family farm with his brother Asa.[15] He would later return to Boston to pursue a career in photographic handwriting analysis and live out his life in nearby Charlestown. Meanwhile, the work habits of Josiah Hawes were consistent and constant: opening the studio six days a week for most of fifty-eight years.[16] What has been largely overlooked is that Hawes himself had a restless, wandering nature. It was this common trait that probably had more to do with his initial friendship and association with Albert Southworth than any other single factor. After all, before meeting his future partner and brother-in-law he had spent over a decade traveling around New England, first giving lectures on electricity with his friend Paul Dodge and later as a self-taught itinerant portrait artist and painter. Much later, in the 1860s, well into his middle years, Josiah would again outfit a traveling wagon, this time for the purpose of making and selling circular and stereoscopic views of Boston and its environs.[17] His frequent trips upcountry to the Samuel Southworth farm are well documented in the local Bradford, Vermont, paper, first called *Stanton's Bradford Opinion* and later *The Bradford Opinion,* and there is additional photographic documentation of time spent in the country.[18] He would eventually die during a trip to Crawford Notch, New Hampshire, an ambitious outing for a man of ninety-three, indicating that he never lost his love of travel.

But we wander from the subject at hand, namely the consequences of the exhibition and sale at Holman's Print Shop. The November 1934 sales are fully documented in an itemized accounting dated December 1, 1934.[19] Fourteen photographs, not all daguerreotypes, went to twelve individuals. A Franklin Pierce daguerreotype, for example, sold for $25; a Horace Mann daguerreotype brought $50. An additional twenty-two daguerreotypes were purchased by I. N. Phelps Stokes, a New York City print collector. With the exception of a daguerreotype of Daniel Webster, for which he paid $250, the daguerreotypes sold for $5 to $60 each, less a lot discount. The total sales were $1,024.50, half of which went to the Hawes children. Stokes would go on to purchase another thirty-five daguerreotypes, and about half of these were not included in the exhibition.[20] He would in turn donate the entire lot to the Metropolitan Museum in 1937. Between 1938 and 1939 the Hawes children would donate another five daguerreotypes to the Metropolitan. Sixty-one of the sixty-two newly acquired daguerreotypes were exhibited in a 1939 show commemorating the centenary of photography. Only the daguerreotype of John L. Tucker (plate 17 in *The Spirit of Fact*) was omitted from the exhibition.[21]

After the November 1934 sale Holman continued to act as an agent for the Haweses. He answered a variety of inquiries regarding specific items in the studio collection. They range from follow-up correspondence with Stokes ("I shall keep my eye peeled for the Lincoln. It's news to me that Hawes made a photo of him."[22]) to the more personal Godwin Earl request: "I had a beautiful portrait of Mr. Hawes which he presented to me about 1885 but it burned up in a fire I had. If you can furnish me another I shall be happy. It is a full face and very distinguished. I loved Mr. Hawes as I would my own father, and I did lots of work for him in the 80's."[23]

After Stokes made his selection on behalf of the Metropolitan, a group of daguerreotypes were returned to the Haweses by Holman on February 7, 1940.[24] This particular group would comprise part of a larger group later donated to the Boston Museum of Fine Arts in memory of their father. The

Hawes children also retained a group of portraits, some of which would later be donated to the Museum of Fine Arts, with others passing to surviving family members. The largest family group would go to Edward McKean Hawes and in turn to Edward Laurie Hawes. After the Hawes children made their selection, the remaining images were made available through Holman for purchase. According to Albert Raborn Phillips, Jr., he saw what remained of the collection at Holman's Print Shop on October 24, 1942, after graduating from midshipmen's school in New York.[25] Phillips bought a quarter-plate tinted daguerreotype of a woman (inventory no. 321) on his first visit to the shop, and two days later was driven by Mr. and Mrs. Holman to Sagamore Beach on the Cape to see Edward Hawes at his summer home.[26] Hawes, the last surviving child of Josiah, would die a month later.

Phillips, through Holman, would add another thirty-three Southworth and Hawes daguerreotypes to his collection, including some of the best remaining examples. Additional items from the studio collection, including two unexposed double whole plates and tin and wooden storage boxes of the type used by Hawes were acquired by Phillips and are currently in the collection of Matthew Isenburg, as are most of the daguerreotypes selected by Phillips. Phillips's collection, consisting of hundreds of daguerreotypes, miscellaneous photographs, a complete daguerreian outfit and other daguerreotype and wet-plate cameras and equipment, and about a hundred books from 1839 to date, were offered for sale as a whole only at about $2,400 in June 1953.[27] The collection went unsold. It would later be purchased sometime before 1965 by Harry Gross of Eugene, Oregon, for about $5,000. When Joe Buberger and Matthew Isenburg acquired the Gross Collection toward the end of 1979, the Southworth and Hawes daguerreotypes that Phillips had purchased from Holman were still in the garage that housed the Gross Collection.

Other enthusiastic pioneer photography collectors found their way to Holman's cluttered shop. The most noteworthy and serious of these collec-

tors was Alden Scott Boyer of Chicago. On November 13, 1943, Boyer began filling small notebooks with miscellaneous information from the Southworth and Hawes studio manuscript materials at Holman's Print Shop.[28] In Book 3 he writes, "I went to N.Y. and then to Boston where I stayed 2 weeks reading the mss. of S&H . . . I spent some time in the Library there, but daily was at Holman's Print Shop 9 to 5." Before leaving for New York he would buy sixty-six whole-plate Southworth and Hawes daguerreotypes from the Holmans, for the son, Richard B., was now also involved in the business. He would eventually buy around 1,200 Southworth and Hawes daguerreotypes in all, a Grand Parlor Stereoscope and the trunk full of manuscript materials at Holman's. His was the finest private collection of historical photography in the United States, and in 1951 he donated his collection to George Eastman House, then in its second year of public operation.[29]

Meanwhile, the estate of Edward Southworth Hawes was being settled. Marshall H. Gould, a longtime family friend, retired lawyer, and fellow Mayflower descendant, had prepared Marion's and

Anon. (U.S.), sixth plate. Portrait of William Stewart. Stewart was related to Southworth through marriage and traveled with him and Albert Hawes, Josiah's younger brother, to California on board the Regulus, which carried the Bunker Hill Trading & Mining Association. In addition to Southworth and Albert Hawes, the ship's manifest also lists Levi French of Boston and A. J. Gould of Andover as daguerreotypists. One can only speculate as to who might have made this image. Collection of Greg French.

Albert Southworth and Josiah Hawes (U.S.), whole plate. Courtesy of the Metropolitan Museum of Art, Gift of Dr. S. Hawes and Miss Marion Augusta Hawes, 1939 (39.22.2).

Albert Southworth and Josiah Hawes (U.S.), quarter plate. Flower Study. Courtesy of Daniel Wolf, Inc., New York.

Edward's wills on the same day in 1940.[30] In 1943, Marshall H. Gould and Edward M. Hawes presented the Boston Museum of Fine Arts a gift of 108 daguerreotypes from Edward Southworth Hawes in memory of his father, Josiah Johnson Hawes. Twenty-one were delivered as they appeared framed at Holman's November 1934 show, 25 were in cases, and 62 were in six storage boxes from the studio and remain unframed to the present. The remaining daguerreotypes and "set plate photographs" at Holman's Print Shop were valued at $470, as part of the schedule of personal property detailed in Edward's probated will. Some pages later, on page 17 of Schedule B, a loss on the sale of this itemized lot is reported at $370, and dated August 28, 1943. Since Boyer did not enter the picture until some months later, it seems likely that the Holmans paid $100 for that part of the studio collection which had not been taken to 90 Bay State Road. It was from this lot that Boyer would purchase 1,200 daguerreotypes and the trunk full of related manuscript materials. However, it was not until 1977, when Richard Holman's health problems finally forced the closing of Holman's Print Shop, that approximately 800 glass negatives and possi-

bly some of the furniture from the Southworth and Hawes studio were finally sold with the rest of Holman's business to Bill Greenbaum, a print dealer from Gloucester. The negatives, many of which were Hawes's Boston scenic photographs, were in turn sold to two businesswomen, Gates and Tripp, who sold historical photographs at Faneuil Hall. Unable for financial reasons to promote the sale of prints made from the Hawes negatives, Gates and Tripp sold the collection to Boston realtor and collector Thomas Lee, who in turn donated them to the John F. Kennedy Library, where they represent the richest and perhaps least studied of the Hawes photographic legacy.[31]

During early negotiations involving the Gross collection, in another part of the country, Robert A. Sobieszek completed an appraisal of "The Edward L. Hawes Collection of Photography and Related Material," dated February 28, 1979.[32] Edward L. Hawes had sold a small group of daguerreotypes to Al Siegle of Chicago some years earlier, a lot which included the half-plate daguerreotype of a bare-chested Albert Southworth later purchased by Gilman Paper Corporation for $36,000 at a May 16, 1980, Christie's sale. Largely on account of Beau-

Albert Southworth and Josiah Hawes (U.S.), quarter plate. Collection of Matthew R. Isenburg.

mont Newhall's association with Eastman House and early enthusiasm for Southworth and Hawes daguerreotypes, other items from the family collection were given or loaned to that museum. At the time of the Sobieszek appraisal, Edward still owned sixty daguerreotypes, numerous paper photographs, albums, paintings, manuscript materials, studio posing furniture—in short, the heart of the studio collection, the things of greatest family interest to the Hawes children. A significant portion of these inherited materials became available soon after their appraisal, and the majority were purchased by Matthew Isenburg, whose Southworth and Hawes collection is the best in private hands.

The careful reader will have noted that there is a discrepancy between the tens of thousands of daguerreotypes and negatives that Josiah Hawes claimed were in his studio collection and the approximately 1,400 daguerreotypes and 800 nega-

tives traced to their present custodians. It seems fitting to close this work-in-progress with some of the most plausible explanations for these widely different numbers. The following speculations are based primarily on bits and pieces of information gleaned from George Eastman House manuscript materials and ten years of field research:

1. Josiah Hawes traded and sold pieces from his collection during his lifetime. He corresponded with photography collectors, including other professional photographers and academics.

2. Hawes gave photographs away.

3. He may have reused old plates during his daguerreian revival period in the 1890s.

4. The present location of Albert Southworth's personal photographs and his share of the studio collection, if he or his heirs in fact claimed a share, is unknown.

5. The records of Holman's Print Shop regarding

Albert Southworth and Josiah Hawes (U.S.), quarter plate. Bust of Clytie. Collection of Matthew R. Isenburg.

the final fate of the studio collection following Edward's death are incomplete, nonexistent, and/or unknown at this writing.

Even so, through a fortuitous set of circumstances involving a diverse group of dedicated family members and friends, dealers and collectors, and museum personnel, the Southworth and Hawes studio collection is remarkably intact. It is a visible diary of genius. There is a tendency in our age to take technological advancements for granted. They have surpassed us and race onward. We forget, as Steven Rose observed, that we have daguerreotypes by serendipity.[33] Their discovery was accidental, by a difficult process that resisted standardization and soon was outmoded altogether. Daguerreotypes require special study and lighting. They are meant to be hand-held. They are intimate, subtle, and mysterious. They do not easily lend themselves to museum exhibition and gallery lighting. Unless you

have looked at a Southworth and Hawes daguerreotype by early light, you have not seen a daguerreotype. Josiah Hawes was a master of light. His work required it. Until his legacy receives the attention and care it deserves, we have yet to understand photographic genius in one of its earliest expressions. What is needed is to see daguerreotypes again with the newborn eyes of first discovery.

NOTES

1. Mrs. D. T. Davis, "The Daguerreotype in America," *McClure's Magazine* 8 (November 1896): 16.

2. Rachel Johnson Homer, *The Legacy of Josiah Johnson Hawes* (Barre, Mass.: Barre Publishers, 1972), p. 9.

3. Charles LeRoy Moore, "Two Partners in Boston" (Doctoral thesis, University of Michigan, 1975), 1: 151.

4. Ibid., p. 224.

5. Biographical information on the Hawes children from obituaries in Samuel Southworth family newspaper clippings scrapbook, author's collection.

6. Southworth and Hawes MSS Collection, George Eastman House, Rochester, N.Y.

7. A. Lincoln Bowles, "A Famous Boston Studio," Boston *Sunday Herald,* March 12, 1893, clipping property of Professor Edward L. Hawes, Springfield, Ill., copy courtesy of Matthew Isenburg and John Wood.

8. Louis A. Holman to the Haweses, account of the November 1934 sales, December 1, 1934, George Eastman House MSS.

9. Holman to I. N. Phelps Stokes, letter dated December 9, 1934, George Eastman House MSS, as quoted by Moore, "Two Partners," 1: 170.

10. Marion A. Hawes's will, property of Professor Hawes, family papers.

11. George Eastman House MSS.

12. Albert S. Southworth to Nancy Niles Southworth, November 29, 1940, George Eastman House MSS.

13. Moore, "Two Partners," 1: 42.

14. Nancy S. Hawes to Albert Southworth, May 12, 1850, George Eastman House MSS.

15. Albert S. Southworth, Southworth Farm Journal, author's collection, courtesy of Mrs. Gertrude Mallary, Bradford, Vermont.

16. Bowles, "A Famous Boston Studio."

17. J. J. Hawes stereograph, collection of Matthew Isenburg.

18. J. J. Hawes stereographs, collections of E. L. Hawes, Matthew Isenburg, and the author.

19. Holman letter to the Hawes children, George Eastman House MSS.

20. I. N. Phelps, *The Hawes-Stokes Collection of American Daguerreotypes by Albert Sands Southworth and Josiah Johnson Hawes* (New York: Metropolitan Museum of Art, 1939), p. 1.

21. Robert A. Sobieszek and Odette Appel, *The Spirit of Fact* (Boston: David R. Godine, 1976), p. 21.

22. Holman to Stokes, George Eastman House MSS.

23. Godwin Earl to Holman, August 5, 1940, George Eastman MSS.

24. Holman to Marion and Edward Hawes, George Eastman House MSS.

25. Albert Raborn Phillips, Jr., handwritten inventory, Los Angeles, Matthew Isenburg Collection, copy courtesy of Joe Buberger.

26. Phillips inventory, p. 30.

27. Paul Vanderbilt, *Eye to Eye,* Bulletin of the Graphic History Society of America, no. 1 (June 1953), copy courtesy of Henry Deeks.

28. George Eastman House MSS.

29. Walter Clark, "George Eastman House—Its Technology Collections," copy courtesy of Grant Romer.

30. Edward S. Hawes's will, copy in author's collection.

31. Information courtesy of Stephen Rose, telephone interviews, February 16 and 23, 1988.

32. Copy in author's collection, courtesy of E. L. Hawes.

33. Telephone interview, February 23, 1988.

Beard and Claudet

A Further Inquiry

Roy Flukinger

Years ago an acquaintance of mine here at the University of Texas who possessed the requisite degrees in the physical sciences as well as a naturally organized and fully curious mind was able to construct a private economic plan to support himself comfortably for the future. He was, therefore, able to leave his job and pursue full-time the career he had always dreamed of—becoming an independent inventor. Throughout this time he has done very well too. He has invented or improved upon several processes and techniques. He has published the results of his research extensively and has accepted numerous invitations to lecture and demonstrate his experiments. His track record of significant improvements in such diverse areas as metallurgy, optics, chemistry, and physics has been exemplary. Within the photographic sciences he has produced work of rather astounding variety—everything from an improved dusting-on technique for making photoceramics to an intriguing process for making daguerreotypes on glass surfaces. In the latter instances he has always been forthcoming in sharing both his research information and the images produced therefrom, and we have been glad to build up a small collection of his imagery and research notes here at the Photography Collection.

In passing I once asked my friend why, in the course of his very open attitude to sharing his results, he did not seek to patent any of his work. After all, it seemed that his time and energy should be of such importance that no one could find fault with his wanting to protect his efforts and interests in these projects. His answer was as customarily precise and well considered as his research: he had no interest in patenting his work because most patents were only capable of guaranteeing a lifetime of litigation within various courts throughout the world. The patent, he felt—and apparently it is an opinion shared among a significant percentage of the scientific community—was not a practical step in the discipline of independent scientific inquiry; rather, it was a formal commitment to a legal structure which could easily become a millstone around the researcher's neck. My friend saw his professional commitment being toward science, and the last thing he wanted to do was spend a considerable part of his lifetime being tied up within the courts and bureaucratic structures trying to protect one or more patents which might be only marginally lucrative at best.

Whenever I find myself studying the early decades of British photography I often reflect upon my friend's observations. For, throughout the early history of photography in England, what should have been years of unbounded experimentation, image-making, and commercial challenge were all too often colored by some aspect of two of the worst patent-infringement conflicts in the medium's history. When the definitive legal history of photography has been set down we will have ample evidence of the individuals, cases, decisions, agreements, and compromises from which to draw firm conclusions. What we will never know is the loss in terms of human enterprise and creativity that years of litigation

Observe, the merchant's function . . . is to provide for the nation. . . . That is to say, he has to understand to their very root the qualities of the thing he deals in, and the means of obtaining or producing it; and he has to apply all his sagacity and energy to the producing or obtaining it in perfect state, and distributing it at the cheapest possible price, where it is most needed. . . . . . . Two main points he has in his providing function to maintain: first, his engagements . . . ; and, secondly, the perfectness and purity of the thing provided; . . . —John Ruskin, Unto This Last and uncertainty created: what businesses never grew, which photographers never flourished, how many works were never produced because of the presence of legal fiat or the fear of economic ruin. That the adverse consequences would have both personal and professional implications was another of the unavoidable aspects of these patent wars.

The two major patent battles involved the two photographic processes most prevalent in England during the 1840s. The first centered around the attempts by William Henry Fox Talbot, the inventor of the photographic drawing and calotype/salt print processes, to confine under his control the licensing and future application of all negative-positive photographic processes. From 1841 to 1851 Talbot filed four separate patents which attempted to encompass all present and possible future modifications of the negative-positive process. Before the matter was resolved in the 1850s Talbot had had many injunctions served against practicing amateur photographers, had won an unpopular decision in one major case, and had lost the support and sympathy of many of the most important British photographers of this period.[1]

The second, equally bitter patent dispute of this period revolved around the other major early photographic process—the daguerreotype. The genesis of this battle was Louis Jacques Mandé Daguerre's decision in 1839 to patent his invention in England. For a two-year period between June 1839, when Daguerre engaged the British patent agent Miles Berry, and 1841, when Richard Beard (in March) and Antoine François Jean Claudet (in June) opened the first and second public daguerreotype studios in London, a complex tapestry of individuals, discussions, agreements, and legal actions evolved on the British photographic scene. The resultant timeline of events and parade of personalities marked an intricate and often confusing period in the evolution of the daguerreotype in Great Britain. It is a knotty problem which current photohistorians have only now begun to unravel. By mid-1841 it had become clear, however, that the continuation of the struggle

over patent rights for the next few years would be centered largely around the first commercial daguerreotypists on the London scene, Beard and Claudet. For a decade which nearly paralleled the period of Talbot's patent applications Beard would be the leading figure and Claudet the earliest and most vocal of his opponents in the dispute over whether or not a single individual had total control in England of the commercial rights to the daguerreotype.[2]

Richard Beard (1801–1885), the son of a grocer, had his first taste of successful commercial management by running the family firm in the 1820s. Taking advantage of the expanding industrial movement in Britain, he moved to London in the early 1830s and became a notable figure in the coal trade. Obviously on the lookout for future enterprises, he began his speculation in patents in 1839 with a process for color printing calicoes and other fabrics. Two years later he negotiated his two agreements with Berry as well as with Daguerre and Joseph Isidore Niepce, becoming the sole patentee for the daguerreotype process in England, Wales, and the colonies of the Empire. He opened three highly successful daguerreotype portrait studios in London in 1841 and 1842, and sold licenses for operation and helped to establish several other daguerreotypists' studios throughout England during the early 1840s. Beard was not a photographer himself, and the daily operation and management of those studios which carried his name was delegated to a number of operators—including John Frederick Goddard, T. R. Williams, and John Johnson—who went on to further their own careers. To protect his interests and those of his licensees he instigated a number of injunctions and legal cases against potential infringement of the patent rights, including most notably an unsuccessful case against Claudet (1841–43) and a successful one against John Wharry Egerton and others (1845–49). His son, Richard Beard, Jr., followed him into the family business and after the father's bankruptcy filing of 1849 continued to stay on in photography for another decade. During this period Richard Beard remained active with his son's business as well as numerous other enterprises ranging from "galvanism" to the rubber trade. Of Beard's four London studios, the last had closed its doors by 1869, if not earlier.

Antoine François Jean Claudet (1797–1867) was the son of a Lyon banker and entered the glass manufacturing business at an early age. He moved to London in 1827 and became a successful importer and manufacturer of glass objects. In 1839, hearing of the daguerreotype process from his friend Noel-Marie Paymal Lerebours, he journeyed to France, sought out Daguerre, and learned the process firsthand from the discoverer; later that year he acquired from Daguerre himself the first license to practice daguerreotypy in England. Although he experimented with speeding up the process and sold daguerreotypes out of his shop, Claudet did not open a commercial studio until three months after Beard in 1841. Following the period of his litigation with Beard, he maintained and expanded his daguerreotype portrait studios, even to the extent of introducing calotype–salt print portraiture at the urging of his friend William Henry Fox Talbot. He continued in the photographic profession, publishing and lecturing on a variety of topics relating to the technical development and artistic growth of the medium. In 1851 Claudet moved his operation to a specially designed studio/showroom in Regent Street; it became a showplace for photographers and countless fashionable patrons as well as the center for his continuing interest in daguerreotypy and commercial portraiture. Shortly following his death in 1867 the establishment was entirely destroyed by fire.

Until recently the historiography of photography has been markedly prejudicial in terms of analyzing the Beard-Claudet conflict and its relationship to the entire story of daguerreotypy in England. At its mildest this reaction of the past generation of photohistorians has been to relegate Beard and his first daguerreotype studio in England to a passing reference while focusing upon Claudet as one of the leading early photographic pioneers. At its more extreme, however, we have witnessed some

Antoine Claudet, sixth plate. Portrait of an unidentified gentleman, ca. 1843. Gernsheim Collection, Harry Ransom Humanities Research Center, University of Texas at Austin.

historians who have been far too willing to cast the relationship into black and white instead of varying shades of gray. To them Beard was merely a grasping businessman who loved profit, not photography, and who was willing to try to crush struggling artists like Claudet underfoot if necessary. In this more romanticized version, Claudet's winning of the appeals case and Beard's later bankruptcy filing are seen as proof that the good guys triumphed over corporate evil. Indeed, this seemed to be underscored by the very nature of the photograph itself, for countless portraits of Claudet's noble and aristocratic face have come down to us over the years, while only in 1981 was a portrait of Beard finally discovered.[3]

Some of the range of the past critical interpretation may indeed be justified. Claudet was a photographer while Beard, despite the fact that he undoubtedly took the time to study the process for which he held the patent, ran the enterprise and hired photographers to operate his galleries. Whereas Beard could count on the loyalty of most of his operators, Claudet had the deeper roots as well as more personal contacts within the immediate photographic community.[4] Finally, as the case

Richard Beard, ninth plate. Portrait of an unidentified youth, ca. 1842. Gernsheim Collection, Harry Ransom Humanities Research Center, University of Texas at Austin.

went through four judges and took a full two years, one is not surprised to find bitterness and acrimony lasting for several more years thereafter. Thus, although Beard has left us no written record of the case or his reactions to it, many of his licensees and photographers have not commented favorably upon Claudet's character or actions.[5] Likewise, Claudet has not written favorably about Beard, labeling him as late as 1867 a "wide-awake speculator."[6] There is also little doubt that Claudet took a swipe at Beard in 1847 while giving a lecture on photographic process to an august gathering of the Royal Society of Arts:

> . . . but the perfection of an art cannot be prevented by the fear of rendering it difficult, and it is to be desired that it should not be practised except by active and enterprising minds, who, for the sake of doing well, will never be stopped by any difficulty. In Photography the difficulties are very great, although it is generally imagined that it is merely a mechanical operation, which depends solely upon the possession of a patented apparatus, with which we expect to become painters of miniatures, as the organ boy becomes a musician by turning the handle of his instrument.[7]

Throughout these legal battles, personality conflicts, ethical debates, and historical interpreta-

tions and reinterpretations, I have always tended to view Richard Beard and Antoine Claudet as being representative of the two major movements that encompassed photography during its earliest years. On the one hand, there is the entrepreneurial approach, manifested in a desire to promote and find commercial utility for the new photographic technologies within an evolving society; on the other, there is the challenge for the natural philosopher, concerned with exploring the potentialities of the new art and striving to enhance or improve upon its qualities. Both functions were clearly evident in the Victorian era and both led to countless economic, cultural, scientific, and artistic successes during that time.

Now, however, the more I look at the two competitors the more I am struck not by their differences but rather by their similarities. Both were independent businessmen who had a number of years of successful experience behind them before entering the photography business. Both entered the profession during its earliest public years, determined—each in his own particular style—to succeed with the new art. Members of the growing middle classes, they were of the later generations spawned by the Industrial Revolution which had begun in the mid-eighteenth century. They were familiar with the entrepreneurial challenge of refining a specific product, defining the potential market for such an item, and using promotion and the advertising media to effectively combine the two. Both aimed for innovation within their operations as well: Beard through a revolving studio and external mirrors which increased the operating time of his facility, and Claudet through his pioneering work with painted backdrops to transform the look and feel of the traditional studio portrait. Finally, both were responsible for technical and scientific improvements of the medium: Beard through his sponsorship (and sometimes patenting) of the credited work of such associates as Wolcott, Goddard, and Johnson; Claudet through several of his own personal experimental, technological, and consumer-oriented innovations.

When viewed from a different historical angle, even the matter of patent speculation must give us pause. The concept of the application of a patent to protect one's possible commercial interests dated back to the seventeenth century. As the economy of the nation evolved from an agrarian base to an industrial "revolution," the perceived need for patent control and protection also grew. Continuing improvements, whether in the production of raw materials or the manufacture of either specialized or everyday goods, were becoming a daily economic reality. Many investors looked toward the patent market, with its lucrative potential in multiple licensing, as a faster and more efficient way to turn a profit.[8]

At the height of the Industrial Revolution speculation in patents had become a standard, if somewhat chancy, profession, and gentlemen like Richard Beard often kept an ear to the ground and an eye on the future. In this instance it is important to note that speculation on the daguerreotype patent in England had first centered around Claudet rather than the man who would soon be his competitor. Indeed, at the time he purchased his license from Daguerre, Claudet also retained from the inventor first-refusal rights for purchasing the patent rights for England. Only his inability to pay the £800 in 1841 prevented him from edging out Beard. It is interesting to speculate upon how Claudet would have handled matters in England had he, rather than Beard, had the exclusive control of the daguerreotype.

Finally, there is the eloquent visual testimony which remains—the extant daguerreotypes from both sets of studios which have survived and come down to us today. It is, admittedly, a difficult challenge because the question of studios, or in the case of Beard and Claudet a series of studios, leaves the matter of individual artistry totally unsettled. We cannot tell which individual—owner, operator, or assistant—produced which image, much less who the subject may be. Nor can we draw any lasting conclusions about the artistic or sociological intentions of the owners or their staffs. Rather, we must be content to examine the existing range of available daguerreotype portraits only to shape some basic generalities from which comparisons might be made.

We know, for example, that Claudet has been credited with being the first portraitist to utilize painted backdrops. In so doing he tended to soften the impact of a portrait of the isolated human face. In addition, Claudet seems to have tended to use props and curtains surrounding his fuller figure studies, thereby placing them in a more harmonious environment. Such a proximate sensibility was derived from the portrait-painting aesthetic of the day, as opposed to the miniature painted portrait, which was the artistic medium that the daguerreotype originally supplanted. Most of the Claudet daguerreotypes reflect an aura perhaps of wealth and success, but most certainly one of economic stability and social permanence—quite typical of the clientele which the daguerreotypist obviously sought to attract to his major studios in the Adelaide Gallery and in Regent Street. In his later stereographs and still lifes Claudet was able to be slightly more adventuresome in terms of arrangement and framing; his portraiture, however, reflected what his customers most likely wanted: security, symmetry, and stability.

Beard's galleries, starting with his first at the Royal Polytechnic, seem to have been founded with an absolute allegiance to the initial principle of early photographic portraiture: to record the facial (and often figural) features of his sitters. (The unstated codicil to this rule was, of course, to make the features as flattering as possible for the sake of sales, the influence of the miniature painted portrait still being most evident.) As a result of this rather immediate concern for producing true likenesses, one tends to feel a stronger presence from Beard's subjects—an almost "documentary" intimacy if you will. The feel of his daguerreotypes is rougher, often with figures off center, heads tilted slightly, lighting appearing harsher, and subjects rather subtly defying the conventional pictorial framing of the day. Even in the portraits with backdrops and props (for Beard was not averse to using the good ideas of his competitors) one feels that the sitters are not so much arranged within the environment as simply put there. The resulting intimacy, oftentimes seeming to propel them through the cover glass, is a noteworthy quality of the talents of Beard's operators. As a result his body of subjects, while dressed for the most part in their best finery, appear to possess a firmer resolve; can we be so bold as to suggest that it is before Beard's cameras that the faces of England's growing middle class first came to be revealed to us?

I find much to commend in the characters and aims of both Richard Beard and Antoine Claudet—perhaps because they were both the inevitable products of their age. History often has a way of treating even the fairest of men unfairly. Circumstance and happenstance, deliberate planning and free will, all may contribute to a particular series of events which lead to a less than perfect conclusion. In such cases it is often easiest just to assess some blame somewhere and to try and go on to the next incident or circumstance. But in doing so I believe we stand to shortchange not only Beard and Claudet but, even more so, our own chances of trying to further understand the complex and wondrous circumstances of photography's nascence and early youth. And that, in turn, increases our tendency to want to trivialize not only the amazing artistic and technological medium which they chose to promote and explore and attempt to understand, but also our basic struggle to learn all that we can about photography itself.

Perhaps, in the final analysis, their significance comes down to this: they both cared strongly and clearly for the daguerreotype and each chose, in his own particular style and manner, to champion—steadfastly, energetically, perhaps even passionately—its impact on the world. In doing so, both became more successful than even they might have hoped to be.

NOTES

1. For further details see Helmut Gernsheim, *The Origins of Photography* (London: Thames and Hudson, 1982), pp. 181–232; H. J. P. Arnold, *William Henry Fox Talbot: Pioneer of Photography and Man of Science* (London, 1977); and Gail Buckland, *Fox Talbot and the Invention of Photography* (Boston: David R. Godine, 1980).

2. Some of the best accounts of this complex period can be found in R. Derek Wood, "The Daguerreotype Patent, the British Government, and the Royal Society," *History of Photography* 4 (January 1980): 53–59; Bernard V. and Pauline F. Heathcote, "Richard Beard: An Ingenious and Enterprising Patentee," *History of Photography* 3 (October 1979): 313–29; Helmut Gernsheim, *The Origins of Photography*, pp. 121–49; and Helmut and Alison Gernsheim, *L. J. M. Daguerre: The History of the Diorama and the Daguerreotype* (New York: Dover, 1968), pp. 143–70.

3. "Richard Beard: Correspondence from Bernard V. and Pauline F. Heathcote," *History of Photography* 5 (July 1981): 268.

4. It is ironic that one of Claudet's closest friends, William Henry Fox Talbot, was himself engaged at this very time in trying to legally control and patent all negative-positive photographic processes in England.

5. For example, see the comments of Alexander S. Wolcott in "Photography in Its Infancy," *American Journal of Photography* 3 (October 1, 1860): 142–43, and of John Frederick Goddard in Jabez Hughes, "The Discoverer of the Use of Bromine in Photography: A Few Facts and an Appeal," *Photographic News* 7 (December 11, 1863): 593.

6. "A Chapter in the Early History of Photography," *Photographic News* 12 (August 21, 1868): 404.

7. Antoine Claudet, "Progress of Photography. Read to the Meeting on the 17th February, 1847," *Journal of the Society of Arts* (1847): 204–205.

8. For a closer analysis of these and other attendant economic considerations, see E. J. Hobsbawm, *Industry and Empire: An Economic History of Britain Since 1750* (London: Weidenfeld & Nicolson, 1968).

Delicate and Complicated Operations

The Scientific Examination of the Daguerreotype

M. Susan Barger

"M. Arago, however, formally declared the positive inability of the combined wisdom of physical, chemical, and optical science, to offer any theory of these delicate and complicated operations, which might be even tolerably rational and satisfactory."

Thus ran part of *The Athenaeum*'s report of the joint meeting of the French Académie des Sciences and the Académie des Arts held on August 19, 1839.[1] That day François Arago, the perpetual secretary of the Académie des Sciences and director of the Paris Observatory, introduced the daguerreotype process on behalf of its inventors, Louis Jacques Mandé Daguerre and Isidore Niepce, who represented his deceased father and Daguerre's former partner, Nicéphore Niepce. The meeting, held at L'Institut and attended by hordes of spectators curious to hear about the mysterious method for drawing with light, had followed months of publicity about this important discovery that had aroused the interest of both the artistic and the scientific communities.

Daguerreotypy, like all forms of photography after it, was at the same time an art, a science, and an applied technology. Artists and scientists alike embraced the new discovery with great fervor. However, far more has been written about the application of the daguerreotype to art and to the production of images for commerce than about the scientific inquiry into and applications of the process. Very shortly after the introduction of the process, scientists devised ways to make daguerreotypes using microscopes and telescopes; they also devised ways to make daguerreotypes out in the field. Daguerreotypes were used by scientists to record events and to document discoveries. Occasionally, items in the history of science mention these applications, but they have not received a great deal of attention.

Even less has been written about the scientific investigation of the daguerreotype process and the efforts to understand or to improve the process. There are several very good reasons for this. Science, as we now know it, was just coming into its own during the period when the daguerreotype process flourished. The scientific tools for examining the image and for determining how it worked were primarily limited to the light microscope and to careful observations. What few improvements and additions there were to the daguerreotype process after it was first announced were not the result of scientific insight per se but rather of experimentation in the practice of the process. Lastly, there were no other photographic processes derived from the daguerreotype. Thus, after it was no longer used, there was little incentive to investigate how it worked. In spite of this, time and again scientists have turned to the daguerreotype process as a scientific curiosity, as a specific method for data collection, and as a model to derive some fundamental information about the photographic process itself. The daguerreotype has not been so willing to give up its secrets and thus has remained a challenge awaiting a solution.

In the late 1960s and early 1970s photography began to enjoy a new popularity. Photographs achieved a status in collectibles and began to fetch handsome prices on the auction block. The interest in historical photographs, including daguerreotypes, increased—and with it a new recognition of the need to preserve photographic materials as an irreplaceable record of our past. These factors combined to encourage new scientific investigations of the various photographic processes in order to develop better methods for the care of photographs based on a modern understanding of their properties. The prime interest of this essay is to describe the research done on the daguerreotype process at the Materials Research Laboratory (MRL) of Pennsylvania State University from 1979 through 1984. This work was done by me and my colleagues and is the largest scientific study of the daguerreotype to date. The results have brought about an entirely new way of looking at and caring for daguerreotypes.

Before describing our work, I would like to acknowledge the scientific work done by others on the daguerreotype process over the last two decades. The two major scientific papers published in this century before the beginning of the MRL work both appeared in the 1970s. The first of these was written by Irving Pobboravsky and was the subject of his master's thesis, "Study of Iodized Daguerreotype Plates."[2] The second was a paper by Alice Swan, the then conservator for the International Museum of Photography at George Eastman House, done with Dr. Chuck Fioro and Dr. Kurt Heinrich from the National Bureau of Standards. Swan and her colleagues were not the first to look at daguerreotypes using a scanning electron microscope; however, their 1979 paper, "Daguerreotypes: A Study of the Plates and the Process," was the first extensive examination of daguerreotype image structure and deterioration published in this century.[3] Several other minor papers have also received some attention over the last two decades. These include other work by Pobboravsky and Swan as well as the work of Prohaska and Fisher,[4] Brodie and Thackray,[5] and others.

I had gone to Pennsylvania State University in 1977 in order to spend time seriously thinking about how photographs deteriorate during the process of natural aging. I was working in the Materials Research Laboratory, and during the summer of 1979 began work on the materials characterization of the daguerreotype process as the focus of my doctoral studies which were completed in 1982. The daguerreotype work continued for two years after the completion of my dissertation. The ultimate aim of the study was to decipher the daguerreotype so that better methods of preservation could be devised. The initial efforts of the study were to ask (and, I hoped, answer) some very basic questions. What is a daguerreotype? What is it about its chemistry or physical structure that makes a daguerreotype a daguerreotype? What makes daguerreotypes different from other photographs? Once these things were understood, would it be possible to use experimental evidence to develop improved methods for daguerreotype care?

Questions similar to these had been asked many times before. The major difference between previous studies and the MRL study was the experimental point of view. The latter investigation used an interdisciplinary approach, treating the subject as a materials problem and not as a specifically chemical or physical problem or as a purely photographic one.

A few definitions are in order. Materials are substances from which things are made, and these include everything from wood, glass, ceramics, and metals to new materials like semiconductors and superconductors. The more traditional disciplines of chemistry and physics make certain underlying assumptions about materials—namely, that they are homogeneous, isotropic, and continuous. That is, it is assumed that materials are the same throughout, that their properties are the same in all directions, and that a hunk of material is contiguous throughout its mass. This framework is an agreed-upon simplification which is useful in formulating theories and looking at the work at hand, whether it be chemistry or physics or some other similar discipline.

Materials science is a relatively new discipline.

Materials scientists look at the world and see that materials are neither homogeneous nor isotropic nor continuous. Instead of throwing up their hands and retreating to a more idealized construct, these scientists use the tools of the chemist, the physicist, and others to look at properties of materials as whole systems—as they exist and not as they can be idealized. This, then, is an applied science. Usually the applications are in making new materials, and recently this area has attracted a great deal of attention and is referred to as the "Materials Revolution." The same tools that are used to understand new materials can also be used to look at old ones and to understand the process of aging and degradation of materials. This, of course, is the aim of those scientists and conservators seeking to preserve patrimony. The daguerreotype study at MRL started with this conceptual foundation in order to make a new attempt at answering old questions.

It was clear from the outset that two kinds of samples would be needed. First, we would need vintage daguerreotypes from as many locations as possible. Second, we would need to have new daguerreotypes to use both for destructive testing and as monitors for how daguerreotype images are formed and how they change over some known time. The study collection of vintage daguerreotypes provided a physical reference of what daguerreotypes are and how they have aged. We took the stance that in the absence of exact written records these objects themselves carried the record of their own history and treatment. Our aim was to find the Rosetta stone that would allow us to read what time had recorded.

During the first summer and over the succeeding years about 150 vintage daguerreotypes were gathered. These came from various sources—some were purchased and some were gifts. All were carefully chosen and checked to make sure that the total sample was representative and also that no daguerreotypes of great value were inadvertently used as sacrificial lambs.

In order to make sure that the new daguerreotypes were as similar as possible to the vintage ones, we decided that daguerreotype plates needed to be made in the laboratory following nineteenth-century methods and carefully controlling the quality of the materials used in plate making. A procedure for electroplating daguerreotype plates was adopted that involved electro-etching copper plates, electroplating the etched plates in a silver cyanide plating solution based on the earliest silver electroplating formulae from the early 1840s, and, lastly, mechanically polishing the silver surface.[6]

Once these experimental plates were made, two-thirds were sent to Irving Pobboravsky to be made into daguerreotype step tablets. Step tablets are the photographic scientist's way of producing standard samples that can be compared one to another. The remaining plates became the raw materials for making daguerreotypes in the laboratory.

A daguerreian outfit based on nineteenth-century designs with halogen fuming boxes, buffing paddles, and a mercury pot was made for the experiments. Making daguerreotypes is easier said than done, and even with the help of Irving Pobboravsky and Ken Nelson it took many months for me to produce even the faintest image in the laboratory. Almost all of the daguerreotypes produced in the lab throughout the experiments were step tablets. My intention was to understand the daguerreotype process as it was practiced during the nineteenth century and not to become a daguerreian artist nor to improve the daguerreotype process.

Along with the preliminaries of gathering and making samples, a massive survey was begun that covered the contemporary literature of the daguerreian era and subsequent historical literature concerned with the production and scientific analysis of the daguerreotype during the daguerreian era and beyond. The survey also covered the extraction, refining, and finishing of silver, copper, and gold during the daguerreian era (including silver-plate manufacture); the source and use of other chemicals used in the daguerreotype process (like iodine, bromine, and sodium thiosulfate); and the science and technologies that influenced the daguerreotype or its production in both direct and indirect ways. This historical background aided the subsequent scientific study in many surprising ways.

Once we had learned to interpret the nineteenth-century scientific record on its own terms and to apply that information to our own empirical observations, we found new ways to confirm nineteenth-century observations and also became sensitive to important early observations that had been overlooked in earlier histories.

As a viewer holds a daguerreotype and moves it back and forth in the light, the image blinks back and forth from a negative to a positive. This most striking mirrorlike appearance is the single characteristic that sets daguerreotypes apart from other photographs and that must be retained when they are preserved. The source of these visual qualities had been described in a general way by previous workers during both the nineteenth and twentieth centuries. The black portions of the image are essentially the bare, polished daguerreotype plate and the white portions are made of small particles dispersed on that polished plate. When light is reflected off the bare plate away from the viewer, no light reaches the eye and this portion of the image is perceived as black. Conversely, light is scattered in all directions by the image particles, and when the viewer holds the daguerreotype in the proper way those portions of the image are perceived as white by comparison with the dark areas.

The first MRL experiments were directed at trying to model and quantify this generalized concept of daguerreotype appearance. The main task was to discover the relationship of the physical structure of a daguerreotype to its optical behavior. This was approached on two fronts. The first approach was to use a variety of spectrographic methods to measure the optical properties of the daguerreotype, and the second was to map and analyze both the daguerreotype plate and the particles that form the image.

Optical properties are simply the behavior of a material when it is illuminated by some sort of radiation. When visible light is the illuminant, optical properties are related to how an object appears to a viewer. Daguerreotypes were examined using a goniophotometer and an optical reflectance spec-

trometer. The goniophotometer measures reflectance as a function of angle of illumination. Not surprisingly, these measurements confirmed the angular dependence required to see light and dark areas in the daguerreian image. They also indicated that daguerreotypes are usually covered with complex thin films, including what we call tarnish, which affect how they appear.[7]

The optical reflectance spectrometer was used to measure the total reflectance from various image areas without regard to angle, using a range of illumination from the ultraviolet through the visible and near-infrared regions of the spectrum.[8] These measurements showed that highlight regions of daguerreotypes typically have a bell-shaped reflectance curve that is centered over the visible region of the spectrum. This is the kind of spectrum that would be expected for a surface with microscopic roughness of the size that would scatter visible light. If a daguerreotype was gilded, the position of these reflectance curves was centered around 550 nanometers and the spectrum was closely matched to the light sensitivity of the human eye.[9] Overexposed daguerreotypes, commonly called "blue front" daguerreotypes, had curves that were centered in the blue portion of the visible spectrum (around 400 nanometers). In all cases the height, but not the shape, of these reflectance curves was altered by the degree of whiteness observed. Thus, shadow areas produced flat curves in the visible region of the spectrum and white areas produced bell curves over the same region.[10]

Once the optical properties of the daguerreotype had been measured, it was necessary to determine the daguerreotype image structure. The mapping of the image was first approached as a metallurgical problem. Plate cross sections were prepared and polished. However, this method yielded little useful information because daguerreotype image particles are too small and too easily altered during polishing to be successfully investigated in cross section. The real key to mapping the image structure was the use of scanning electron microscopy. In all, several scanning electron microscopes were used to examine the daguerreotype image structure. One of the microscopes had a computer-controlled electron beam so that the microscope could be used to count and sort image particles according to their chemical compositions. This made it possible to determine average image particle sizes and numbers per unit area for different image areas. A profilometer was used to measure the height of image particles and to compare their sizes and spacings against the scanning electron microscope measurements.

Thousands and thousands of image particles were analyzed using this combination of instrumentation. Statistics were kept on the size, spacing, number, and chemical composition of image particles in areas of the daguerreotype image. We found that image particles in highlight and midtone regions of the image ranged over 0.1–1 micrometer in diameter and spacings between particles. These particles were generally rounded or slightly polygonal, but it was noted that there was some range in the shapes that image particles exhibit. The number of particles varied such that the whitest image areas have as many as 200,000 image particles per square millimeter and other image areas have progressively fewer and more widely spaced image particles. Over the same square-millimeter area, shadow areas have only fifty to one hundred large (10–50 micrometers in diameter), odd-shaped particles, which were named shadow particle agglomerates.

Interestingly, the statistical distribution curves of image particle sizes derived from particle counting matched the diffuse reflectance curves obtained for each specific image area. A unifying physical model was devised based on these findings. This Physical Model has been consistently applied to account for all observed daguerreotype optical properties, including those associated with aging, in terms of microstructure only.

The most surprising finding about the image particles on daguerreotypes was their widely varied chemical composition. It had always been assumed that the particles making up the daguerreian image would be composed of a single silver mercury amal-

gam. Not only is there no single composition, there is actually very little mercury present in the image particles of daguerreotypes. Shadow particle agglomerates have some mercury, but smaller particles have almost none. Gilded daguerreotypes usually have no mercury present, except possibly as traces in the shadow particle agglomerates.

We found that while the image on a freshly made, but ungilded, daguerreotype can be wiped off with the slightest touch, as a daguerreotype ages its image particles become mechanically more robust. This is a characteristic of amalgams and is due to mercury loss over time. The process is called age hardening. Age-hardened image particles also expand slightly as a result of the aging. During the gilding process they undergo a rapid hardening caused by the replacement of mercury with gold. Since gold atoms are slightly larger than mercury atoms, gilded image particles are correspondingly larger than those that are ungilded. We also found that gold from gilding is not present as a thin layer over the surface of the entire daguerreotype plate, as had been previously thought.[11]

The definition that was derived from these findings is as follows: A daguerreotype is a photographic image on a silver plate which is made of metal image particles whose size and spacings are on the order of visible light. The image is visible to the observer because of varying amounts of light scatter and specular reflectance from the plate surface. This definition is very useful because it leads to several important conclusions about daguerreotypes and, ultimately, about the requirements for their preservation. The first conclusion is that the physical structure of the image is what defines a daguerreotype and not its chemical composition. It is this overall physical structure alone that is responsible for the unusual appearance of daguerreotypes. Surprisingly, both direct analytical evidence from image-particle compositions and the Physical Model indicate that a specifically chemical solution is not a suitable approach to daguerreotype care. Rather, the maintenance of the physical structure of the daguerreotype image is paramount to its preservation. This means that it is of great importance to understand how the image structure is formed and how the processes of aging and past preservation and cleaning treatments alter the physical structure of daguerreotypes.

To a certain extent, it is necessary to understand how the daguerreotype image is formed before going on to look at how these images age. The main reason for this is to sort out what gives rise to the characteristic daguerreian image structure and to understand which structures are the result of image processing and which are the result of aging. The study of image formation also elucidates how the daguerreotype is related to the more conventional forms of photography. In this vein, the two most interesting questions about daguerreotypes are: What is the role of mercury in the formation of the image—is it a developer, as tradition holds, or does it have some other function? and What is the contribution of bromine and other halogens in shortening exposure times?

A portion of my experiments on image formation repeated some experiments on photographic development done by James Waterhouse during the 1890s.[12] He used prepared daguerreotype plates to investigate what occurs during photographic development. It has long been assumed that the mercury in the daguerreotype process merely acts like one type of conventional photographic developer and that therefore it should be possible to make daguerreotypes without using mercury. When Waterhouse tried using conventional developers to make daguerreotypes, he reported that he made images but that they did not look like daguerreotypes. In order to understand what Waterhouse found and to help shed new light on image formation, a new set of experiments on image formation was conducted, using both the developers he used and more modern photographic developers.

All of the test developers produced images on the daguerreotype plates, but none of them produced daguerreotypes. Scanning electron microscopy showed that these developers produced image microstructure of filamentary bundles that were like those that would be expected for conventional black and white films. These experiments confirmed that it is relatively easy to produce images on a silver plate, but that it is not easy to produce daguerreotypes.

If conventional developers don't produce daguerreotypes, how are image particles formed and what does mercury contribute to their formation? In photography, a developer is strictly defined as an agent that causes the reduction of silver halide to silver at latent image sites—the specks of silver formed as a result of light exposure in a camera. We could find no evidence in our experiments that mercury vapor acts as a reducing agent. Instead, mercury appears to act merely as a vapor phase solvent which aids the formation of the silver crystals we call image particles. The size of these particles is dependent upon the amount of silver that is present in the halogen layer on the daguerreotype plate. Further, bulk silver in the plate itself does not seem to be directly involved in the image-formation process.

We found that different daguerreotype microstructure can be produced by altering the method by which the daguerreotype is sensitized before camera exposure. The question arose as to whether the use of bromine or chlorine actually increased photographic speed of a daguerreotype or if it had some other role? These halogens do slightly increase the "photon-catching" efficiency or speed of the daguerreotype system, but not sufficiently to account for the decrease in exposure times attributed to their use. The real role of bromine and other halogens used for accelerators appears to be to increase the availability of silver that can be used to form image particles.

Normal plate preparation is carried out in subdued light so that the daguerreotypist can monitor the color (and therefore the thickness) of the silver halide layers as the plate is passed over iodine and bromine vapors in the fuming boxes. Since these layers are light-sensitive, some photolytic silver is formed as the light-sensitive layers are built up on the plate. The final iodine treatment is carried out

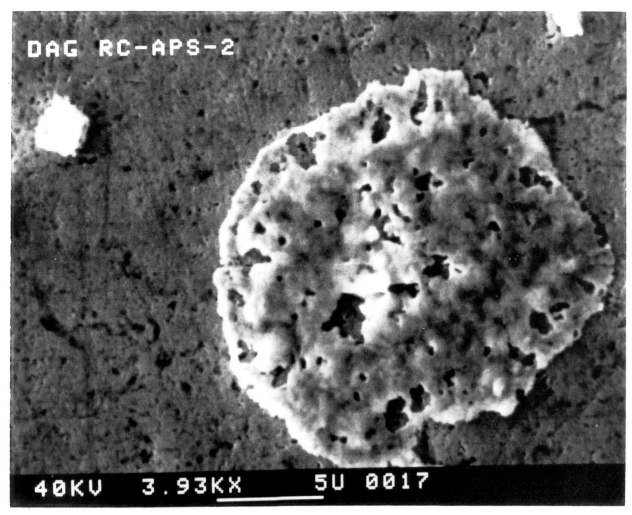

Micrograph 1. This secondary electron image is dominated by the ungilded, shadow particle agglomerate on the right side of the field. A second image particle is the white cube also visible in the micrograph. The overall texture of the plate is due to the etching of the daguerreotype surface when it was cleaned with a thiourea cleaner. The scale bar is equal to 5 micrometers.

in total darkness, and some but not all of the photolytic silver formed during random exposure to light is converted back to silver iodine. During camera exposure more photolytic silver is formed, but it is distributed in proportion to the intensity of light striking the prepared plate surface. These last atoms of silver are called the latent image.

When the exposed plate is treated with mercury vapor, image particles are formed at latent image sites. However, the size and number of image particles is controlled by the presence of photolytic silver made available in the mercury vapor solvent for crystal formation. Given the same light exposure, daguerreotypes sensitized using only iodine (singly sensitized) have comparatively fewer and smaller image particles than multiply sensitized daguerreotypes which were treated in the traditional three-step process to iodine, bromine, and iodine vapors. Similarly, daguerreotypes multiply sensitized in total darkness have fewer image particles than those sensitized in subdued light. The major contribution of multiple sensitization is that it improves the possibility of forming the optimal microstructure which will produce the best visible image. Multiple sensitization does effect some real increase in photographic speed, but its most important feature is its contribution to building better image microstructure.[13]

Image formation is a crystal-growing process. The skill and patience spoken of by nineteenth-

Micrograph 2. The dark mottled areas on the daguerreotype surface in this secondary electron image are etched areas caused by glass corrosion debris that fell to the plate surface. The white form in the center of the field is a sulfur-rich silicate growth. Two shadow particle agglomerates are visible— one directly above the silicate growth and one in the lower left quadrant of the view. The scale bar is equal to 10 micrometers.

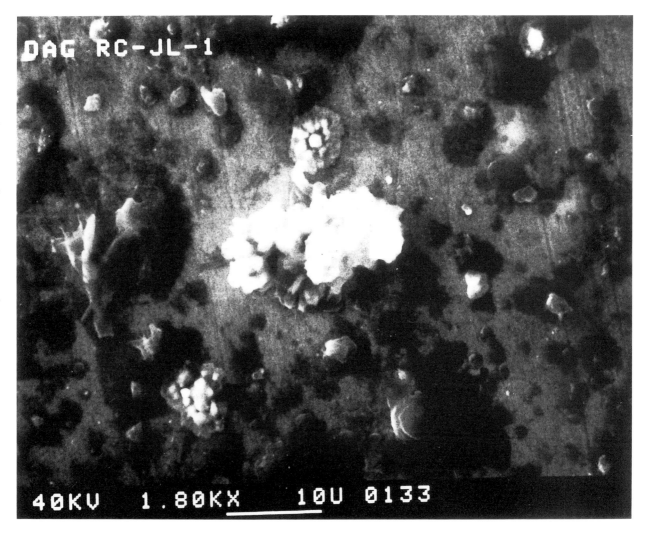

century workers is a real phenomenon. It turns out that it is rather easy to make image particles, but it is not so easy to make them the proper sizes and spacings needed to produce an image that we can see. There is a skill and intuitive understanding of the process that comes into play that is difficult to grasp until one has made successful images—and equally difficult to impart to others once one has. This, of course, is like the difference between having the recipe for a soufflé and actually making a successful soufflé.

As daguerreotypes age, colored tarnish films develop first at the edges of the plate, then at the mat edge, and then gradually encroach over the whole image. It had long been held that because daguerreotypes are made on silver and since they darken with age their behavior must be like common silverware—the tarnish must primarily be silver sulfide and, perhaps, silver oxide. Using scanning electron microscopy and energy dispersive x-ray spectroscopy along with other surface analytical techniques such as secondary ion mass spectroscopy, Raman spectroscopy, and Auger electron spectroscopy to identify what is present on aged daguerreotypes, we found that the tarnish is made up of many compounds. It was proved to be chemically very complicated, and we began to use the more general term "corrosion" to convey this notion. Our results

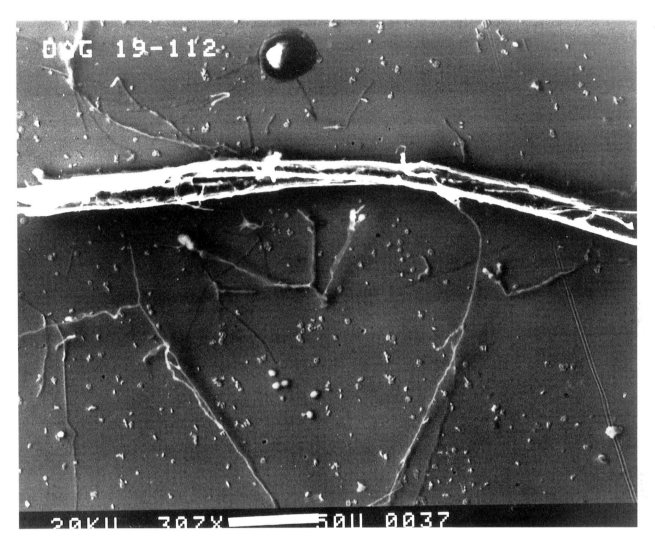

Micrograph 3. This is a secondary electron image of a mid-tone image area of a daguerreotype. The fibrous bundle across the field of the micrograph, the weblike threads, and the black spot (upper center) are all debris on the plate surface derived from corrosion of the daguerreotype's cover glass. The small white particles scattered over the ground are image particles. The scale bar is equal to 50 micrometers (0.5 millimeter).

showed that while silver sulfide is present in daguerreotype tarnish it is only a minor corrosion product as long as an individual daguerreotype has been kept cased with a cover glass, tape, and a mat. When daguerreotypes have been kept cased, the major corrosion product observed is silver oxide. We also saw a wide variety of corrosion films and debris that were the result of remnants left by cleaning solutions or that were caused by the deterioration of the daguerreotype cover glasses.[14]

The traditional potassium cyanide or thiourea cleaning solutions leave films of silver cyanide or silver-thiourea complexes and silver phosphate on the daguerreotype surface. These films are not re-moved even by extended washing. The compounds themselves are corrosion products and they tend to color with age. For instance, the dramatic clouding-over observed on daguerreotypes cleaned during the last thirty years in thiourea is the result of the reaction of silver-thiourea complexes with water in the atmosphere. In addition, these solutions etch the daguerreotype surface, thereby irreparably altering its appearance. The change in the image structure caused by these cleaners results in what is perceived as "image fading" in daguerreotypes.[15]

The effects of glass corrosion were a totally unexpected finding.[16] Weeping cover glasses on daguerreotypes is an old problem, but it was never really thought to cause harm to daguerreotypes. The presence of silica on daguerreotype surfaces had been reported by our group; by Swan, Fioro, and Heinrich; and by others. I was trying to verify the Swan, Fioro, and Heinrich observation that one of the major sources of damage to daguerreotypes was caused by the presence of molds on the daguerreotype surfaces. Upon analysis, these "molds," which are very common on aged daguerreotypes, were composed of silica, potassium, calcium, and sodium. These elements are glass formers. I tried without success to find the presence of DNA or RNA, or spores, or to culture these "molds." Finally, I was forced to conclude that these growths were silicates, and could not possibly be living species.

This sparked a deeper investigation into the glasses found on daguerreotypes and into the aging processes of the glasses and their effect on daguerreotypes. The major conclusion drawn from this part of the study is that the primary cause of corrosion on daguerreotypes is related to the aging of their cover glasses. Most of the debris found on daguerreotypes, instances of catastrophic etching observed on plates, and many of the other common corrosion products come from glass decomposition. Glass corrosion is partly the result of unstable glass formulae; however, it is primarily a result of the geometry of the daguerreotype package.

All of the findings from these investigations formed the basis of a new approach to the prevention of deterioration of daguerreotypes and a new definition of possible safe cleaning methods. The key to the daguerreian image is in its very narrowly defined microstructure. Because the size and spacing of the image particles is critical to producing visible light scatter, any slight alteration of the microstructure can, and does, cause large visual changes in the daguerreian image. The same holds true for alterations of the shadow areas. Thus, any acceptable cleaning method would have to remove tarnish and debris without altering the image particles, etching the plate surface, or depositing new corrosion products on the daguerreotype surface.

In the spring of 1982 we reported the use of physical sputtering with hydrogen/argon plasmas as a possible method of cleaning daguerreotypes.[17] Shortly before the report of our findings, Vincent Daniels of the British Museum had published a related paper on the use of plasma reduction to do the same thing.[18] These methods were also investigated by other workers during the same period.[19] Over the next two years we carried out further investigations aimed at making these observations into practical cleaning methods for daguerreotypes.

Certain problems inherent to the sputtering process could not be overcome. The wide variety of corrosion products found on daguerreotypes made it difficult to design a combination of gases to use in the sputtering chamber that would remove tarnish safely without damaging the plate surface. All of the groups that worked on these methods had encountered a persistent problem with the appearance of faint white films on daguerreotypes that had been sputter cleaned. These films turned out to be unavoidable pitting of the daguerreotype plate caused by the susceptibility of silver to sputtering. We also felt that sputtering was an expensive, "high tech" solution and as such would probably not be adopted for general use. We finally concluded that this method should be reserved for special cases, such as the cleaning of highly colored daguerreotypes that could not be wetted during treatment.

A new cleaning method based on the electrochemical properties of silver and the daguerreotype corrosion products evolved during this time. This method was the result of the collaborative effort of Ajay Giri, William B. White, and me, at MRL, and Thomas M. Edmondson, a photographic conservator then from Connecticut. The four of us, working together, devised and tested the new electrocleaning method. During trials of the process, over one hundred daguerreotypes were treated and subjected to scanning electron microscopy and spectrographic examination in order to monitor the effects of the treatment on the daguerreian microstructure.

In the electrocleaning process the daguerreotype

is a stationary electrode in an electrochemical cell. A silver wand, used as a second movable electrode, directs the cleaning effect to specific areas of the daguerreotype plate. The daguerreotype is placed in an ammonium hydroxide bath which acts as the electrolyte of the cleaning cell. Corrosion is both carried away by the silver oxide solvent action of the ammonium hydroxide and broken up by the changing polarity of the wand electrode versus the daguerreotype. Not only does the new method successfully remove tarnish and preserve the image microstructure, it also appears to heal slightly the etched surface of previously cleaned daguerreotypes. Further, no new corrosion products are left on the surface of daguerreotypes cleaned using this method.

In spite of everything, daguerreotypes are tough and can withstand a lot of abuse. This is lucky because the more valuable a daguerreotype the more likely it is to have been repeatedly cleaned in cyanide and thiourea over the years. The damage done by those cleanings can *never* be repaired. We recommend electrocleaning if a daguerreotype is obscured by tarnish.[20]

Daguerreotypes should be packaged with a modern glass and a mat (preferably a nineteenth-century mat or a mat of modern, unbuffered board) and sealed with a good archival paper tape. Modern window glasses are orders of magnitude more stable than any nineteenth-century cover glasses. The daguerreotype should ideally be kept in a stable environment with low relative humidity (under 30% RH), but it is far more important to have a stable relative humidity free from fluctuations than to have a low relative humidity. Fluctuations in relative humidity encourage glass corrosion.

Most important, the seal on a daguerreotype should not be considered static. The geometry of the daguerreotype package drives glass corrosion on the inside of the package and any glass, no matter how stable, will begin to corrode in time. The daguerreotype package is very protective and glass is a good material to use in the package. It has a high degree of clarity, is readily available and inexpensive, does not outgas, and is not easily abraded. The glass on a sealed daguerreotype should be checked from time to time and at the first signs of glass corrosion it should be replaced with a new glass. This might need to be done every twenty to thirty years.

Late in 1982 William F. Stapp of the National Portrait Gallery was beginning to put together an exhibition on the work of Robert Cornelius, the first American portrait photographer. He asked me if the findings from the MRL study could be applied to decipher how a daguerreotypist worked. I thought it might be possible if a variety of daguerreotypes made by the same person over a period of time could be analyzed. Stapp was able to obtain over half of the known Cornelius daguerreotypes for me to look at.

The following spring Stapp brought the daguerreotypes to MRL and for one week we sat at the scanning electron microscope and examined the Cornelius plates, the Joseph Saxton daguerreotype, and several other very early daguerreotypes. It was a remarkable time. We often had four or five people from the laboratory sitting with us during the day and watching as the work progressed. Over two hundred micrographs were taken during that time. After Stapp left I laid the micrographs out on a large table and, using information from dated daguerreotypes, the chemical data, and the recorded image microstructure, I was able to make a chronology for the undated Cornelius daguerreotypes. What was most remarkable was that the Saxton and Cornelius image microstructure structures matched image microstructure which had been produced in the laboratory using specific processing regimes. The Physical Model and our experimental work was a Rosetta stone and it was the work of Cornelius that allowed for the verification of that fact. It is not often that a scientist receives verification of his work in such a splendid way.[21]

All in all, this study was the most massive examination of the daguerreotype process ever undertaken. It provided a great deal of new information about the properties of daguerreotypes, how they deteriorate, and methods for their care, as well as fundamental information about how they are formed. More important, it has provided a model for a fruitful method of investigating the deterioration of photographic materials as we continue the search for new measures for their preservation. Photographs differ from other materials in that their image is formed as a result of the interaction of light with a photosensitive material followed by some subsequent treatment to form a characteristic microstructure. The optical properties of this microstructure are what give rise to what the viewer sees as the image. This is quite different from a drawing or a painting in which an image is applied to some suitable support material. In the photograph, it is paramount to preserve the image microstructure as well as the other materials that carry and support the image as a whole. In the drawing, the materials that make up and carry the image are one and the same.

Some of the most interesting findings are those that help to place the daguerreotype process in the context of the rest of photography. The evidence shows that the daguerreotype is a very narrowly defined process which was not amenable to many additions. It is related to the rest of photography only in that the image is initiated by the formation of latent images within a silver halide matrix. Daguerre was very lucky when he chanced upon the use of mercury. The method of crystal growth using mercury vapor in this system just happens to produce image particles that are the right size to scatter visible light and, thus, to produce a visible image. Indeed, if the particles were slightly larger or slightly smaller than they are, even though an image might be produced, we would not be able to see it.

Further, since the image particle size is just below the limits of resolution of a light microscope, this precluded the extensive examination of the daguerreian image structure until the advent of the scanning electron microscope. Thus, the daguerreotype was a difficult puzzle to solve, but not because of limitations on the part of those who previously investigated the process. Rather, it was because of limitations of the extensions and tools available to examine and characterize materials.

NOTES

1. *The Athenaeum,* no. 617 (1839): 636–37.

2. Irving Pobboravsky, "Study of Iodized Daguerreotype Plates" (M.S. thesis, Rochester Institute of Technology, 1971).

3. Alice Swan, C. E. Fioro, and K. F. J. Heinrich, "Daguerreotypes: A Study of the Plates and the Process," *Scanning Electron Microscope* 1 (1979): 411–23.

4. R. Prohaska and A. Fisher, "X-Ray Response of Daguerreotype Photographic Plates," *Applied Physics Letters* 40 (1982): 283–85.

5. I. Brodie and M. Thackray, "Photocharging of Thin Films of Silver Iodide and Its Relevance to the Daguerre Photographic Process," *Nature* 312 (1984): 744–46.

6. M. Susan Barger, "The Daguerreotype: Image Structure, Optical Properties, and a Scientific Interpretation of Daguerreotypy" (Ph.D. dissertation, Pennsylvania State University, 1982).

7. M. Susan Barger and W. B. White, "The Optical Characterization of the Daguerreotype," *Photographic Science and Engineering* 28 (1984): 172–74.

8. M. Susan Barger, R. Messier, and W. B. White, "Non-Destructive Assessment of Daguerreotype Image Quality by Diffuse Reflectance," *Studies in Conservation* 29 (1984): 84–86.

9. This is also called the "luminous efficacy" curve for human vision.

10. M. Susan Barger, R. Messier, and W. B. White, "A Physical Model for the Daguerreotype," *Photographic Science and Engineering* 26 (1982): 285–91.

11. M. Susan Barger, R. Messier, and W. B. White, "Gilding and Sealing Daguerreotypes," *Photographic Science and Engineering* 27 (1983): 141–46.

12. James Waterhouse, "Some New Methods of Developing Daguerreotype Plates," *British Journal of Photography* 45 (1898): 686; James Waterhouse, "Teachings of Daguerreotype," *British Journal of Photography* 46 (1899): 740–45, 756–57.

13. M. Susan Barger, "Image Formation in Daguerreotypes," in preparation. The work on image formation has been written up in several places—in my dissertation, in my essay in the Cornelius catalogue, and in passing in various of our other papers. A formal discussion of the image formation work was presented at the

annual meeting of the Society of Photographic Scientists and Engineers in San Francisco in May 1983.

14. M. Susan Barger and W. F. Stapp, "Daguerreotype: A Precautionary Discussion of Deterioration, Cleaning, and Treatment," in *Preprint Volume for the 7th Triennial Meeting of the Committee for Conservation of I.C.O.M.* (Copenhagen, 1984), pp. 84.14.8–84.14.12.

15. M. Susan Barger, A. P. Giri, W. B. White, and T. M. Edmondson, "Daguerreotype Cleaning," *Studies in Conservation* 31 (1986): 15–28; corregendum, *Studies in Conservation* 32 (1987): 141–43.

16. M. Susan Barger, Deane K. Smith, and W. B. White, "Characterization of Corrosion Products on Old Protective Glass, Especially Daguerreotype Cover Glasses," *Journal of Materials Science* (1988), in press.

17. M. Susan Barger, S. V. Krishnaswamy, and R. Messier, "The Cleaning of Daguerreotypes I. Physical Sputter Cleaning: A New Technique," in *AIC Preprints* (Washington, D.C.: American Institute for Conservation of Historic and Artistic Works), pp. 9–20; M. Susan Barger, S. V. Krishnaswamy, and R. Messier, "The Cleaning of Daguerreotypes: Comparison of Cleaning Methods," *Journal of the American Institute for Conservation* 22 (1982): 13–24.

18. V. Daniels, "Plasma Reduction of Silver Tarnish on Daguerreotypes," *Studies in Conservation* 26 (1981): 45–49.

19. M. S. Koch and A. Sjogren, "Behandlung von Daguerreotypien mit Wasserstoffplasma," *Maltechnik Restauro* 90 (October 1984): 58–64.

20. Electrocleaning is a safe and effective method for cleaning and there is some evidence that it may make daguerreotypes less vulnerable to recorrosion. While I have no reservations about recommending electrocleaning for daguerreotypes, being of the if-it-ain't-broke-don't-fix-it school I tend to be very conservative about cleaning daguerreotypes. Tom Edmondson, on the other hand, feels very strongly that when it is known that a daguerreotype has been previously cleaned in thiourea or cyanide cleaners, that daguerreotype should be electrocleaned to remove the corrosion products left by the previous cleaners. He feels that the evidence of prophylactic benefits attendant with cleaning using this method is substantial and that this should be acted upon.

21. William F. Stapp (with Marion S. Carson and M. Susan Barger), *Robert Cornelius: Portraits from the Dawn of Photography* (Washington, D.C.: Smithsonian Institution Press, 1983); M. Susan Barger and W. F. Stapp, "The Evolution of the Daguerreotype Art of Robert Cornelius: A Scientific Retrospective by Scanning Electron Microscopy," in Pamela A. England and Lambertus van Zelst, eds., *Application of Science in Examination of Works of Art: Proceedings of the Seminar, September 7–9, 1983* (Boston: Research Laboratory, Museum of Fine Arts, 1985), pp. 164–73.

Heavy Lightness, Serious Vanity

Modern Daguerreotypy

Grant B. Romer

All lovers of the daguerreotype are spellbound beings. Once having been struck with its ineffable beauty, they must pursue, they must possess something of its mystery for themselves. No other of the many appealing photographic processes charm like the daguerreotype; hence the specializing collectors, dealers, and historians who are its ardent devotees.

Virtually all of the daguerreotype's becharmed admirers dream, at one moment or another, of having the ability to create daguerreotypes. This usually remains a fantasy. The few who attempt to act immediately confront substantial barriers. Where does one obtain a supply of plates? Where can daguerreian equipment be purchased? Where does one find pumice, rouge, lampblack? Those undaunted by such problems are frightened away by the vaporous, stinking red specter of bromine and the shimmering insidious phantom of mercury. Possessing such substances in tightly stopped bottles is problem enough; releasing them into one's own breathing space is terrifying. Thus, most must be content with owning the images and objects of the daguerreotype, wrapped in the romantic notion of the daguerreotype as a "lost art." They are fond of explaining its absence from the contemporary scene with such commonly heard offerings as "Modern chemicals are too pure," or "The secrets of the daguerreotype are buried with the masters of the art." This is much more satisfying than admitting it is just too difficult and dangerous to make daguerreotypes.

However, if an international call were made for those who work with the process to show themselves, dozens of individuals would appear with handfuls of silvered plates bearing images of their own production. Most would be unknown to each other as well as to a wider community. What is to be made of these individuals, working in clandestine isolation? What value does their work have?

Many collectors and scholars are aware of the existence of contemporary daguerreotypists. Indeed, it is a fact that there have always been practitioners of the process beyond the era of its commercial demise in the 1860s. Some collections hold examples of such late productions. For instance, the Eastman House collection holds examples made by J. J. Hawes in the 1880s, M. J. Steffens in the 1890s, Charles Tremear in the 1930s, and Harvey Zucker and Irving Pobboravsky in the 1970s. The St. Louis Historical Society possesses a great number of late daguerreotypes made by Thomas Easterly. No matter how beautiful and provocative the later daguerreotypes are, they are generally viewed as mere curiosities. Clearly, the current valuation of a daguerreotype is dependent upon the era of its production. The idea that daguerreotypes have been made beyond the 1850s, and are being made today, is disturbing to some collectors and historians. In their minds, there is something not quite authentic about such images. Indeed, some question the validity of making daguerreotypes today. (Ironically, the same people are willing to commission portraits of themselves, their lovers, children, pets, and daguerreian cameras.) Such attitudes are understandable in light of monetary investment in daguerreotypes. There have been examples of modern productions being passed as vintage items, and rare cases of outright attempts at forgery. Thus, the contemporary maker of daguerreotypes is not the darling of collectors. This is unfortunate, because it withholds the patronage of the audience best equipped to appreciate and encourage the contemporary daguerreotype.

Surely, some collectors would be willing to pay a price commensurate with a choice production of the daguerreian era if the quality of the modern daguerreotype were comparable. Admittedly, most modern productions are sick sisters of the radiant beauties of the past. Even when of high quality, these images appear disturbingly new. They present faces which only their parents can love. Making a daguerreotype does not make one a daguerreotypist, and most daguerreotypes produced today do not constitute a respectable manifestation of the craft. One cannot talk of the "contemporary daguerreotype" in the same way one might of the "contemporary lithograph." However, it would be wrong to ignore or dismiss such work and its creators. Certain individuals have achieved something which warrants them a place in the history of the process. They have a valid contribution to make to the common understanding of the elusive essence of the daguerreotype's appeal. They have a unique connection to the process. Collectors gather the sheer veils and subtle reflections of the process, virtual souvenirs of its presence. Historians trace its footsteps. But modern workers hold the very hand of the daguerreotype—and some even receive its caresses.

If there is something magical in the daguerreotype, and all agree that there is, then those who make daguerreotypes, no matter how poorly, are magicians in a sense. For them, daguerreotypy is a kind of mystery school wherein one may gain hidden knowledge and transform oneself. To successfully make a daguerreotype is to gain the password of the first degree and initiation into an august occult society. The entered apprentices of the da-

guerreotype know the very same emotions as the first experimenters with the process. They can understand how the faintest shadow of an image can be the cause of the greatest sensation of excitement and triumph. They know secrets, they wield powers, they are forever bonded with souls long gone from this world. Their own elevated sense of self-worth is, of course, not shared by those who have not had the same experience. But that matters little. What they have learned is its own reward. No one who has not soiled himself with jeweler's rouge, worked his arms sore in polishing a plate to a mirror finish, had his nostrils fill with the peculiar odor of iodine, can understand the thrills of the process. No one who has not poured a puddle of mercury, heated it with a flame, watched an image gradually materialize, and when done, laid first eyes upon a new, naked daguerreotype can realize the full poignance of its otherworldly beauty. One's vision is transformed by such experiences. Eyes, so prepared, see a daguerreotype like no others.

To become a daguerreotypist today is considerably harder than it was in the 1850s. At that time there were experienced instructors, a ready supply of high quality supplies, and financial reward for work. The details of the process are really relatively simple, which is why blacksmiths, barbers, and shoemakers could be taught its rudiments in a day. However, they then had to work hard at the craft to gain control of it in order to make a living by it. The modern worker has no teacher, nor ready supply of essentials, nor hope of gaining a financial return for his or her labors. Therefore, few go beyond the first degree of experience. They discover that summoning the Daguerreian Muse is one thing; making her stay is another. Many abandon further efforts after rudimentary success, filled with pride in their special, though neophyte, status.

The initiates of the second degree are far fewer in number. These individuals, through disappointment and frustration, gain sober and deep respect for those who have gone that way before them. They develop true admiration and understanding of daguerreian achievement. In every image they

Irving Pobboravsky (U.S.), quarter plate. White Birch. Collection of John Wood.

can sense the daguerreotypist who brought it into existence. They discover that daguerreotypy is an uphill battle. Problems are encountered and must be solved. Supplies of consistent quality must be secured, efficient methods of polishing evolved, equipment refashioned, and constantly shifting variables responded to in daily practice.

Time, money, and labor are rapidly lost in misjudged exposures, ruined plates, and fruitless experiments. Worst of all is the experience of having a success and being unable to repeat it, even though every operation is conducted as before. Those who do manage to establish some control often find themselves creatively exhausted in the process, without the strength to produce decently conceived images. Curiously, many of the subjects of modern daguerreotypes parallel the banalities found in holograms. Each worker of this degree may produce a stunning image or two which goes beyond the power

of the daguerreotype to render almost any subject interestingly. For this, they count themselves lucky, if they are wise.

The world possesses perhaps only two master daguerreians, although both would deny that they held the third and final degree. Nonetheless, they have studied the grammar of the daguerreotype, have achieved control of it, and have stated something of substance in that most subtle language. Their work speaks of the essence of the daguerreotype. It must be seen in the original to be understood. No reproduction, no matter how fine, can convey that message, for it can be no more than the shadow of something which is all light.

Irving Pobboravsky and Patrick Bailly-Maitre-Grand are well known by daguerreian cognoscenti, yet remain unknown in the truest sense, as is befitting keepers of occult knowledge. Both share a background in the sciences and have been drawn

The Illustrations

The daguerreotype is an unreproducible image. The very best possible copy on paper is only a vague approximation of what a daguerreotype actually looks like. Paper simply cannot so catch the light and so seduce the eye. Without holding a daguerreotype in your hands, there is no way to see the incredible play of light and color on the plate itself. That ocular drama is the very definition of daguerreotypy. A copy of a daguerreotype is like a translation of a poem: we can get the message but not the music, the sense but not the sound, the outlines but not the rhythms. All the subtleties and the magic are either lost or changed. But if we can't read the original, what a wonderful thing it is to have a translation, and if we can't hold the original, what a wonderful thing it is to see a copy.

This selection of copies attempts to present the daguerreotype solely as an art form and to suggest and perhaps even define through the selection the aesthetics of the form. Several kinds of images have been excluded from this book or given only slight representation. There is only one gold-mining scene here. There are few views of the West, no American street scenes, few occupational portraits, and few famous people. In other words, the kinds of images that make up the bulk of Beaumont Newhall's wonderful *Daguerreotype in America* are barely represented in this book at all. It is not that I personally like one kind of image but dislike another. The daguerreotype is collected and valued today for a variety of reasons—historical, cultural, social, artistic, and so forth—and each of them is important.

But what is here represents a conscious effort to separate art from what is clearly and exclusively history, documentation, and social commentary.

This is not always an easy task. Many of the pieces I have included were not originally intended to be art, but the distancing of time and our eye has redefined them. I tried to select pieces that clearly have that power of art, the power to rivet our gaze and demand of our eyes that they return again and again to gaze deeper and deeper and reward that deeper, more thoughtful looking not only with continued pleasure but with expanded insight, with deeper understanding of man and nature and the fellowship and interaction between the two. That is the power and the grace of art and what I find present in each of these daguerreotypes.

In the list of images that follows, I have for the sake of simplicity adhered to the nineteenth-century terms instead of using the more precise measure of inches or millimeters, except in the case of "La Locomotive." There were variations in sizes; plates were occasionally trimmed; some European plates do not conform to the standard American sizes; and modern daguerreotypes do not exactly conform to the older sizes. However, in general, the designation of whole plate indicates $6\frac{1}{2} \times 8\frac{1}{2}$ inches or 165×215 mm; half plate indicates $4\frac{1}{4} \times 5\frac{1}{2}$ inches or 108×140 mm; quarter plate indicates $3\frac{1}{2} \times 4\frac{1}{4}$ inches or 82×108 mm; sixth plate, which was the most common size, indicates $2\frac{3}{4} \times 3\frac{1}{4}$ inches or 70×82 mm; and ninth plate indicates $2 \times 2\frac{1}{2}$ inches or 51×65 mm.

1. Albert Southworth and Josiah Hawes (U.S.), whole plate.

Hawes considered this image not only his masterpiece but "the finest [daguerreotype] in the world." Certainly it is one of the masterpieces of Western art. Collection of Matthew R. Isenburg.

2. Albert Southworth and Josiah Hawes (U.S.), whole plate.

Twenty years before Julia Margaret Cameron, Southworth and Hawes had captured the style. Note the weightlessness of the book in the hand, added to the way the dress folds off the shoulders and body. This suggests that the subject was possibly lying down and the daguerreotype taken from above, a technique common to modern fashion photography but, like so much of Southworth and Hawes's work, a radical and innovative departure from accepted nineteenth-century photographic conventions. The central scratch seen on so many of Southworth and Hawes's major works is the result of two things. The device they used for holding the plate during buffing caused it to protrude slightly at the center; then in later years Hawes kept his personal collection unglassed in the original plate boxes. These two facts, coupled with an old man's unsteady hand, led to this mark common on so many of the greatest plates. Collection of Matthew R. Isenburg.

3. Albert Southworth and Josiah Hawes (U.S.), whole plate.

This study in black and white is the finest known example of contrasting background to bring out foreground and feature in portraiture. The girl's crown of dark hair is silhouetted against a light gray background that magically changes to black when highlighting facial features. Collection of Michael Isenburg.

4. Albert Southworth and Josiah Hawes (U.S.), whole plate.

This beautifully tinted and vignetted portrait-bust daguerreotype is of an unidentified minister. Note how the background enhances the image. Collection of Matthew R. Isenburg.

5. Albert Southworth and Josiah Hawes (U.S.), whole plate.

This portrait is greatly enhanced by Southworth and Hawes having positioned the sitter at a higher elevation than the camera. The most delicate blue tinting was used on the liner and ribbon of the bonnet, and the face was framed within it. Collection of Matthew R. Isenburg.

6. Irving Pobboravsky (U.S.), quarter plate. Young Beech Branches.

This image has all the poetry of Sudek's photographs; however, Pobboravsky, who lives in Rochester, New York, is relatively unknown as an artist because he has devoted himself to the daguerreotype. In the world of glitter and hype, it is difficult to build a reputation out of unique images, even if they are of excellent craftsmanship. Pobboravsky's work has been exhibited at Marcuse Pfeifer Gallery in New York, the International Museum of Photography at George Eastman House, "the photography place" in Philadelphia, and in a one-man show at McNeese University. He has been the subject of a television program produced by Japan Broadcasting Corporation, and his work has been discussed in a variety of essays, particularly Grant Romer's "The Daguerreotype in America and England after 1860" (*History of Photography* 1 [July 1977]: 201–12). His work is in many private collections and the permanent collection of the International Museum of Photography at George Eastman House. Collection of the artist.

7. Hermann Carl Eduard Biewend (Germany), half plate. Harz Landscape near Königshütte.

Dr. Biewend was one of the great amateur daguerreotypists, and his portraits of his wife and children are quite well known. This landscape taken on June 27, 1854, is a prime example of his surviving work. Collection of Robert Lebeck.

8. Baron Louis-Adolphe Humbert de Molard (France), half plate. View of Lagny on the Marne.

Baron Humbert de Molard was possibly the best of the French amateur daguerreotypists and photographers. This image of Lagny, where twenty-five or so of his daguerreotypes are preserved in the municipal museum, resembles his later works on paper. (See Philippe Neagu and Jean-Jacques Poulet-Allamagny, *Anthologie d'un Patrimoine Photographique, 1847–1926.*) On the reverse the Baron wrote: "Lagny, Septembre 1846, 18 secondes, Eau-bromine." Trying to fix the movement of those washerwomen on the Marne with an eighteen-second exposure was no easy task. Collection of Robert Lebeck.

9. Anon. (U.S.), quarter plate.

Highly prized for their historical importance, California gold-mining scenes are among the most sought-after daguerreotypes. Few, however, are of this quality. The care that went into the composition and coloring of this piece makes it nearly unique in a genre primarily distinguished for documentation and reportage, not for aesthetic content. Courtesy of LaPlaca Productions.

10. Anon. (U.S.), half plate. Preston's Livery Stable, Yuba, California.

Apart from its historical significance as an important document of the early West and the effect of the Gold Rush, this is an important image in the history of the art of the daguerreotype because it is a beautiful American scenic daguerreotype. Collection of Stephen Anaya.

11. Platt Babbitt (U.S.), whole plate. Niagara Falls.

Babbitt was *the* photographer of Niagara Falls and probably the inventor of vacation photography. Collection of Matthew R. Isenburg.

12. Anon. (China), sixth plate. Portrait of Tsow Chaoong.

Though Jules Itier daguerreotyped in China in the early 1840s, that work appears to be lost. This daguerreotype dated 1847 predates by several years what had been thought to be the earliest surviving image made in China. It is on a slightly smaller than normal sixth plate housed in a case made for that exact size and sealed with yellow rice paper. Laid in the case is a nineteenth-century calling card printed "Tsow Chaoong / Canton" in both English and Chinese with an inscription in English "for Miss Percival, / With Tsow Chaoong's / Compliments 1847." Collection of Richard Segan.

13. Anon. (U.S.), quarter plate. Iroquois Maiden.

An image of great importance. Though unidentified and in a different pose, the same elegant Iroquois maiden appears in a woodcut in Minnie Myrtle's *The Iroquois; or, The Bright Side of Indian Character* (New York: Appleton & Co., 1859). By the time this image was made, the Iroquois were feeling the effects of America's genocidal policy toward the Indian. As early as 1807 Baron Hyde de Neuville found New York's once-proud Iroquois reduced to squalor and "stagnating in misery." Collection of David Belcher.

14. John H. Fitzgibbon (U.S.), three-quarter plate. Portrait of Kno-Shr, Kansas Chief.

The plate is inscribed "Kno-Shr Kansas Chief / Daguerreotyped by Fitzgibbon / Presented to G. V. Brooke by / J H Fitzgibbon, St. Louis April 4th 1853." Though Fitzgibbon was St. Louis's leading daguerreotypist, he traveled widely and visited the various Indian nations in order to compile a collection of Indian portraits, which Marcus Root praised for their "delineation, depth, tone, and beauty." Collection of Gilman Paper Company.

15. Patrick Bailly-Maitre-Grand (France), 30 × 160 cm. La Locomotive.

Bailly-Maitre-Grand is one of France's leading painters and photographers and its greatest living daguerreotypist. His work has been the subject of one-man shows at the Musée National d'Art Moderne at Centre Georges Pompidou, Musée Nicéphore Niepce, Musée d'Art Moderne de Strasbourg, Marcuse Pfeifer Gallery, Galerie Michelle Chomette, and the French Cultural Center in Prague and is in the permanent collections at Centre Pompidou, the Bibliothèque Nationale, the Cabinet des Estampes Strasbourg, the Musée Nicéphore Niepce, the Centre National d'Etude Spatiale, and the Ecole Nationale de Photographie. He has been the subject of many articles, and he has appeared on the cover of *Match* in the process of making a daguerreotype. This image, over five feet long and nearly one foot wide, was produced on eight separate plates. Bailly-Maitre-Grand has produced other large-format daguerreotypes, including a two-foot-square image of the moon constructed of six plates on a swinging panel so that three can be juxtaposed at right angles to the other three, thereby causing the moon to appear in three dimensions. That image was purchased by CNES, the French equivalent of NASA. It and "La Locomotive" are his master-

pieces. This particular locomotive is a model 5.231 H8 type Pacific (c. 1920) from the Musée du Chemin de Fer de Mulhouse. The daguerreotype, made in 1986 and 1987, was exhibited in November 1987 at the great exhibition in Cormeilles-en-Parisis on the occasion of the bicentennial of Daguerre's birth. Collection of Count Geoffroy de Beauffort.

16. Irving Pobboravsky (U.S.), quarter plate. 17 Church St., Scottsville.

Pobboravsky's daguerreotypes of houses and the industrial landscape impose elegance and order on America. Collection of the artist.

17. Patrick Bailly-Maitre-Grand (France), half plate.

In this image typical of Bailly-Maitre-Grand's work we see the eye of a contemporary Atget at work. Collection of the artist.

18. Anon. (France), three-quarter plate. Vaucenans.

A carefully composed garden scene in the Jura near St. Amour. Collection of John Wood.

19. Wilhelm Schonfeldt (Russia), half plate.

Russia, unlike the United States, lacked a large middle class who could afford daguerreotypes. It appears that few daguerreotypists operated there and that little of their work survived the social upheavals of this century. This aristocratic lady of St. Petersburg in her green bonnet, though photographed before Chekhov's birth, looks as if she could have stepped from one of his stories. Collection of John Wood.

20. Anon. (France), stereoscopic daguerreotype.

One of the most atypical and imaginative nude studies of the daguerreian era. Collection of Uwe Scheid.

21. Anon. (France), stereoscopic daguerreotype.

Though somewhat typical in posing of the nude studies of the period, this girl looks more like a figure from Gauguin than from a daguerreotype. Courtesy of LaPlaca Productions.

22. Irving Pobboravsky (U.S.), quarter plate. Young Tree.

This is one of Pobboravsky's masterpieces, exhibiting perfection both in craft and in composition. A cursory glance at Pobboravsky's trees suggests that he is drawn either to examples like this one or to dense and gnarled examples. At base, however, in his work they are the same. Pobboravsky's aesthetics and his world view were both highly influenced by the German photographer Karl Blossfeldt, whose *Uniformen der Kunst* suggests that apparent simplicity is wondrously complex and that in the most complicated patterns of nature there reside simple and harmonious forms. Collection of the artist.

23. Anon. (Australia), quarter plate.

A river in Victoria inspired this lyrical daguerreian landscape. One wonders if this might be an Australian gold rush image because gold was discovered in great quantities in Victoria in 1851. Or is this a farm scene, and are those sheep grazing on the other side of the river? Collection of Robert Lebeck.

24. Anon. (U.S.), quarter plate.

A portrait of innocence and beauty, probably the daguerreotypist's daughter. This pure and lovely image is one of the great American daguerreotypes. Collection of Charles Swedlund.

25. Charles Williamson (U.S.), sixth plate.

Williamson of Brooklyn was distinguished for his portraits of mothers and children, and his are among the best daguerreotypes in that genre. Collection of John Wood.

26. Anon. (U.S.), sixth plate. Portrait of Uncle George and Gus.

A portrait of such tremendous sensitivity that it reaches out to us with both the power of art and that unique power of photography which constantly reminds us that what we see actually happened. Collection of Wm. B. Becker.

27. Anon. (U.S.), sixth plate.

A convincing portrait that can stand alongside the best portraits of both centuries. Collection of George S. Whiteley IV.

28. Antoine Claudet (England), stereoscopic daguerreotype.

English daguerreotypes were often over-tinted, and Claudet, though a fine photographer and a student of Daguerre, was often guilty of garish uses of color or of allowing his operators to apply color crudely. Only Kilburn's studio at its worst could be worse than Claudet's at its worst; however, Kilburn, too, created many fine daguerreotypes. Another problem with Claudet's work, especially in stereo, is that his plates appear to have been among the most poorly buffed of any daguerreotypist; consequently, his daguerreotypes often look as if they are scratched or streaked. This bride, however, is perfection itself. Collection of Mark Koenigsberg.

29. Jeremiah Gurney (U.S.), sixth plate.

Gurney was one of the leading New York daguerreotypists, and this is one of his most graceful and finely tinted images. Courtesy of LaPlaca Productions.

30. Larcher (France), stereoscopic daguerreotype.

From a series of nine stereoscopic daguerreotypes of this family on the grounds of their estate by Larcher of Bordeaux. All nine are sensitive, moving studies, and the individuals are handled more delicately than is usually seen in the French daguerreotype, which tends to present the portrait with more monumentality than delicacy. Such delicacy as is seen in the posing of the girl and the maid in the doorway is usually reserved for landscape views. Collection of John Wood.

31. Mathew Brady (U.S.), half plate.

This intense portrait of a mature-looking young boy, as fine an example of Brady's work as we have, is of a completely different order from most of his commercial work. Courtesy of LaPlaca Productions.

32. Anon. (France), half plate. Portrait of Curé Paulin of Tremblay.

This is most likely Auguste Paulin, whose book *Leçons de cosmographie ou de géographie astronomique avec les solutions de cinquante problèmes sur les globes et les sphères* was published in nearby Nantes. Though an amazing portrait for several reasons, one of its most interesting features is that it appears to have been made in a studio. If so, it is an amusing prospect to think of the good curé so passionate about his armillary spheres and books that he would carry them to a studio to be photographed. Collection of John Wood.

33. Anon. (U.S.), sixth plate.

As simple yet dramatic a postmortem as one might imagine. The drama here derives from that simplicity, from the child himself. Grieved parents looking on, the clutched bouquet, or any of the other elements often found in the postmortem could not intensify the loss of this child. Collection of John Wood.

34. Albert Southworth and Josiah Hawes (U.S.), quarter plate.

This portrait features a style and type of tinting so unusual in technique that the viewer does not realize at first it is a daguerreotype. As in so many tinted images by Southworth and Hawes, the picture can only be seen as a positive because the tinting is so prominent that it excludes the possibility of being viewed as a negative regardless of the light source. One can surmise that the mottled or stippled effect seen in this image carries the blurred fingerprints of Nancy Southworth Hawes, Southworth's sister and Hawes's wife, who did the studio tinting. Collection of Matthew R. Isenburg.

35. Albert Southworth and Josiah Hawes (U.S.), whole plate.

Another classic example of the work of Southworth and Hawes. Collection of the Metropolitan Museum of Art, Gift of I. N. Phelps Stokes, Edward S. Hawes, Alice Mary Hawes, Marion Augusta Hawes, 1937. (37.14.20).

36. Albert Southworth and Josiah Hawes (U.S.), whole plate.

By using an illustrated book as a central theme of interest, Southworth and Hawes created an informal yet perfectly composed image. Collection of Matthew R. Isenburg.

37. Albert Southworth and Josiah Hawes (U.S.), whole plate.

Southworth and Hawes were famous for their bridal portraits and were probably the first photographers to recognize the potential lucrative market for such images. Here is a prime example of their work in that genre. Courtesy of LaPlaca Productions.

38. Anon. (U.S.), half plate.

A powerful image. Daguerreian profiles are relatively rare, and close-ups are even rarer. Regardless of whether this image was the daguerreotypist's or the sitter's doing and regardless of whether it might even be a cut-down whole plate, such a profile made so close up exhibits a kind of artistic vision unknown in photography until Helmar Lerski, though its roots clearly reside in early Renaissance portraiture. Collection of David Belcher.

39. Anon. (U.S.), sixth plate.

A simple but beautiful image in every respect. Collection of George S. Whiteley IV.

40. Anon. (U.S.), quarter plate.

The composition of this portrait is natural, casual, and totally inspired. Collection of Joan Murray.

41. Anon. (U.S.), sixth plate.

A masterfully composed image. Collection of Mark Koenigsberg.

42. Albert Southworth and Josiah Hawes (U.S.), quarter plate.

Relaxed and pensive, this young girl looks as if she were standing in a garden, not a studio. Collection of Matthew R. Isenburg.

43. Anon. (U.S.), sixth plate.

It may come as some surprise that this little girl, so spontaneous and unlike the figures in most daguerreotypes, is identified on the back of the plate as being William Foster Lipton. It is dated April 1854. Collection of Dafydd Wood.

44. Anon. (U.S.), quarter plate.

A vital image, rather unusual because it has a later feel than the 1850s about it. Collection of Mark Koenigsberg.

45. Anon. (U.S.), sixth plate.

This young machinist with his rolled shirt-sleeve, firm grip, and intense look is as richly sensual an image as daguerreotypy was capable of producing. It is more than a picture of this particular man; it is an icon of America on the verge of the Industrial Revolution—a superb American occupational portrait. Collection of Paul Katz.

46. Frederick Coombs (U.S.), quarter plate.

A classic portrait of a frontiersman. Coombs began his career with a gallery in St. Louis (1846–47), moved to Chicago (1848–49), and was then drawn West with the Gold Rush to San Francisco, where he operated a gallery until 1851. Collection of Count Geoffroy de Beauffort.

47. Albert Southworth and Josiah Hawes (U.S.), whole plate. Portrait of Erastus Hopkins.

This image is actually half of a whole-plate stereoscopic pair. Hopkins, a leader of the Free Soilers, who were pledged to bring the Mexican Territory into the Union as free, not slave, states, was a lank and lean Yankee, and Hawes played to this characteristic, utilizing it in order to give added stature to the man. He did this by incorporating as many vertical lines as possible into the portrait. First, the unusual standing pose accentuated by legs parallel but apart added even more thinness to an already thin frame. The book held on end by a long thin arm heightened the statement. The book rests on a pedestal table, and finally the great column thrusts upward to the edge of the plate. There are few daguerreian portraits composed with such care and obvious forethought. And it is clearly one of the first photographs to make a deliberate political statement. Hawes wanted Hopkins to appear larger than life, and one can imagine that when the portrait was viewed in the Grand Parlor Stereoscope, that is the exact effect he achieved. Collection of Matthew R. Isenburg.

Detail from Plate 50.

48. Anon. (U.S.), half plate.

Daguerreotypes of armed soldiers, hunters, frontiersmen, and toughs, though rare, are not uncommon; this image, however, seems a thing apart from that genre. These clearly dangerous yet attractive characters are hard to classify. The younger man is probably the brother or son of the older one, whose somewhat frightening demeanor he is trying to copy. Collection of Mark Koenigsberg.

49. Anon. (U.S.), sixth plate. Telegraph Lineman.

This portrait of a lineman with pole-climbing rigging and clamps is historically an important image in that it fuses the two most revolutionary inventions of the era—the telegraph and the photograph. Collection of Terry Toedtemeier.

50. Anon. (U.S.), quarter plate (enlarged).

One wonders what is happening in this intriguing image of a fort. Are the two men on horses greeting each other? Did a firing squad just execute three men, one naked and with his back turned (see detail)? Why is there a grave beside the reviewing stand in the center of the fort? And what is that pile of things close to the upper right of the grave? Collection of Count Geoffroy de Beauffort.

51. Anon. (U.S.), sixth plate.

Though obviously meant to be a kind of comic picture, this compelling image is one of the great American daguerreotypes. Unlike the usual novelty image, which finally is only a piece of kitsch, this sculptural portrait is a haunting picture of violence and sensuality. Collection of Mark Koenigsberg.

52. Anon. (U.S.), half plate.

Another powerful and penetrating portrait. Collection of Mark Koenigsberg.

53. Anon. (U.S.), sixth plate.

Everything about this image works and everything about it is beautifully balanced. Though somewhat contrived, it has a feeling of authenticity right down to the sitter's feet on the chair rung. The man was probably a traveling patent medicine "doctor." He is poor, but there's no look of the yokel here; this man is bright, not unsophisticated, and struggling to make it. And he has made it to the point that he can at least afford a daguerreotype of himself. This image is an interesting companion piece to Cornelius's great portrait of Dr. Boye mixing chemicals. Collection of Mark Koenigsberg.

54. Anon. (U.S.), quarter plate.

Possibly an elegantly dressed machinist, or possibly the inventor. The handsome young man looks quite modern to us because of his mustache, which was a rarity in the daguerreian era. Writing on "The Lost Art of the Daguerreotype" in *Century Magazine* in 1904, Abraham Bogardus noted, "The mustache was then seldom seen. A man wearing one on the street was the subject of remark, and the boys were always ready to 'guy' him." Collection of Nicholas Graver.

55. Anon. (U.S.), sixth plate.

Few portraits convey a greater sense of self-confidence than this image of a black man. Considering the status of the Negro in nineteenth-century America, it is as remarkable a historic document as it is a work of art. Collection of George S. Whiteley IV.

From
L'Illustration,
July 1, 1848.

La barr..ode de la rue Sain'-Maur-Popincourt le dimanche matin,
d'après une planche daguerréotypée par **M. Thibault**.

56. Anon. (U.S.), half plate. Portrait of Dan Rice.

This intense portrait, possibly by Southworth and Hawes, is, surprisingly, of a famous nineteenth-century clown. Collection of Richard and Christine Rydell.

57. John Plumbe (U.S.), half plate. The United States Capitol.

This architectural tour de force taken by Plumbe in 1846 is one of the two earliest known photographic views of the building. The other example, which is in the Library of Congress, is static by comparison.

From
L'Illustration,
July 1, 1848.

La barricade de la rue Saint-Maur-Popincourt le lundi après l'attaque,
d'après une planche daguerréotypée par M. Thibault.

The focus here is critically sharp and allows for minute examination of the construction details. The image possesses a heightened feeling of depth and balance because it was taken from an angle that allows both the side and face of the building to be seen. Collection of Matthew R. Isenburg.

58. Anon. (France), half plate.

A lovely image of a house on a rocky shore in Brittany. Note the lobster traps. Collection of Robert Koch.

59. Anon. (France), whole plate. Breton Village.

This is one of the most beautiful of French daguerreotypes, a work comparable in its brilliance and calm to Clausel's famous "Landscape near Troyes." This is not a piece of documentation. The daguerreotypist was clearly composing a picturesque image and attempting to create a work of art. Collection Centre Canadien d'Architecture / Canadian Centre for Architecture, Montreal.

60 and 61. Thibault (France), three-quarter plates. The Revolution of 1848.

These two daguerreotypes constitute the first examples of photography being used for war reportage. They are before-and-after pictures of the attack at the barricades of Rue St. Maur during the bloody "Days of June" of the 1848 Revolution. The great Paris weekly *L'Illustration* sent a daguerreotypist named Thibault to photograph the barricades before the attack on Sunday, June 25, and after the attack on Monday, June 26, with the express purpose of immediately publishing the images. They appeared as wood engravings in their exact dimensions in *L'Illustration* of Saturday, July 1. It was a first in journalism. Among the hundreds of engravings having to do with these events published by *L'Illustration*, these are the only two bearing the description of being made from daguerreotypes. They were again reproduced in 1848 in the monumental volume *Journées Illustrées de la Revolution de 1848*, edited by *L'Illustration*. These two daguerreotypes also happen to predate Bayard's view of barricades near the Madeleine, a photograph that had been thought to be the only image of the 1848 Revolution. Though credited to Thibault, they are signed "Richebourg," for whom Thibault likely worked. Collection of Count Geoffroy de Beauffort.

62. Jules Janssen (France). The Transit of Venus (Note by M. Susan Barger).

Four times every 243 years, Venus appears to transit the solar disk much like the moon does during a solar eclipse. These rare astronomical events, each called the Transit of Venus, occur in pairs separated by eight years. The last Transits of Venus were in 1874 and 1882 and the next will be shortly after the turn of the twenty-first century, in 2004 and 2012. The perceived significance of these events was that it was thought that by timing the Transit of Venus across the solar disk from limb to limb, in several widely spaced observation sites, the exact distance between the sun and the earth could be calculated. Thus, scientific teams were sent out during each of the last four Transits to make these measurements. In every case the data gathered was insufficient to determine the distance because of limitations in the equipment available, weather problems, and other variables. The sun-earth distance has since been found by other means and the significance of the Transit of Venus has been diminished.

Because of the advent of photography, the nineteenth-century Transits of Venus were especially important. There was an international effort, headed by Warren de la Rue, the English Astronomer Royal, to coordinate the photographic activities of various investigation teams sent out by England, Germany, France, and the United States. Photography enabled the members of these teams to record the Transit of Venus as the event was occurring. The hope was that these photographs could later be used to determine the exact time Venus touched and let go of the edge (or limb) of the solar disk. Because it would be necessary to make exact measurements from these photographs in order to make the sun-earth distance calculations, there was a great deal of interest in assessing the dimensional stability of wet collodion films before and after processing and drying. Obviously, if an image made while the collodion was wet changed during drying, measurements made on that plate would not be meaningful.

In France, one of the members of the photographic advisory team was Hypolyte Fizeau, the director of L'Observatoire in Paris. Fizeau suggested that the daguerreotype process was suitable to make images of the solar disk, that it was a dry photographic process, and thus there would be no worry about dimensional alteration. Fizeau was uniquely qualified to make such a statement. In 1845 he and Léon Foucault had used the daguerreotype process to make the first photographs of the solar disk. Fizeau taught the members of the French Transit of Venus teams to make daguerreotypes and the process was, thus, revived for the 1874 Transit.

The facts mentioned above were reported in the French reports on the Transit of Venus, *Recueil de Mémoires, Rapports et Documents Relatifs à l'Observation de Passage de Vénus sur le Soleil* (Paris: L'Institut de France, 1876), and in various histories of astronomical photography. However, I had never seen or heard of any of these daguerreotypes having survived. In 1984 I went to Paris to look for various scientific daguerreotypes that had been mentioned in nineteenth-century reports and that I hoped were now squirreled away in the different archives and collections in Paris. In particular, I was hoping to find any evidence that daguerreotypes had really been taken during the Transit of Venus.

For the better part of a week I visited collections and was able to look at most of the daguerreotypes I had hoped to see. I asked many people if they knew anything about any Transit of Venus daguerreotypes, and everyone I asked said how wonderful it would be if there were such images, but no one had ever seen them. It was very discouraging. On my last day I decided to walk over to L'Observatoire to see if I could find anything. I presented myself at the gate, gave the gatekeepers a formal letter of introduction I had with me, and asked if it would be possible to visit the library. I was soon taken to the original observatory building and met by the librarian.

In my best French I explained that I was there looking for daguerreotypes of the Transit of Venus and that I thought these could have been made by any of several people I had on a list. The librarian said, "Non, non, non, c'est Janssen." She and I went back and forth several times about these names because Janssen was not on my list. Suddenly she said, "Venez avec moi!" and headed down a wide hallway into an open gallery. She pointed into one of the vitrines, saying, "Le voilà!" There was the Transit of Venus daguerreotype. It was as you see it in this illustration.

This daguerreotype was taken by Jules Janssen, using his *revolver photographique,* a rotating camera that he invented in 1873. This camera used a circular daguerreotype plate that was rotated past the lens at regular intervals. The image that you see is like separate frames of cinematic film. The fin-like shape in the image is a portion of the disk of the sun and the small dark circle is Venus as it makes contact with one of the limbs of the solar disk and begins its transit. The oval cutout and the notch in the inner edge of the daguerreotype plate were there to attach the plate to the mechanism that moved it past the lens of the telescope. Collection L'Observatoire de Paris.

63. J.V. (Europe), whole plate.

This architectural daguerreotype of great power is dated 14 Juin 1842. The French spelling of June leads one to assume it is a French image, and it could be, though it certainly does not seem to be from Paris. Further, the clock tower that appears to be strung with laundry has more of an Eastern European feel about it than a French feeling. Though it isn't Prague, it looks more like something from Prague than from Paris. It could, however, be Brno, where Jan Vrba made daguerreotypes in the early 1840s. If it is by Vrba, that would explain the initials "J.V.," which are not those of any known French daguerreotypist or photographer working as early as June 1842. Collection of Robert Koch.

64. Frederick De Bourg Richards (U.S.), half plate. Portrait of Lola Montez.

Though lacking the insouciance of her famous portrait with cigarette in hand by Southworth and Hawes, Richards has far better captured her beauty in this very painterly image. A variant of this pose, made at the same sitting and entitled "The Lace Shawl," is illustrated by Bogardus in his 1904 essay in *Century Magazine* entitled "The Lost Art of the Daguerreotype." Collection of Paul Katz.

65. Anon. (France), stereoscopic daguerreotype.

Painting, Ingres in particular, and not contemporary daguerreian imagery and practice was the inspiration in this image possibly by Moulin or d'Olivier, both of whom used mirrors in a similar fashion. Collection of John Wood.

66. Anon. (France), oversized stereoscopic daguerreotype.

This image is 3¾ × 6 inches as opposed to the previous image, which is 2¾ × 5 inches. It is a most atypical nude, austere and cool and looking far more like someone Lempicka or Romaine Brooks might have painted than Ingres, far more Art Deco than Second Empire, and far more erotic than the majority of daguerreian nudes. Collection of Robert Koch.

67. Charles and Henry Meade (U.S.), quarter plate.

A strong, well-made portrait. Collection of Joan Murray.

68. Anon. (England), quarter plate. Portrait of M. and Mme Georges Dufaud and family.

The quintessential Victorian image, this daguerreotype is housed in a leather case stamped "Howell James & Co Regent St." Messrs. Howell and James operated a fancy goods emporium in Regent Street, Weston-super-Mare, and evidently had a staff pho-

tographer. Arthur Gill wrote, "Judging by the clothes, I would say it was taken in the mid to late 1840s. If it was taken in the 1850s all the women are wearing very old-fashioned dress." The daguerreotypist was most likely Thomas Sims, who in 1847 had been licensed by Thomas Sharp to operate a studio in Weston-super-Mare. A note in the case reads: "Monsieur Georges Dufaud & wife, daughters & granddaughters. Great grandfather of Florence Esdaile wife of J. Kennedy Esdaile & daughter of George Crawshay." This suggests that they were not French tourists but actual residents. Collection of John Wood.

69. Anon. (U.S.), sixth plate.

This is certainly one of the strangest of daguerreotypes. It suggests Botero's paintings or Bernard Faucon's photographs. One cannot tell if the child is a painting or a doll. Everything is very delicately tinted; the chessmen are red and white; a daguerreotype case rests on the table. Though one does not ask what art *means*—and it is clearly a conscious attempt on the part of the daguerreotypist to make a work of art—one cannot keep from wondering what the artist was trying to do or say. Collection of Paul Missal.

70. Elliot (England), stereoscopic daguerreotype.

This lovely genre study would not seem at all unusual thirty or forty years later, but in daguerreotype it is very much a surprise. Collection of Mark Koenigsberg.

71. Anon. (England), ninth plate (enlarged).

This remarkable still life was probably made in Ledbury, for that single word is written on the reverse. It is an early piece, possibly as early as 1842; the central object of the composition, a Gothic revival jug by Charles Meigh, was registered that year. Collection of Robert Harshorn Shimshak.

72. Jean-Gabriel Eynard-Lullin (Switzerland), half plate.

A beautiful still life by the great Swiss amateur. Collection of the J. Paul Getty Museum.

73. Anon. (France or U.S.), quarter plate.

Though the passe-partout frame suggests a French origin, the trees above the lady in the gazebo appear to be filled with Spanish moss, which is not found in France. It may be a Southern, possibly even a New Orleans image. That would explain the moss and account for the frame. There has always been great intercourse between France and New Orleans, and a daguerreotypist like Jules Lion, who was born in France, often returned. A New Orleans provenance might also account for the folksy floral backing paper, which is original to the image and unlike anything I have ever seen on a French daguerreotype. Collection of Paul Katz.

74. Kenneth E. Nelson (U.S.), half plate. View on Parliament Hill and Ottawa River.

Not only is Ken Nelson one of the best American daguerreotypists, he is also a fine actor who portrayed the daguerreotypist in *Emily Dickinson* on the PBS television series *Voices and Visions*. Nelson has had a one-man show at Northlight Gallery, Arizona State University in Tempe, and has had work exhibited at the International Museum of Photography at George Eastman House. He is the author of a practical text on the making of daguerreotypes (see Bibliography). Collection of the artist.

75. Anon. (U.S.), sixth plate.

If a picture of a pig might be called beautiful, then this is it. Much of the beauty of the image, of course, comes from the wonderful verticals and horizontals of the fence and the framing of the pig. She stands in corncobs and her baby is blurred, just as the baby in countless daguerreotypes of mothers and children is. Collection of Charles Swedlund.

76. Anon. (U.S.), quarter plate.

American scenic daguerreotypes seldom have the lyricism of this pastoral scene. Collection of George S. Whiteley IV.

77. Louis-Auguste Bisson (France), quarter plate. Portrait of Jess.

Though the Bisson brothers are primarily remembered for their architectural and Alpine studies, they opened one of the first daguerreotype studios in Paris and produced superior work. This image from 1841 by the older of the two brothers is a particularly fine study of form and shadow. Collection of Robert Lebeck.

78. Platt Babbitt (U.S.), whole plate. Niagara in Winter.

This image obviously was created simply to be a work of art. The other great winter scenes of Niagara, possibly also by Babbitt or by Southworth and Hawes, are in a vertical format for use in the Grand Parlor Stereoscope. This image is unique in Babbitt's work. Though it could have been commissioned by someone, it seems to possess no commercial *raison d'être*. Collection of the J. Paul Getty Museum.

79. Anon. (U.S.), whole plate.

One wonders what it is that is being documented in this strong architectural daguerreotype. Is it the conversation of the two ladies in the doorway, the houses, the office of Dr. H. B. May, or the shop of J. Wood, the butcher, or possibly the builder whose sign can be partially read? Collection of Julian Wolff.

80. Anon. (U.S.), quarter plate.

This ordnance sergeant in the 7th New York Regiment of the National Guard is considerably more handsome and considerably more formal than the individuals one usually finds in military daguerreotypes. Collection of George S. Whiteley IV.

81. Anon. (U.S.), quarter plate.

A vigorous image of a musician playing his clarinet. Collection of Allen Phillips.

82. Anon. (England), three-quarter plate.

The designer and his chair in a beautifully balanced composition. Collection of Gail Gomberg Propp.

83. Anon. (Italy), sixth plate.

A strong image suggestive of the work of Antonio Sorgato. Collection of Paul Katz.

84. Samuel Root (U.S.), quarter plate. Portrait of Malvina Pray Florence.

Samuel Root and his brother Marcus were two of the most honored of American daguerreotypists. Here Root has captured in a striking profile the face of a nineteenth-century actress. The National Portrait Gallery owns a lithograph of Miss Florence after a daguerreotype by the Meade brothers. Collection of Paul Katz.

85. Anon. (U.S.), sixth plate.

This self-possessed black woman in typical Louisiana Creole headgear wears three rings, a gold watch and chain, gold earrings, and a commanding look. Collection of Paul Katz.

86. Albert Southworth and Josiah Hawes (U.S.), quarter plate. Portrait of Lajos Kossuth.

An unusual spotlight-style vignette gives this famous Hungarian patriot a look of importance reflected in his visionary stare. A letter in the Isenburg Collection from Hawes to his wife tells of how Kossuth simply appeared at the studio one day and wanted his daguerreotype made. Hawes exposed seven plates, though it did not seem Kossuth intended to pay for any of them, and Kossuth finally talked Hawes into giving him one. In an interview years later with Lincoln Bowles, Hawes also admitted that Kossuth had talked him into buying some Hungarian Fund bonds, which, of course, eventually proved to be worthless. Collection of Matthew R. Isenburg.

87. Anon. (U.S.), half plate.

A beautiful child in a stylish composition. Collection of Gail Gomberg Propp.

88. Anon. (U.S.), half plate.

Another portrait of great charm. Collection of Joan Murray.

89. Anon. (U.S.), half plate.

A vivid portrait of a cowboy. Collection of the J. Paul Getty Museum.

90. Jesse Whitehurst (U.S.), half plate.

A most important piece of photographic Americana. Here are some of our first get-rich-quick boys. Collection of Gail Gomberg Propp.

91. William and Frederick Langenheim (U.S.), half plate.

Few portraits by the Langenheims can surpass this one for its composition and relaxed feeling. Its rich gray tones, which, of course, cannot be seen in a black and white reproduction, add to the somber mood and seem to heighten the possibility that this might be a mourning picture of some sort. Its distinct European look is seldom seen in the American daguerreotype. Collection of Gilman Paper Company.

92. Anon. (U.S.), half plate.

These three women in mourning bring the Fates to mind. Collection of George S. Whiteley IV.

93. Anon. (U.S.), sixth plate.

This moving image of a family gazing on the portrait of the father, who obviously has died, is a powerful study in sorrow and restraint. The daughter's hand on her face and her other hand lightly touching the portrait is not only the physical center of the image but its emotional center as well. Collection of Julian Wolff.

94. Anon. (U.S.), quarter plate.

An amazing, unsettling postmortem. Collection of Robert Harshorn Shimshak.

95. Grant B. Romer (U.S.), half plate.

Grant Romer, one of the finest of American daguerreotypists, has here created a work of perfect technical and emotional balance. Not just objects but light, too, are set in balance. The darker half of the image is more illuminated than the lighter half, and the ominous imagery of skull, sphere, and column gives way to a kind of grinning black humor as the skull peeks out over the top hat and flourished ribbon. It is just the kind of ribbon one might find bearing some message or motto on a crest or shield; however, Romer has deliberately left it blank and has left the message to his viewers. Romer has written, "I learned what a daguerreotype was at the age of 13 in 1959. I saw an actual example for the first time in a Civil War museum in Gettysburg in 1961. I bought my first daguerreotype in 1970. I made my first daguerreotype in 1976. From that time I have owed my professional existence to the daguerreotype as a writer, lecturer, and conservator of the daguerreotype. I am currently the Conservator of Photography at the International Museum of Photography at George Eastman House. I

would say I have had every daguerreian thrill there is to have." Collection of the artist.

96. Vincent Chevalier (France), half plate. La Bernadière, 1839.

This is one of the two or three most important of extant daguerreotypes. It is the first still-surviving photograph of people, Daguerre's famous daguerreotype of a man getting his shoes shined having been destroyed through cleaning. It is also one of possibly only two, though perhaps four (depending on the attribution of two plates at the Canadian Centre for Architecture), of the surviving work by the great optician Vincent Chevalier (1770–1840), who with his son Charles (1804–1859) made both Niepce's and Daguerre's first lenses and cameras, including the 1826 camera that Niepce used to make the first photograph. Chevalier was responsible for the two inventors meeting each other and, therefore, indirectly responsible for the invention of the daguerreotype. It is signed "Vincent Chevalier Nr. 69, Quai de l'Horlage, Paris." Number 69, later changed to number 29, became the address of the well-known studio of Richebourg, Chevalier's student. The Chevaliers are often erroneously referred to as brothers, even in some of the standard histories of photography. For a complete genealogy and a history of the firm, one should consult the *Dictionnaire de Biographie Française* (vol. 8, p. 1053) or Josef Maria Eder's technical history of photography. Collection of Robert Lebeck.

97. Baron Louis-Adolphe Humbert de Molard (France), half plate. Self-Portrait.

The baron's insightful eye, which was responsible for some of the finest daguerreotypes and photographs made in nineteenth-century France, is turned inward upon himself, and the result is one of the most penetrating self-portraits of the nineteenth century. Here is the photographer, inventor, chemist, magician even; here is the look of a man who does many things well and who knows it. Collection of Gilman Paper Company.

98. William and Frederick Langenheim (U.S.), half plate. Frederick Langenheim Looking at Talbotypes of Himself.

This may well be the greatest of the Langenheims' daguerreotypes and is without doubt the most interesting, being a self-portrait within a self-portrait. Here Frederick Langenheim studies portraits of himself, his brother, and others. The portrait, made about 1849, is also a study in irony because the Langenheims' faith in Talbot and the talbotype led them to bankruptcy and the collapse of their firm. A talbotype version of the same image exists in the New York Public Library. Collection of Gilman Paper Company.

99. Albert Southworth and Josiah Hawes (U.S.), half plate. Self-Portrait of Southworth.

A moving portrait of Southworth grown older, plumper, and more tired. Courtesy of Museum of Fine Arts, Boston.

100. Josiah Hawes (U.S.), quarter plate. Self-Portrait.

Almost fifty years after the passing of the daguerreotype's popularity, Hawes personified his love of that first process in this haunting self-portrait. Alone in a studio that at one time had been an artistic center, the old man pulls the string to capture his final adieu on silver. Collection of Matthew R. Isenburg.

Contributors

Ken Appollo, a self-styled itinerant historian, holds a degree in history from Wesleyan University and supports a variety of research projects (ranging from his ongoing work on Southworth and Hawes to a book on organ grinders and street musicians) by dealing in rare nineteenth-century photographs and historical documents. Appollo lives in Portland, Oregon.

M. Susan Barger is research professor in the Department of Materials Science and Engineering at Johns Hopkins University. She directs the Surface Analytical Laboratory and is involved in a joint program with the Smithsonian's Conservation Analytical Laboratory for the training of conservation scientists. She was the first Mellon Fellow in Preservation Science in the Preservation Research and Testing Laboratory of the Library of Congress, is the author or coauthor of over a dozen journal articles on the daguerreotype, and the coauthor of *Robert Cornelius: Portraits from the Dawn of Photography* and *The Daguerreotype: Nineteenth Century Technology and Modern Science.* She holds a doctorate from Penn State.

Janet E. Buerger, associate curator of photographic collections, International Museum of Photography at George Eastman House, and lecturer in extension, Harvard University, holds a doctorate in art history and archaeology from Columbia. She has been the recipient of a number of grants and fellowships including four Smithsonian Institution grants for research, three Metropolitan Museum of Arts grants, a postdoctoral fellowship at Harvard, and a National Museum of American Art/Smithsonian Institution Visiting Fellowship. She is the author of *French Daguerreotypes, The Last Decade: The Emergence of Art Photography in the 1890s,* and *The Era of the French Calotype,* as well as articles on subjects as diverse as Degas and medieval pottery.

Roy Flukinger is curator of the photographic collections of the Harry Ransom Humanities Research Center at the University of Texas in Austin. He is the author of *The Formative Decades: Photography in Great Britain, 1839–1920,* coauthor of *Paul Martin: Victorian Photographer,* coeditor of the two-volume *Texas: A Photographic Portrait,* and author of many articles on photographic history. He has been curator for over a dozen major exhibitions.

Matthew R. Isenburg is one of America's foremost daguerreian scholars. A successful businessman, he has taken off from his professional activities for as long as three years at a time in order to devote himself to photographic research in this country and in Europe. Isenburg is the coauthor of *Photographica* and has assembled the country's largest privately owned library of original documents, manuscripts, correspondence, and primary research materials related to nineteenth-century photography.

Ben Maddow is the author of poems, plays, a novel, and some of the most acclaimed screenplays of our time. He wrote *A Sunday Between Wars,* a social history of the United States between 1865 and 1917, and the standard books on Edward Weston, Max Yavno, and W. Eugene Smith. His biography of Smith, *Let Truth Be the Prejudice,* won the International Center for Photography's first prize and was designated "Book of the Year." His book *Faces: A Narrative History of the Photographic Portrait* is considered by many to be the finest photographic criticism that has been written.

Grant B. Romer is conservator of the Photographic Collections of the International Museum of Photography at George Eastman House. He is well known as a writer on the daguerreotype and is a coauthor of *The Erotic Daguerreotype.* He has presented major papers at the Victoria and Albert Museum, the Tokyo Polytechnic Institute, the American Academy in Rome, Conseijo Mexicana, the Metropolitan Museum of Art, the Museum of Fine Arts (Caracas), the National Photographic School in France, and the National Museum of Photography in England. He has held both a Fulbright Commission Grant in Art and Art History and a Japan Foundation Grant. He is also one of America's finest daguerreotypists.

Alan Trachtenberg is one of the nation's leading photographic historians and literary critics. He holds a doctorate in American studies and is professor of American studies and English at Yale. He is the author of *Brooklyn Bridge: Fact and Symbol,* the editor of several critical anthologies, and author of works on Lewis Hine, Hart Crane, and others.

John Wood, director of the Master of Fine Arts Program in Creative Writing at McNeese State University, holds a doctorate in English literature as well as degrees in philosophy and creative writing. His poems have appeared in *Poetry, Antaeus,* the *Southern Review,* and elsewhere, and a portfolio of them with accompanying woodcuts by Harold Swayder and an introduction by Allen Ginsberg was published in a limited edition by Apollyon Press. He has had several grants for photohistorical studies and has published essays on Restoration drama, eighteenth-century fiction, and modern poetry.

Selected Bibliography

The most important task the serious student of any art form faces is to see as much of the art as possible and to be thoroughly familiar with the critical and historical literature of the field. This bibliography, therefore, includes the standard scholarship but also works of limited scholarly importance, though of great visual importance—and perhaps only for the inclusion of a single image. I have tried to prepare the kind of bibliography I wished someone might have given me when I first became interested in the daguerreotype. Though some of these books are out of print, all are available through interlibrary loan.

I have included a few important auction catalogues that are not difficult to obtain from the original galleries or from photographic book dealers. I have excluded histories that repeat the same old images and facts, and I have also excluded journal articles, simply because they are usually more difficult to obtain, even though they are the source of some of the best scholarship on the daguerreotype. A formal, scholarly bibliography would cite both, but this does not purport to be a scholarly bibliography—merely an aid to those wishing to learn about the daguerreotype and to see, though secondhand, as many as possible. I have indicated with an asterisk the twenty most basic books such an individual might wish to be familiar with.

* Adam, Hans Christian, Grant B. Romer, and Uwe Scheid. *The Erotic Daguerreotype.* Forthcoming. A photographic survey of over five hundred images and a major essay.

After Daguerre: Masterworks of French Photography from the Bibliothèque Nationale. New York: Metropolitan Museum of Art in association with Berger-Levrault, 1980. Reproduces some daguerreotypes but more valuable for its information on various daguerreotypists who went on to work on paper.

Auer, Michel. *The Illustrated History of the Camera.* Boston: New York Graphic Society, 1975. Reproduces a few daguerreotypes, including a pre-1839 image by Daguerre.

* Barger, M. Susan, and William B. White. *The Daguerreotype: Nineteenth Century Technology and Modern Science,* Washington, D.C.: Smithsonian Academic Press, 1989. The history of the scientific investigation and use of the daguerreotype from 1839 to the present.

Becchetti, Piero. *Fotografi e fotografia in Italia, 1839–1880.* Rome: Edizioni Quasar, 1978. An important work but with few interesting daguerreotypes.

* ———— and Carlo Pietrangeli. *Roma in Dagherrotipia.* Rome: Edizioni Quasar, 1979. A major study with many important illustrations.

* Bernard, Bruce. *Photodiscovery: Masterworks of Photography, 1840–1940.* New York: Abrams, 1980. Visually the best anthology of photographs of all time. Reproduces seventeen major daguerreotypes in color, a few of which are reproduced elsewhere but not as finely as here. Insightful notes on the images.

Bibliothèque Nationale. *Daguerre et les premiers daguerreotypes français.* Paris, 1961. Contains a short introduction by Jean Adhemar and Beaumont Newhall. No illustrations, but valuable information and descriptions of images in the show from public and private collections.

Bovis, Marcel, and François Saint-Julien. *Nus d'Autrefois, 1850–1900.* Paris: Arts et Métiers

Graphiques, 1953. Reproduces nineteen daguerreotypes, though with some censoring at times.

Buckland, Gail. *First Photographs: People, Places, and Phenomena Captured for the First Time by the Camera*. New York: Macmillan, 1980. Reproduces many fine daguerreotypes, some in color, the majority not seen elsewhere.

* Buerger, Janet. *French Daguerreotypes*. Chicago: University of Chicago Press, 1988. The standard study of the work of the Parisian daguerreotypists.

Burns, Stanley. *Masterpieces of Medical Photography*. Pasadena: Twelvetrees, 1987. Not a very happy book to look at, but with excellent commentary on the images and three interesting daguerreotypes.

Christ, Yvan. *L'Age d'Or de la photographie*. Paris: Vincent, Freal, 1965. A beautiful little book with several wonderful daguerreotypes, including one of a man with his mouth open wide.

Christie's East. *Nineteenth and Twentieth Century Photographs*. Sale No. 228 (November 10 and 11, 1981). Includes a half plate of New York City (lot 33), several Southworth and Hawes images (lots 34–37), a most interesting Hesler (lot 41), and a Babbitt (lot 42).

———. *Nineteenth and Twentieth Century Photographs*. Sale No. 281 (May 26, 1982). Includes a pornographic daguerreotype and a daguerreotype of a man sleeping (lots 28 and 29).

———. *Nineteenth and Twentieth Century Photographs*. Sale No. 5215 (November 8, 1982). Includes an image of two Canadian Indians in mock fight (lot 79).

* Constantini, Paolo, and Italio Zannier. *I Dagherrotipi della Collezione Ruskin*. Florence and Venice: Alinari and Arsenale, 1986. Reproduces over one hundred daguerreotypes of Italy and Switzerland from John Ruskin's famous collection.

Daguerre, L. J. M. *An Historical and Descriptive Account of the Daguerreotype and the Diorama*. Introduction by Beaumont Newhall. New York: Winter House, 1971. Text in French and English with reproductions of thirty-four daguerreotypes, some found nowhere else.

* von Dewitz, Bodo, and Fritz Kempe. *Daguerreotypien*. Hamburg: Museum für Kunst und Gewerbe, 1983. A well-illustrated catalogue of one of the great public collections.

* Dröscher, Elke. *Kindheit im Silberspiegel*. Dortmund: Harenberg, 1983. Eighty fine color reproductions of daguerreotypes of children. A beautiful and inexpensive book.

Eder, Josef Maria. *History of Photography*. Translated by Edward Epstean. New York: Dover, 1978. The great technical history of photography with several chapters on the daguerreotype, first published in 1905.

Finkel, Kenneth. *Nineteenth-Century Photography in Philadelphia*. New York: Dover, 1980. Includes quite a few fine daguerreotypes.

Flukinger, Roy. *The Formative Decades: Photography in Great Britain, 1839–1920*. Austin: University of Texas Press, 1985. Reproduces and discusses three daguerreotypes.

Ford, Colin. *Portraits*. London: Thames and Hudson, 1983. Includes a reproduction of Southworth and Hawes's "Boston Beauty" in color as well as several other fine daguerreotypes.

Freyermuth, Gundolf, and Rainer Fabian. *Der Erotische Augenblick*. Hamburg: Stern, 1984. Reproduces fifteen daguerreotypes in color and includes several in large format.

Gautrand, Jean-Claude. *Paris des Photographie*. Paris: Contrejour, 1985. A beautiful but expensive book with some fine daguerreotypes reproduced.

———. *Le temps des pionniers*. Paris: Photo Poche, 1987. This collection of the Société Française de Photographie includes three daguerreotypes and the best reproduction of Foucault's famous grapes.

* Gernsheim, Helmut and Alison. *L. J. M. Daguerre: The History of the Diorama and the Daguerreotype*. New York: Dover, 1968. The standard work on Daguerre, with quite a few good reproductions.

* Gernsheim, Helmut. *The Origins of Photography*. London: Thames and Hudson, 1982. The revised third edition of Helmut and Alison Gernsheim's *History of Photography* with an added chapter on the Italian daguerreotype by Daniela Palazzoli. A major work on the daguerreotype and the calotype, including many reproductions.

Gilbert, George. *Photography: The Early Years*. New York: Harper & Row, 1980. Includes a chapter on the daguerreotype with some good reproductions.

Goldsmith, Arthur. *The Camera and Its Images*. New York: Ridge Press, Newsweek, 1979. Includes excellent reproductions and in some cases the very best of some well-known daguerreotypes such as Carl

Biewend's wife and children, Baron Jean Gros' "Pont d'Alexandre," and four from the Galerie Historique originally in Werner Bokelberg's collection.

Greenhill, Ralph, and Andrew Birrell. *Canadian Photography, 1839–1920.* Toronto: Coach House Press, 1979. The standard work on early Canadian photography, with fine text and eight daguerreotypes.

Hales, Peter. *Silver Cities: The Photography of American Urbanization, 1839–1915.* Philadelphia: Temple University Press, 1984. Reproduces many fine daguerreotypes, including two in panorama format.

Heilbrun, Françoise, and Philippe Néagu. *Musée d'Orsay: Chefs-d'oeuvre de la collection photographique.* Paris: Philippe Sers, 1986. A stunning book with twenty-two daguerreotypes, including previously unpublished works of Gros, Itier, Molard, Millet, Feuardent, etc.

Heyert, Elizabeth. *The Glass-House Years: Victorian Portrait Photography, 1839–1870.* Montclair and London: Allanheld & Schram/George Prior, 1979. A good text with quite a few reproductions.

Horan, James D. *Mathew Brady: Historian with a Camera.* New York: Crown, 1955. Reproduces quite a few Brady daguerreotypes.

* Hough, Robert. *Forty Daguerreotypes from the Bokelberg Collection.* Edinburgh: Scottish Arts Council, 1980. An amazing collection of daguerreotypes.

Howarth-Loomes, B. E. C. *Victorian Photography.* New York: St. Martin's Press, 1974. Includes a chapter on the daguerreotype and reproduces many images found nowhere else.

Jammes, Andre, and Eugenia Parry Janis. *The Art of French Calotype.* Princeton: Princeton University Press, 1983. Reproduces Baron Gros' daguerreotype of his salon with several other daguerreotypes on view.

Jensen, Oliver, Joan Paterson Kerr, and Murray Belsky. *American Album.* New York: American Heritage and Ballantine Books, 1970. Includes several interesting and curious daguerreotypes: an armed gold miner, a Gurney-Fredericks half plate of a man with a carnation in his mouth, and others.

Johnson, Robert, and Robert Shimshak. *The Power of Light: Daguerreotypes from the Robert Harshorn Shimshak Collection.* San Francisco: Fine Arts Museum, 1986. Reproduces twenty-four daguerreotypes, including a wonderful Plumbe of a church.

Johnson, William S. *An Annotated Bibliography of the History of Photography.* Vol. 1, *Prehistory to 1879.* Boston: G. K. Hall & Co., 1988. A major source book for the scholar.

* Kempe, Fritz. *Daguerreotypie in Deutschland.* Seebruck: Heering Verlag, 1979. The standard book on the German daguerreotype, a major study with many wonderful reproductions, including the Pero views of Lübeck.

Köhler, Michael, and Gisela Barche. *Das Aktfoto.* Munich: Bucher, 1986. A study of the nude with an essay on the daguerreotype by Hans Christian Adam. Reproduces eight daguerreotypes, including one modern example by Shinkichi Tajiri.

Koltun, Lilly, ed. *Private Realms of Light: Amateur Photography in Canada, 1839–1940.* Ontario: Fitzhenry-Whiteside, Markham, 1984. A beautiful book but with little to say about the daguerreotype.

Lecuyer, Raymond. *Histoire de la photographie.* Paris: Baschet, 1945. A sumptuous photohistory book, with several fine reproductions of daguerreotypes.

Lemagny, Jean-Claude, and André Rouillé, eds. *A History of Photography.* Translated by Janet Lloyd. Cambridge: Cambridge University Press, 1987. Includes a short but interesting discussion of the daguerreotype by Bernard Marbot, curator of early photography at the Bibliothèque Nationale, and several daguerreotypes finely reproduced.

Lewinski, Jorge. *The Naked and the Nude: A History of the Nude in Photographs, 1839 to the Present.* New York: Harmony Books, 1987. Not a book for the beginning student of photohistory. It is riddled with errors; however, there are four very good color reproductions of daguerreotypes.

Macdonald, Guy. *Camera: Victorian Eyewitness.* New York: Viking, 1979. Text of English television series on photohistory with several interesting daguerreotypes.

McElroy, Keith. *Early Peruvian Photography.* Ann Arbor: UMI Research Press, 1985. Includes a chapter on the daguerreotype and several reproductions of daguerreotypes by B. F. Pease and others.

* Maddow, Ben. *Faces: A Narrative History of the Portrait in Photography.* Boston: New York Graphic Society, 1977. The most intelligent statement that has yet been made on the subject of photography.

Maddow's discussion of the daguerreotype is outstanding.

Masterworks of Photography from the Rubel Collection. Sacramento: Crocker Art Museum, 1982. Exhibition catalogue reproducing daguerreotypes seen elsewhere except for a sixth plate of a nude at a mirror.

Meredith, Roy. *Mr. Lincoln's Camera Man: Mathew B. Brady.* New York: Dover, 1974. Reproduces some Brady daguerreotypes.

Moore, Charles LeRoy. *Two Partners in Boston: The Careers and Daguerreian Artistry of Albert Southworth and Josiah Hawes.* Ann Arbor: University Microfilms, 1975. A fine, though not definitive, study of Southworth and Hawes; includes many reproductions, but in Xerox.

Morand, Sylvain. *La Mémoire Oubliée: Du Daguerreotype au Collodion.* Strasbourg: Musées de Strasbourg, 1981. Reproduces some of the daguerreotypes in the museum's collection.

Munchner Stadtmuseum. *Die Sammlung Josef Breitenbach.* Munich: State Museum, 1979. Reproductions of twelve daguerreotypes, including a southern harbor scene.

Nazarieff, Serge. *Le Nu Stéréoscopique.* Paris: Filipacchi, 1985. Reproduces over seventy stereoscopic daguerreotypes and comes with glasses for viewing.

Nelson, Kenneth E. *A Practical Introduction to the Art of Daguerreotypy in the 20th Century.* Tempe: Arizona State University Press, 1977.

* Newhall, Beaumont. *The Daguerreotype in America.* New York: Dover, 1976. One of the standards in the field and with over one hundred illustrations.

———. *The History of Photography.* New York: Museum of Modern Art. This was first published in 1949, and there have been five editions, so one should peruse the various editions because some of the images change. Recent editions unfortunately exclude Clausel's "Landscape near Troyes," one of the great daguerreotypes of the nineteenth century.

Pare, Richard. *Photography and Architecture, 1839–1939.* New York: Callaway Editions and the Canadian Centre for Architecture, 1982. One of the major photographic books, but with few daguerreotypes.

Parke-Bernet Galleries. *Rare Photographic Images, Apparatus & Literature: The Collection of Sidney Strober.* Sale No. 68 (February 7, 1970). An important catalogue of a famous sale with some fine daguerreotypes reproduced and a foreword by Josephine Cobb.

* Pfister, Harold Francis. *Facing the Light: Historic American Portrait Daguerreotypes.* Washington, D.C.: Smithsonian Institution Press, 1978. One of the classics and a necessity in any library of daguerreian literature.

Pierce, Sally. *Whipple and Black: Commercial Photographers in Boston.* Boston: Boston Athenaeum, 1987. A good study of their work including several excellent daguerreotypes.

Pobboravsky, Irving. *Study of Iodized Daguerreotype Plates.* Rochester: RIT Graphic Arts Research Center, 1971. A major scientific study of the daguerreotype plate.

Pollack, Peter. *The Picture History of Photography.* New York: Abrams, 1958. Includes many important reproductions and much information. Avoid the abridged version.

Pontonniée, Georges. *The History of the Discovery of Photography.* Translated by Edward Epstean. New York: Arno Press, 1973. A reprint without illustrations of the 1925 Paris, Montel, edition; includes much information available nowhere else.

Reinke, Jutta, and Wolfgang Stemmer. *Pioniere der Kamera: Das Erste Jahrhundert der Fotografie, 1840–1900. Die Sammlung Robert Lebeck.* Bremen: Fotoforum Bremen, 1987. Includes over eighty daguerreotypes from Lebeck's famous collection, many in color. There is also a magnificent Southworth and Hawes whole plate of General Wool as well as several views of Rome, a whole plate of the harbor at Sete by François Adolphe Certes, etc.

Riba-Mobley Auctions (South Glastonbury, Connecticut). *Historical Ephemera Auction* (May 31, 1986). An important sale of Southworth and Hawes images and daguerreotypes from the Josephine Cobb Collection.

Rinhart, Floyd and Marion. *American Daguerreian Art.* New York: Clarkson Potter, 1967. Includes some daguerreotypes not in *The American Daguerreotype.*

* ——— and ———. *The American Daguerreotype.*

Athens: University of Georgia Press, 1981. One of the standards in the field and with an extremely helpful appendix listing many of the known American daguerreotypists.

Robinson, William. *A Certain Slant of Light: The First Hundred Years of New England Photography.* Boston: New York Graphic Society, 1980. Includes an 1840 Gouraud still life and several other daguerreotypes, most reproduced elsewhere.

* Rudisill, Richard. *Mirror Image: The Influence of the Daguerreotype on American Society.* Albuquerque: University of New Mexico Press, 1971. Another of the standards that should be in all libraries. Many reproductions and an invaluable annotated bibliography.

Sandweiss, Martha A. *Masterpieces of American Photography: The Amon Carter Museum Collection.* Birmingham: Oxmoor House, 1982. A beautiful book with only seven daguerreotypes but some interesting pieces.

Scheid, Uwe. *Das erotische Imago.* Dortmund: Harenberg, 1984. Includes handsome color reproductions of eleven daguerreotypes.

Sobieszek, Robert, ed. *The Daguerreotype in Germany.* New York: Arno Press, 1979. A reprint of two early and important works: Wilhelm Dost's *Die Daguerreotypie in Berlin, 1839–1860* and Wilhelm Weimar's *Die Daguerreotypie in Hamburg, 1839–1860,* as well as Cephir's short *Daguerreotype War in Hamburg;* some illustrations of important daguerreotypes but most appear in Kempe as well as much of the information.

* Sobieszek, Robert, and Odette Appell with the research of Charles Moore. *The Daguerreotypes of Southworth and Hawes.* New York: Dover, 1980. A revised reprint of *The Spirit of Fact* (Boston: David R. Godine, 1976). The illustrations are wonderful, but Moore's own book is probably a better source of information.

Sobieszek, Robert. *Masterpieces of Photography from the George Eastman House Collection.* New York: Abbeville, 1985. Fine text and illustrations, including Clausel's great "Landscape" in its best reproduction and other fine daguerreotypes.

Sotheby's. *Photography.* Sale No. 5318 (May 7 and 8, 1985). Includes an excellent daguerreotype of an Indian (lot 15), an Austrian daguerreotype (lot 627), and a fine Lorenzo Chase half plate (lot 628).

Sotheby's (London). *Photographic Images.* (November 1, 1985). Includes a major work by Itier (lot 17) and a good selection of stereo daguerreotypes (lots 5–12) of various subjects.

———. *Photographic Images.* (November 6, 1987). Includes three still lifes (lots 17–19) and an 1841 whole plate by Calvert Jones, one of the great calotypists, of Margam, home of Christopher Talbot, Fox Talbot's cousin (lot 63).

* Stapp, William, Marion S. Carson, and M. Susan Barger. *Robert Cornelius: Portraits from the Dawn of Photography.* Washington: Smithsonian Institution Press, 1983. An important historical and scientific study of the work of Cornelius and containing excellent reproductions of his work.

Stenger, Erich. *Die Photographie in Munchen, 1839–1860.* Berlin, 1939. Another important German study but eclipsed by Kempe.

Sullivan, Constance. *Nude Photographs, 1850–1980.* New York: Harper & Row, 1980. Includes eleven daguerreotypes and the best reproductions of some of them, also a perceptive essay by Ben Maddow.

* Taft, Robert. *Photography and the American Scene.* New York: Dover, 1964. A reprint of the classic 1938 work, a major study.

Weiermair, Peter. *Das Verborgene Bild.* Vienna: Ariadne, 1987. A history of the male nude in photography with reproduction of three daguerreotypes, one appearing for the first time.

Welling, William. *Collectors' Guide to Nineteenth-Century Photographs.* New York: Macmillan, 1976. Includes a daguerreotype of an elephant and some other interesting examples.

Wills, Canfield and Deirdre. *History of Photography.* London: Hamlyn, 1980. Reproduces several daguerreotypes seen no place else, and some of the fakes featured in the case of the Queen vs. Shaw at Manchester Crown Court in June 1979.

Willsberger, Johann. *The History of Photography.* Translated by Helga Halaki. Garden City: Doubleday & Co., 1977. Reproduces two of the greatest gems from the Rudolph Skopec Collection, a nude and a pre-1839 daguerreotype presented by Daguerre to Prince Metternich.

1.
Albert
Southworth
and Josiah
Hawes (U.S.),
whole plate.

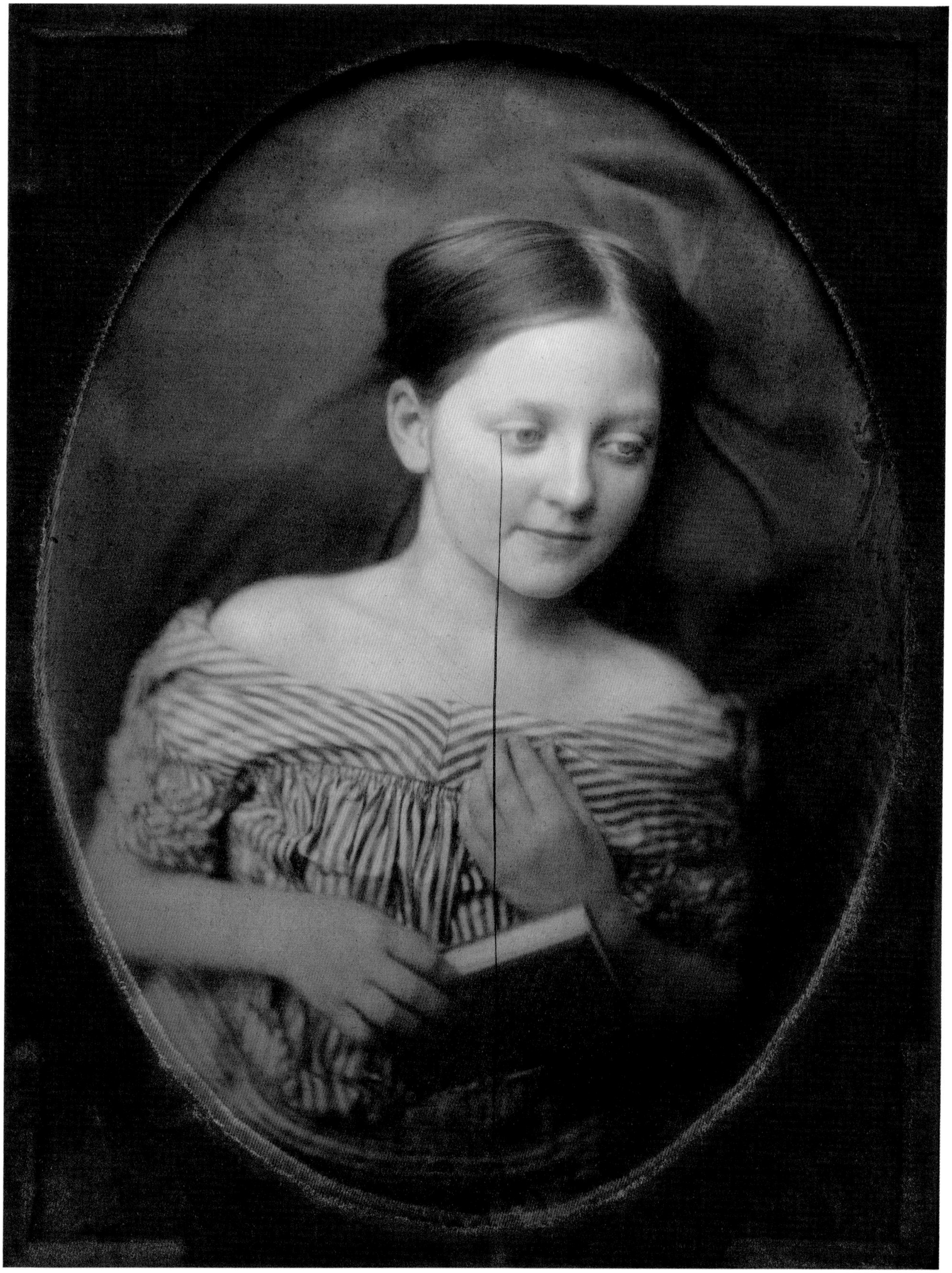

2.
Albert Southworth and Josiah Hawes (U.S.), whole plate.

3.
*Albert
Southworth
and Josiah
Hawes (U.S.),
whole plate.*

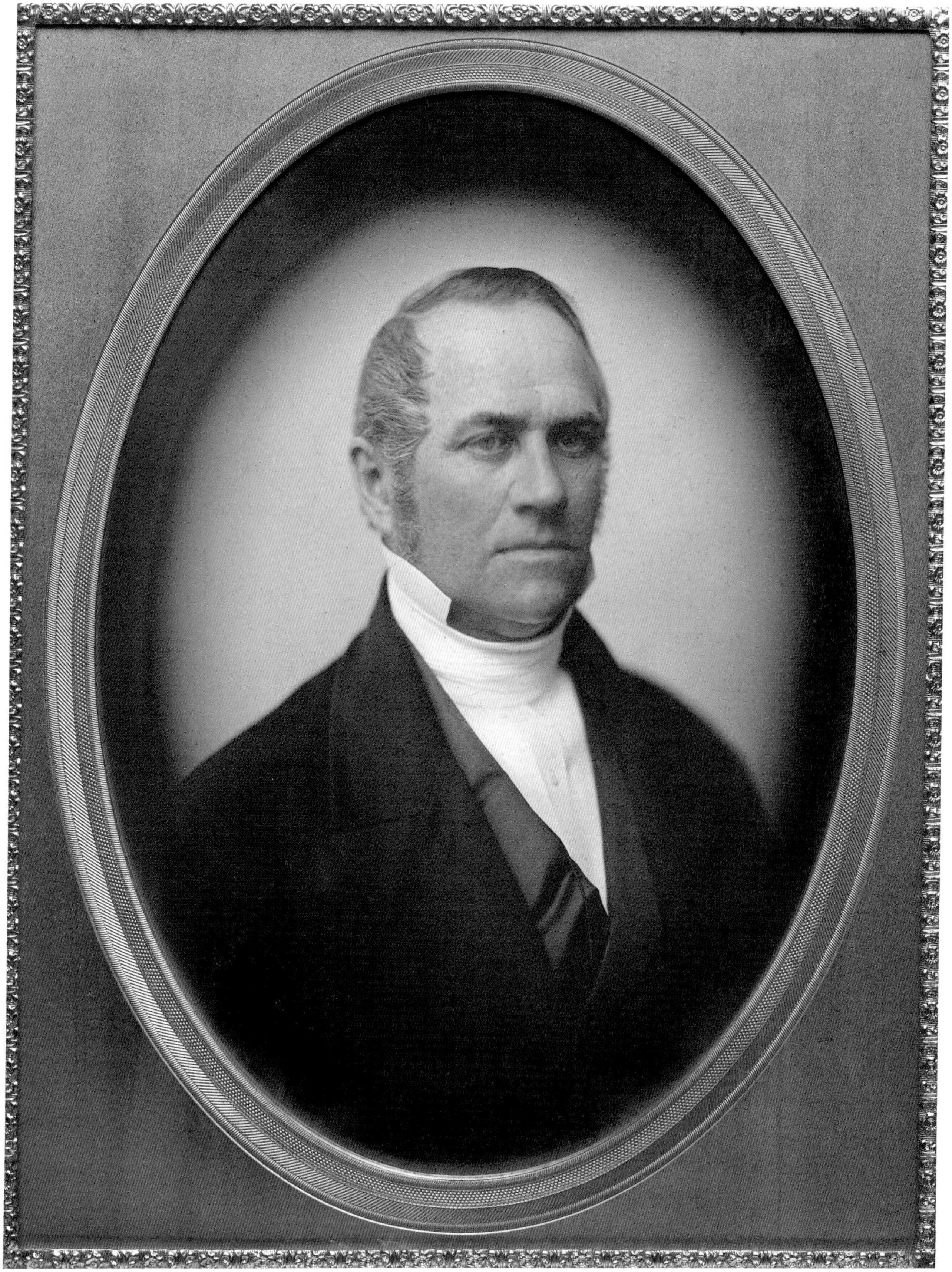

4.
Albert Southworth and Josiah Hawes (U.S.), whole plate.

5.
*Albert
Southworth
and Josiah
Hawes (U.S.),
whole plate.*

6.
*Irving
Pobboravsky
(U.S.), quarter
plate. Young
Beech
Branches.*

7.
*Hermann
Carl Eduard
Biewend
(Germany),
half plate.
Harz
Landscape
near
Königshütte.*

8.
Baron Louis-
Adolphe
Humbert
de Molard
(France), half
plate. View of
Lagny on the
Marne.

9.
Anon. (U.S.),
quarter plate.

10.
Anon. (U.S.),
half plate.
Preston's
Livery Stable,
Yuba,
California.

11.
*Platt Babbitt
(U.S.), whole
plate. Niagara
Falls.*

14.
*John H.
Fitzgibbon
(U.S.), three-
quarter plate.
Portrait of
Kno-Shr,
Kansas Chief.*

15.
Patrick Bailly-
Maitre-Grand
(France),
11¹³⁄₁₆ inches ×
5 feet, 3
inches. La
Locomotive.

16.
Irving
Pobboravsky
(U.S.),
quarter plate.
17 Church St.,
Scottsville.

17.
*Patrick Bailly-
Maitre-Grand
(France), half
plate.*

18.
Anon.
(France),
three-quarter
plate.
Vaucenans.

20.
Anon.
(France),
stereoscopic
daguerreotype.

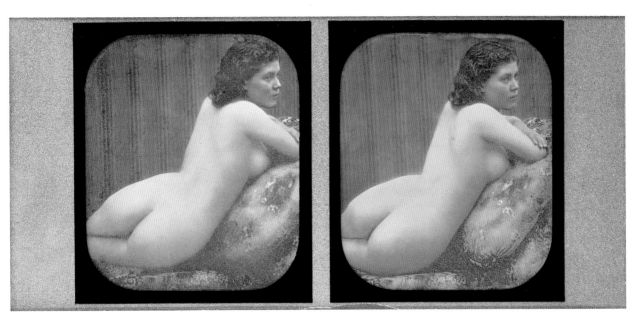

21.
Anon.
(France),
stereoscopic
daguerreotype.

22.
*Irving
Pobboravsky
(U.S.), quarter
plate. Young
Tree.*

23.
*Anon.
(Australia),
quarter plate.*

24.
Anon. (U.S.),
quarter plate.

25.
Charles
Williamson
(U.S.), sixth
plate.

26.
Anon. (U.S.),
sixth plate.
Portrait of
Uncle George
and Gus.

27.
Anon. (U.S.),
sixth plate.

28.
Antoine
Claudet
(England),
stereoscopic
daguerreotype.

29.
*Jeremiah
Gurney (U.S.),
sixth plate.*

30.
*Larcher
(France),
stereoscopic
daguerreotype.*

32.
Anon.
(France), half
plate. Portrait
of Curé Paulin
of Tremblay.

33.
Anon. (U.S.),
sixth plate.

34.
Albert
Southworth
and Josiah
Hawes (U.S.),
quarter plate.

35.
Albert
Southworth
and Josiah
Hawes (U.S.),
whole plate.

36.
Albert
Southworth
and Josiah
Hawes (U.S.),
whole plate.

37.
*Albert
Southworth
and Josiah
Hawes (U.S.),
whole plate.*

39.
Anon. (U.S.),
sixth plate.

40.
Anon. (U.S.),
quarter plate.

41.
Anon. (U.S.),
sixth plate.

42.
Albert
Southworth
and Josiah
Hawes (U.S.),
quarter plate.

43.
Anon. (U.S.),
sixth plate.

44.
Anon. (U.S.),
quarter plate.

45.
Anon. (U.S.),
sixth plate.

46.
Frederick
Coombs
(U.S.), quarter
plate.

47.
*Albert
Southworth
and Josiah
Hawes (U.S.),
whole plate.
Portrait of
Erastus
Hopkins.*

49.
*Anon. (U.S.),
sixth plate.
Telegraph
Lineman.*

50.
*Anon. (U.S.),
quarter plate
(enlarged).*

51.
Anon. (U.S.),
sixth plate.

52.
Anon. (U.S.),
half plate.

53.
*Anon. (U.S.),
sixth plate.*

54.
*Anon. (U.S.),
quarter plate.*

55.
Anon. (U.S.),
sixth plate.

56.
Anon. (U.S.),
half plate.
Portrait of
Dan Rice.

57.
*John Plumbe
(U.S.), half
plate. The
United States
Capitol.*

58.
*Anon.
(France), half
plate.*

59.
Anon.
(France),
whole plate.
Breton Village.

60.
*Thibault
(France),
three-quarter
plate. The
Revolution of
1848: Before
the Attack.*

61.
*Thibault
(France),
three-quarter
plate. The
Revolution of
1848: After
the Attack.*

62.
*Jules Janssen
(France). The
Transit of
Venus.*

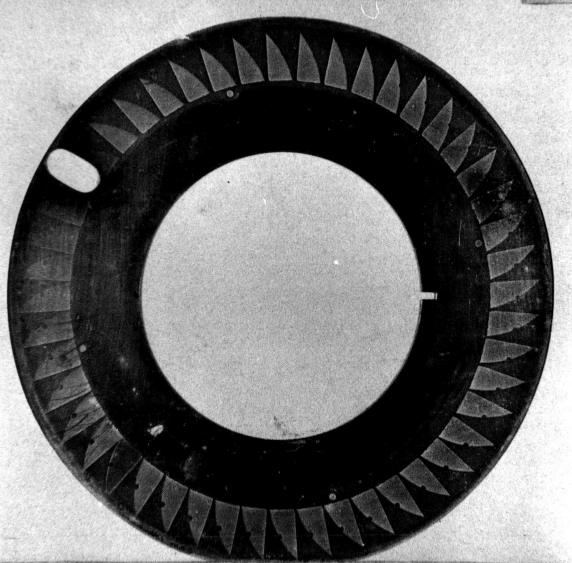

1874. Passage artificiel de Vénus sur le Soleil. Le Révolver photographique est devenu le point de départ d'instruments qui ont servi aux recherches de mécanique animale et en général à l'étude des phases de tout phénomène variant rapidement.

64.
*Frederick
De Bourg
Richards
(U.S.), half
plate. Portrait
of Lola
Montez.*

65.
Anon.
(France),
stereoscopic
daguerreotype.

66.
Anon.
(France),
oversized
stereoscopic
daguerreotype.

67.
Charles and
Henry Meade
(U.S.), quarter
plate.

68.
Anon.
(England),
quarter plate.
Portrait of
M. and Mme
Georges
Dufaud and
family.

69.
Anon. (U.S.),
sixth plate.

70.
Elliot
(England),
stereoscopic
daguerreotype.

71.
Anon.
(England),
ninth plate
(enlarged).

72.
Jean-Gabriel
Eynard-Lullin
(Switzerland),
half plate.

73.
Anon. (France
or U.S.),
quarter plate.

74.
Kenneth E.
Nelson (U.S.),
half plate.
View on
Parliament Hill
and Ottawa
River.

75.
Anon. (U.S.),
sixth plate.

76.
Anon. (U.S.),
quarter plate.

77.
*Louis-Auguste
Bisson
(France),
quarter plate.
Portrait
of Jess.*

78.
*Platt Babbitt
(U.S.), whole
plate. Niagara
in Winter.*

80.
Anon. (U.S.),
quarter plate.

81.
Anon. (U.S.),
quarter plate.

82.
Anon.
(England),
three-quarter
plate.

83.
Anon. (Italy),
sixth plate.

84.
Samuel Root
(U.S.), quarter
plate. Portrait
of Malvina
Pray Florence.

85.
Anon. (U.S.),
sixth plate.

86.
Albert
Southworth
and Josiah
Hawes (U.S.),
quarter plate.
Portrait of
Lajos Kossuth.

90.
*Jesse
Whitehurst
(U.S.), half
plate.*

91.
William and Frederick Langenheim (U.S.), half plate.

92.
Anon. (U.S.),
half plate.

93.
Anon. (U.S.)
sixth plate.

94.
Anon. (U.S.),
quarter plate.

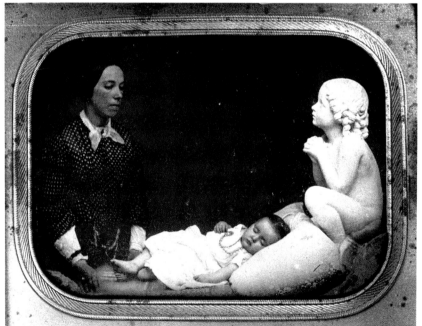

95.
Grant B.
Romer (U.S.),
half plate.

96.
Vincent
Chevalier
(France), half
plate. La
Bernadière,
1839.

97.
Baron
Louis-Adolphe
Humbert
de Molard
(France),
half plate.
Self-Portrait.

98.
William and Frederick Langenheim (U.S.), half plate. Frederick Langenheim Looking at Talbotypes of Himself.

100.
*Josiah Hawes
(U.S.), quarter
plate. Self-
Portrait.*